*Ora*

Oracle Database 10g New Features

About the Author

Robert G. Freeman has been involved in Oracle for well over a decade (and almost a decade and a half!). Having decided many moons ago that selling trucks was not the life for him, Robert moved into computing. From there he started delving into C programming and then he quickly moved into Unix administration and then to Oracle. As a consultant, Robert has experienced many an interesting assignment all over the United States. Additionally, Robert has spoken at many user groups, both national and international. In his free time (does he have free time?) Robert enjoys being with his new wife (who he totally didn't deserve), his wonderful kids, and Clifford the cat (and no, Clifford isn't eight feet tall). He's also trying to learn French, but is sure he will never get it. Robert welcomes positive e-mails at dbaoracle@aol.com.

About the Contributor

Jonathan Lewis is known internationally as the author of *Practical Oracle8i: Building Efficient Databases* (Addison-Wesley, 2001) and as the designer and presenter of the three-day seminar, "Optimising Oracle – Performance by Design."

Jonathan has an international reputation as one of the leading independent specialists in Oracle database technology, with more than 18 years' experience designing, implementing, and troubleshooting systems around the world.

About the Technical Editor

Pete Sharman has 16 years' IT experience designing, implementing, and managing the performance of Oracle solutions. As a solo consultant and team leader, Pete has provided administrative and technical leadership to leading Internet-based businesses, as well as several Fortune 100 and Fortune 500 companies. He has also completed world-class benchmarks and implementation reviews of the Oracle RDBMS, and performed high-impact performance tuning. A proven technical leader, Pete has acquired expert-level skills in Oracle Parallel Server and Real Application Clusters database design, administration, backup and recovery, operations planning and management, performance management, system management, and security and management of complex data centers.

Currently, Pete is performing the role of Oracle9*i* and Oracle 10*g* Database Global Consulting Lead, acting as an interface between Oracle Development and North America Sales and Consulting. Pete has also passed all the Oracle DBA Certifications (Oracle7, Oracle8, Oracle8*i*, and Oracle9*i*) and was one of the first 20 people in the world to qualify as an Oracle9*i* Certified Master.

Oracle Press™

Oracle Database 10g
New Features

Robert G. Freeman

McGraw-Hill/Osborne

New York   Chicago   San Francisco
Lisbon   London   Madrid   Mexico City   Milan
New Delhi   San Juan   Seoul   Singapore   Sydney   Toronto

The McGraw·Hill Companies

McGraw-Hill/Osborne
2100 Powell Street, 10th Floor
Emeryville, California 94608
U.S.A.

To arrange bulk purchase discounts for sales promotions, premiums, or fund-raisers, please
contact **McGraw-Hill**/Osborne at the above address. For information on translations or book
distributors outside the U.S.A., please see the International Contact Information page
immediately following the index of this book.

Oracle Database 10*g* New Features

1234567890 CUS CUS 01987654

ISBN 0-07-222947-0

Publisher Brandon A. Nordin	**Proofreader** Claire Splan
Vice President & Associate Publisher Scott Rogers	**Indexer** Claire Splan
Acquisitions Editor Lisa McClain	**Computer Designers** Jean Butterfield Kelly Stanton-Scott
Project Editor Janet Walden	**Illustrators** Melinda Lytle Kathleen Edwards
Acquisitions Coordinator Athena Honore	
Technical Editor Pete Sharman	**Series Design** Jani Beckwith Peter Hancik
Copy Editor William McManus	**Cover Designer** Damore Johann Design, Inc.

This book was composed with Corel VENTURA™ Publisher.

This book is dedicated to the people who really matter. To the love of my life (and by the time you read this, my new wife!), Lisa. The truth is, the only reason I got this thing done, instead of finding myself buried somewhere in a deep depression, was because she was there. 2003 was a year of turmoil for me. She came to me late in 2003, and has made 2004 a monumentally wonderful year. Thank you Lisa.

I dedicate this work to my five kids, Felicia, Sarah, Jacob, Jared, and Elizabeth.

Thanks to my Dad. The persistent drive to do and not just sit and observe comes completely from him.

I must admit that in the past, I've been hesitant to include any mention of Heavenly Father or Jesus Christ in my book dedications. It's for purely personal reasons, because I consider my relationship with them to be just that, personal. But, as I reflect over the events of my life recently, and even not so recently, I feel I owe them a public word of thanks for the place they have in my life and the blessings that I have.

Finally, to Clifford the cat, my buddy, confidant, and chief foot warmer, I say, purrrrrr....

Contents at a Glance

Table of Contents

Acknowledgments

ost important, I acknowledge the love of my life, Lisa. To my kids who put up with my absence way too often I think, they must be acknowledged for this sacrifice.

Thanks to the great folks at McGraw-Hill/Osborne's Oracle Press who put up with me and Oracle's beta cycle. You have not lived until you have worked on the beta version of some product and tried to write on it knowing fully well that it's probably going to change by the time you are done writing about it! The folks at Oracle Press stuck it out, waiting to publish this book until after the product actually came out in its final form and the content could be updated. So thank yous go out to Lisa McClain, Athena Honore, Janet Walden, Bill McManus, and Osborne's production department.

A special thanks to Mark Townsend, who served as the Oracle sponsor for this book.

Thanks to Pete Sharman, my technical editor—great job Pete! Pete is a wizzo of an Oracle employee!

Thanks to Jonathan Lewis, who not only added some great insights into the book, but also served as a second technical editor too. Thanks Jonathan!

Krishna Kakatur came to the rescue with Chapter 9 and its OEM content. He did a great job on short notice. Thanks Krishna!

Also, I'd like to acknowledge the good folks that I work with at TUSC. There are just so many of these guys that I dare not name them for fear of missing a name here or there and hurting feelings. I can say that without a doubt there is some incredible talent at TUSC, and I'm happy to be associated with it. Also, thanks to all the clients I've met over the past year at TUSC—I learn much from you!

Introduction

Change has considerable psychological impact on the human mind. To the fearful, it is threatening because it means that things may get worse. To the hopeful, it is encouraging because things may get better. To the confident, it is inspiring because the challenge exists to make things better. Obviously, then, one's character and frame of mind determine how readily he brings about change and how he reacts to change that is imposed on him.

—King Whitney Jr.

ing wasn't a DBA, but he might have been. Technology, and particularly the DBA world, has been about *change* in the last several years. Each year, with a new software release here or a new operating system release there, we have to contend with changes. DBAs are a special lot because we really have to understand all those layers to some degree to really excel at what we do. It's hard work, but it's incredibly rewarding.

Oracle Database 10*g* is all about change. This book, and the other *New Features* books that I've written over the years, is all about change. The Oracle Database product has changed so much in the years that I've worked and written about it, and Oracle Database 10*g* is no exception. There is more change packed into this version than it is possible to write about in these few pages, but I sure tried.

No doubt you will read these pages and say, "Wow, lots of stuff there!" Don't let this overwhelm you; the database proper, in and of itself, still pretty much looks and feels the same. You can install Oracle Database 10*g*, and treat it from the outset much like you would have an Oracle9*i* database. You use SQL*Plus to connect to it (much to the happiness of those who, early on, were subject to the rumor that SQL*Plus was going away!) and you still start it with the **startup** command and shut it down with the **shutdown** command. You can migrate from Oracle8*i* or Oracle9*i* with little effort (but much caution!) and not have to contend with too many of the new features (with a few exceptions, such as the new SYSAUX tablespace). In short, many of these new features are optional to a degree, but offer enhanced performance, easier management, and more functionality.

Also, in this book you will find some great commentary by Jonathan Lewis! Now, if you know Oracle, you probably have at least heard of Jonathan. He is, by all accounts, "Mr. Oracle." I believe that he must dream of online redo log switches in his head by night. Jonathan provides some commentary throughout the book regarding the new features of Oracle Database 10*g*, such as why they were added, how they may be applied, and any potential dangers that they might pose.

This book is written to be a quick-start guide to these features. It's not an exhaustive introduction to each new feature and it's not an OCP prep guide (though I am sure that it will serve as a good study guide to the new features that might be covered in the OCP New Features exam). It's the wading pool for you to walk through before you dive into the adult pool. It's the escalator that runs you by the crown jewels before you actually break into the case and take the ones that appeal the most to you. (Please do note that preparation for the OCP exam is beyond the scope of this book.)

In fact, this book was written long before the OCP for Oracle Database 10*g* ever existed. It was primarily written using the beta version of Oracle Database 10*g*, and then the material was checked against the *production version* of the database. In checking the content against the final release, I came across a few items that are still buggy as of the writing of this book. Keeping this in mind, I present the functionality as it is supposed to work. The OEM material in Chapter 9 is still in a great deal of flux even with the final release. The moral of the story is this: before you decide to use anything discussed within the pages of this book, make sure you test it in your own environment. Lastly, I chose to give more coverage to some material and less to other material based on my assessment of their immediate merit.

Writing Oracle Database 10*g* has been a great experience, and my life has changed so much over the course of this book. I hope you find success as you start to use Oracle Database 10*g*.

CHAPTER
1

Getting Started

- Welcome to Oracle Database 10*g* and the "Grid"
- Upgrading to Oracle Database 10*g*
- The Database Configuration Assistant
- The SYSAUX Tablespace
- Automatic Storage Management
- Oracle Database 10*g* Real Application Clusters

elcome to *Oracle Database 10*g *New Features*! This chapter is the place to start in your effort to learn all about Oracle Database 10*g*. In this chapter, we will first look at the "Grid" and see what it is all about. Then we move on to explain how to upgrade to Oracle Database 10*g*. The following are the specific topics that are covered:

- The "Grid"

- Upgrading to Oracle Database 10*g*

- The SYSAUX tablespace

- Automatic Storage Management (ASM)

Welcome to Oracle Database 10*g* and the "Grid"

Oracle Database 10*g*. If you are wondering what that *g* is all about, it stands for this rather murky concept of the "Grid." As I was writing this book, I asked some fellow DBAs what they thought the Grid was. There were those who had some idea, and those who were not so sure. In fact, I did a search in the Oracle Beta documentation set, and found little or no reference to the Grid. I did determine that the final release will contain a book that provides concept, configuration, and administration guidance for the Grid, however.

A new concept and little documentation—what is a DBA to do? Never fear, *Oracle Database 10*g *New Features* is here! So, what is the Grid? The Grid is all about the synergies that can be achieved by aligning the Oracle technologies with the capabilities of existing and future hardware. As Larry Ellison put it, the Grid is "…capacity on demand made up of low-cost parts." The Grid enables you to do the following:

- **Leverage components made available to the Grid**   Through Oracle Real Application Clusters, Automatic Storage Management (ASM), and Ultra-Large Data Files (all of which are discussed in this book), Oracle allows you to take advantage of your hardware investment in a much more efficient manner.

- **Load-balance across the enterprise**   Oracle Real Application Clusters, Oracle Streams, and Oracle distributed database technologies support this concept.

■ **Share information regardless of its location**   This concept is supported through new transportable tablespace features, Oracle Streams (e.g., Replication), external tables, and distributed SQL queries.

■ **Schedule resources across the Grid**   The new features of the Oracle scheduler and the Oracle Database Resource Manager help the DBA to effectively take better advantage of the Grid.

The Grid may not be 100 percent there with Oracle Database 10*g*, but it's certainly a start. Oracle Database 10*g* is full of new features that more fully align it with the concepts of the Grid. In this book, we will look at these new features, and a number of other new features that make Oracle Database 10*g* an interesting upgrade indeed!

Upgrading to Oracle Database 10*g*

Oracle Database 10*g* provides a fairly easy upgrade path for users of older Oracle Database versions. The following versions can directly be upgraded to Oracle Database 10*g*:

■ Oracle Database 8.0.6

■ Oracle Database 8.1.7

■ Oracle Database 9.0.1

■ Oracle Database 9.2

If your database version is not in the preceding list, then you must first upgrade to one of these versions, after which you can upgrade to Oracle Database 10*g*.

After you are at a supported upgrade level, you can upgrade to Oracle Database 10*g* by using any one of the following four upgrade options:

■ Use the Oracle Database Upgrade Assistant (DBUA). (This was called the Oracle Data Migration Assistant previously.)

■ Perform a manual upgrade.

■ Use **exp/imp** to copy the data in your database to a new Oracle Database 10*g* database.

■ Use the SQL*Plus **copy** command or the **create table as select** command to copy the data from your current database to your new Oracle Database 10*g* database.

NOTE
*Always back up your database before you start
your upgrade!*

The DBUA

The DBUA is a GUI that is designed for upgrading your Oracle database to Oracle
Database 10*g*. You will have the option of starting the DBUA from the Oracle Universal
Installer (OUI) when installing Oracle Database 10*g*. DBUA guides you through the
upgrade of your Oracle database. You can also start the DBUA at any time in stand-
alone fashion (from the command line, just enter **dbua**) to upgrade your database.
From Windows, you can also start the DBUA from the Start menu (either from the
Oracle folder or use Start I Run and click dbua). One nice feature of the DBUA is
that it will offer to back up your database for you. This feature does have some limited
functionality, because backups to removable media are not supported. DBUA supports
both normal database upgrades and Real Application Clusters database upgrades.

CAUTION
*Oracle Database 10*g* only supports a direct
downgrade back to Oracle release 9.2.0.3 or
later. You can use **imp/exp** (Oracle's import/export
utilities), however, to move the migrated database
data to other versions of Oracle Database. I strongly
advise that you test this method of downgrading on
a nonproduction server first, if you plan to use it.*

Performing Manual Upgrades

Manual upgrades (my personal favorite) allow you to use a series of scripts and
utilities to upgrade your database. The summary steps of manual upgrades include

- Develop a test plan to run after your upgrade.

- Back up your database.

- Run the Upgrade Information Tool (UIT), which is a SQL script,
  utlu101i.sql, located in the directory $ORACLE_HOME/rdbms/
  admin. This script analyzes your database before you upgrade it and
  alerts you to any problems that might endanger the successful upgrade
  of your database. If you want your output in XML format, you should
  run utlu101x.sql.

- Upgrade the database. Follow the Oracle upgrade instructions for your specific version and operating system. This step includes the creation of the new SYSAUX tablespace, which is new in Oracle Database 10*g*. (This tablespace is described in detail later in "The SYSAUX Tablespace.")

- Check the component registry (DBA_REGISTRY) to make sure your upgrade was successful.

- Back up your new Oracle Database 10*g* database.

- Run your test plan and validate your upgrade.

About the compatible Parameter

Once you have upgraded to Oracle Database 10*g*, the **compatible** parameter can be set no lower than 9.2.0. Thus, if you are upgrading from 8.0.6, you need to set **compatible** to 9.2.0 before you can open your database under Oracle Database 10*g*. The Oracle upgrade manual (*Oracle 10*g *Upgrade Guide*) provides detailed instructions on setting the **compatible** parameter. Once you are satisfied that the database can operate under Oracle Database 10*g*, you can set the **compatible** parameter to 10.0. Note that, once you set the **compatible** parameter to 10.0, you cannot set it back. This is different than in previous versions of Oracle. Also note that the command **alter database reset compatibility** is now obsolete.

There are a number of other possible upgrade issues that you need to deal with depending on the database features that you are using. I strongly suggest that you carefully review the Oracle Upgrade documentation and that you test your Oracle Database 10*g* upgrades several times before doing one for real in production.

One final upgrade thought—I suggest that you do not use any of the new Oracle Database 10*g* features in a production environment until you have tested the feature thoroughly. While Oracle does its best to regression-test new features, there are always a few kinks to be worked out in the beginning. If you find a new feature irresistible (and after you read this book, I hope you do!), then by all means try it out. Test it over and over to make sure it works the way it's intended, and that it doesn't have some nasty impacts, like causing performance problems or causing your database to crash. Also, check Oracle MetaLink, and even open an Oracle iTAR, before you use a new feature that will be a prominent part of your design.

Other Upgrade Methods

The use of the Oracle **exp/imp** utilities is supported for migrating your Oracle database data to Oracle Database 10*g*. You will use the export utility associated with the version of the database you are currently on (e.g., 8.0.6) to create the dump file. Use the **imp** utility from the Oracle Database 10*g* database to import the dump file created for the

Jonathan Says...
Remember that **sql_trace** (possibly started by a logon trigger that calls the packaged procedure **dbms_support.start_trace**) is your best friend when you are testing. Many of the enhancements and features that appeared in Oracle9*i* Database were supported by PL/SQL packages and recursive SQL. Expect more of the same approach to appear in Oracle Database 10g.

If you switch on **sql_trace** when testing a feature, you may find out what Oracle Database 10g is doing under the covers to support that feature, and discover that a feature that looks good on paper has a nasty side effect that makes it unsuitable for your production system.

Another little trick for discovering hidden costs when you start to test new data structures is to start with a clean schema, create an example of the new data structure, and then query the USER_OBJECTS view to discover what hidden objects Oracle has created to support that structure.

upgrade. The Oracle upgrade manual provides a complete set of instructions on how to perform this type of upgrade.

Finally, you can use the SQL*Plus **copy** command or the SQL **create table as select** command to move your database data to a new Oracle Database 10g instance. Again, the Oracle upgrade manual provides a complete set of instructions on how to perform this type of upgrade.

The Database Configuration Assistant

As an author who admits to hating GUIs, I rather like the Database Configuration Assistant (DBCA). Creation of a small database is a great way to test your new Oracle software install. Oracle Database 10g has added new functionality to the DBCA, including the ability to perform Real Application Cluster database installs and configuration of Automatic Storage Management (a new feature that is described later in this chapter).

The SYSAUX Tablespace

In the previous section you might have noticed that when you upgrade your Oracle database to Oracle Database 10g, you need to create a new tablespace called SYSAUX. Also, when you create your first Oracle Database 10g database, Oracle will create SYSAUX as well. The SYSAUX tablespace is a new tablespace component in Oracle

Database 10*g*. This section first discusses the SYSAUX tablespace and then reviews some Oracle-supplied procedures that allow you to perform maintenance tasks on the SYSAUX tablespace.

Introducing the SYSAUX Tablespace

The SYSAUX tablespace is a new tablespace that is required in Oracle Database 10*g*. SYSAUX is a secondary tablespace for storage of a number of database components that were previously stored in the SYSTEM tablespace. The SYSAUX tablespace is created as a locally managed tablespace using automatic segment space management.

Previously, many Oracle features required their own separate tablespaces (such as the RMAN recovery catalog, Ultra Search, Data Mining, XDP, and OLAP). This increases the management responsibility of the DBA. The SYSAUX tablespace consolidates these tablespaces into one location, which becomes the default tablespace for these Oracle features.

When you create an Oracle database, Oracle creates the SYSAUX tablespace for you by default. If you are using Oracle Managed Files (OMF), then the tablespace is created in the appropriate OMF directory. If you use the **sysaux datafile** clause in the **create database** statement, then the SYSAUX tablespace datafile(s) will be created in the location you define. Finally, if no **sysaux datafile** clause is included and OMF is not configured, Oracle creates the SYSAUX tablespace in a default location that is OS-specific. Here is an example of a **create database** statement with the **sysaux datafile** clause in it:

```
CREATE DATABASE my_db
DATAFILE 'c:\oracle\oradata\my_db\my_db_system_01.dbf' SIZE 300m
SYSAUX DATAFILE 'c:\oracle\my_db\my_db_sysaux_01.dbf' SIZE 100m
DEFAULT TEMPORARY TABLESPACE dtemp_tbs tempfile
'c:\oracle\my_db\my_db_temp_01.dbf' SIZE 100m
UNDO TABLESPACE undo_tbs_one DATAFILE
'c:\oracle\my_db\my_db_undo_tbs_one_01.dbf' SIZE 100m;
```

As stated earlier in this chapter, when you migrate to Oracle Database 10*g*, you need to create the SYSAUX tablespace as a part of that migration. You do this after mounting the database under the new Oracle Database 10*g* database software. Once you have mounted it, you should open the database in migrate mode with the **startup migrate** command. Once the database is open, you can create the SYSAUX tablespace. Here is the **create tablespace** statement that you would use to perform this operation:

```
CREATE TABLESPACE sysaux
DATAFILE 'c:\oracle\oradata\my_db\my_db_sysaux_01.dbf' SIZE 300m
EXTENT MANAGEMENT LOCAL SEGMENT SPACE MANAGEMENT AUTO;
```

The SYSAUX tablespace must be created with the attributes shown in the preceding example. The following restrictions apply to the usage of the SYSAUX tablespace in Oracle Database 10*g*:

■ When migrating to Oracle Database 10*g*, you can create the SYSAUX tablespace only when the database is open in migrate mode.

■ Also, when migrating to Oracle Database 10*g*, if a tablespace is already named SYSAUX, you need to remove it or rename it while you are in migrate mode.

■ Once you have opened your Oracle Database 10*g* database, you cannot drop the SYSAUX tablespace. If you try, an error will be returned.

■ You cannot rename the SYSAUX tablespace during normal database operations.

■ The SYSAUX tablespace cannot be transported to other databases via Oracle's transportable tablespace feature.

Once the SYSAUX tablespace is in place and the database has been upgraded, you can add or resize datafiles associated with a SYSAUX tablespace just as you would any other tablespace through the **alter tablespace** command, as shown in this example:

```
ALTER TABLESPACE sysaux ADD DATAFILE
   'd:\oracle\oradata\my_db\my_db_sysaux_01.dbf' SIZE 200M;
```

Managing Occupants of the SYSAUX Tablespace

Each set of application tables within the SYSAUX tablespace is known as an *occupant*. Oracle provides some new views to help you monitor space usage of occupants within the SYSAUX tablespace and some new procedures you can use to move the occupant objects in and out of the SYSAUX tablespace.

First, Oracle provides a new view, V$SYSAUX_OCCUPANTS, to manage occupants in the SYSAUX tablespace. This view allows you to monitor the space usage of occupant application objects in the SYSAUX tablespace, as shown in this example:

```
SELECT occupant_name, space_usage_kbytes FROM v$sysaux_occupants;
```

In this case, Oracle will display the space usage for the occupants, such as the RMAN recovery catalog.

If you determine that you need to move the occupants out of the SYSAUX tablespace, then the MOVE_PROCEDURE column of the V$SYSAUX_OCCUPANTS view will indicate the procedure that you should use to move the related occupant from the SYSAUX tablespace to another tablespace. This can also be a method of "reorganizing" your component object tables, should that be required.

NOTE
The loss of the SYSAUX tablespace is not fatal to your database. In our testing it appears that the only real impact is that certain functionality related to the occupants of the SYSAUX tablespace is lost.

Automatic Storage Management

Oracle Database 10*g* introduces Automatic Storage Management (ASM), a service that provides management of disk drives. ASM can be used on a variety of configurations, including Oracle9*i* Database RAC installations. ASM is an alternative to the use of raw or cooked file systems and is part of Oracle's overall desire to make management of the Oracle Database 10*g* easier, overall.

ASM Features

ASM offers a number of features, including:

- Simplified daily administration

- The performance of raw disk I/O for all ASM files

- Compatibility with any type of disk configuration, be it just a bunch of disks (JBOD) or complex Storage Area Network (SAN)

- Use of a specific file-naming convention to name files, enforcing an enterprise-wide file-naming convention

- Prevention of the accidental deletion of files, since there is no file system interface and ASM is solely responsible for file management

- Load balancing of data across all ASM managed disk drives, which helps improve performance by removing disk hot spots

- Dynamic load balancing of disks as usage patterns change and when additional disks are added or removed

- Ability to mirror data on different disks to provide fault tolerance

■   Support of vendor-supplied storage offerings and features

■   Enhanced scalability over other disk-management techniques

ASM can work in concert with existing databases that use raw or cooked file systems. You can choose to leave existing file systems in place or move the database datafiles to ASM disks. Additionally, new database datafiles can be placed in either ASM disks or on the preexisting file systems. Databases can conceivably contain a mixture of file types, including raw, cooked, OMF, and ASM files (though the management of such a system would be more complex).

ASM makes adding and removing of disks easy. It will rebalance the data on the underlying disks as they are added and removed. This results in the best possible performance for your database.

ASM is not a replacement for your existing OS file systems. The disks assigned to ASM will not be visible from the OS. Thus, ASM is not going to be used for Oracle software installs, administrative directories, or the location of parameter files.

The ASM Instance

ASM starts with the ASM instance that is responsible for the management of the various disk groups and the associated files. If ASM is being used by a database then the ASM instance must be started before the Oracle database instance is started. The ASM instance has a very small footprint and does not consume much in the way of resources. The ASM instance will mount the disks, create an extent map, and then pass this information on to the Oracle database instance when it is started. Note that ASM has few real "run-time" responsibilities and that all I/O requests to the ASM file system are handled by the Oracle database itself. The only time that ASM gets involved during run time is if there is some disk configuration change. This would include file removal or creation, or addition or removal of a disk.

To create an ASM instance, create a parameter file called init_osm.ora. In the ASM parameter file, you need to set the **instance_type** parameter to a value of OSM. The **instance_type** parameter defines the instances as an ASM instance. Generally, other ASM-related parameters take on default values, which can be accepted. Once the parameter file is created, start the ASM instance, using the **startup** command. Shutting down the ASM instance is done via the **shutdown** command (**normal**, **immediate**, **force**, and **abort** commands are supported). Note that this will result in the shutdown of all database instances related to the ASM instance and that the mode used to shut down the ASM instance will be the same mode used to shut down the associated database instances.

Also, the Oracle Database 10g DBCA can be used to create, configure, and start up an ASM instance. If ASM is already in use, the DBCA will allow you to take advantage of it. If ASM is not installed, you will be given an opportunity to install it.

NOTE
The DBCA will give you an option to create an ASM instance, if one does not already exist! This includes configuration of the parameter file of that instance.

Setting Up ASM Disks

Once the ASM instance is in place, you are ready to set up disk groups. Much like a logical volume in OS logical volume managers, a disk group is a logical collection of a number of physical disk devices. You create a disk group with the **create diskgroup** command. Within the **create diskgroup** command, you define both the main disk group and the failover disk group that is associated with that main group. Here is an example of the creation of a disk group:

```
Create diskgroup disk_group_001
FAILGROUP fail_group_01 DISK
'/dev/disk1', '/dev/disk2', '/dev/disk3',
FAILGROUP fail_group_02 DISK
'/dev/disk5', '/dev/disk6', '/dev/disk7';
```

ASM offers redundancy of data in the definition of the disk groups. This example creates a disk group with two failure groups. Each failure group has three disks assigned to it. Oracle will mirror the two groups, and will stripe Oracle files across one group, and then mirror that to the other group. Normal redundancy, as you see in this example, is the default, and requires that two failure groups be allocated. High redundancy requires three **failgroup** disk definitions. Another option, external redundancy, does not mirror at all in ASM, and rather leaves redundancy to an external entity (such as the disk array that might be mirrored).

When you create a disk group, you can constrain how much space within the disks are allocated to the disk group. This allows you to keep some space in reserve for later use. You cannot allocate more space to a disk group than already exists.

When the disk group is allocated, ASM will balance database files across the disks of that group, and will rebalance the group when disks are added or removed. All of this can take place without needing to cycle the database, thus availability of the database is not impacted.

NOTE
*The **create diskgroup** command is only run from the ASM instance, not from a normal database instance.*

The **alter diskgroup** command is provided to help you manage existing disk groups. The **alter diskgroup** command allows you to add disks to an existing group, remove disks from an existing disk group, and resize disks in an existing disk group. Also, the **alter diskgroup** command allows you to manually rebalance disks and mount or dismount a given disk group.

You can also create directories within your disk groups by using the **alter diskgroup** command, as shown in this example:

```
Alter diskgroup disk_group_001 add directory
'+disk_group_001/data_001';
```

You can also rename and drop directories with the **alter diskgroup** command.

Addressing ASM Disks

Once the disk group is assigned, the Oracle DBA need only refer to the disk group when creating a tablespace. Here is an example:

```
Create tablespace data_tbs datafile '+disk_group_001' size 300MB;
```

Note that in this case we referenced the ASM disk group that we created in the previous section. After this command is issued, Oracle will create the datafile in the disk group assigned, using an OMF-compliant naming convention. If you need to manage these files later on (for example, you need to grow the datafile), you can find the files in the DBA_DATA_FILES or V$DATAFILE views, as you previously did.

ASM and Data Dictionary Views

Several new data dictionary views exist to help you manage ASM. These data dictionary views are available both when connected to the ASM instance as well as to any Oracle Database 10*g* database. Each view is slightly different in its presentation depending on whether the instance you are looking at is an ASM instance or a database instance (and some views are only used in the ASM instance). Let's quickly look at these views.

V$ASM_ALIAS
When you are connected to an ASM instance, the V$ASM_ALIAS view displays a single row for every alias present in every disk group mounted by the ASM instance. This view is not used when connected to a normal database instance (no rows will be displayed).

V$ASM_CLIENT
When you are connected to an ASM instance, the V$ASM_CLIENT view displays a single row for every database instance using a disk group managed by the ASM

instance. When you are connected to a normal database instance and the database has open ASM files, the V$ASM_CLIENT view displays a single row for the ASM instance.

V$ASM_DISK

When you are connected to an ASM instance, the V$ASM_DISK view displays a single row for every disk discovered by the ASM instance, including disks that are not part of any disk group. When you are connected to a normal database instance, the V$ASM_DISK view only displays rows for disks in disk groups in use by the database instance.

V$ASM_DISKGROUP

When you are connected to an ASM instance, the V$ASM_DISKGROUP view displays a single row for each disk group discovered by the ASM instance. When you are connected to a database instance, the V$ASM_DISKGROUP view displays a single row for every ASM disk group mounted by the local ASM instance.

V$ASM_FILE

When you are connected to an ASM instance, the V$ASM_FILE view displays a single row for every ASM file in every disk group mounted by the ASM instance. This view is not used when connected to a normal database instance (no rows will be displayed).

V$ASM_OPERATION

When you are connected to an ASM instance, the V$ASM_OPERATION view displays a single row for every active ASM long-running operation executing in the ASM instance. This view is not used when connected to a normal database instance (no rows will be displayed).

V$ASM_TEMPLATE

When you are connected to an ASM instance, the V$ASM_TEMPLATE view displays a single row for every template present in every disk group mounted by the ASM instance. When you are connected to a database instance, the V$ASM_TEMPLATE view displays a single row for every ASM disk group mounted by the local ASM instance.

This is just a quick introduction to the power of ASM. A small book probably could be written on just this new feature alone. Still, I hope I have gotten you interested in it!

Oracle Database 10*g* Real Application Clusters

Oracle9*i* Database introduced Real Application Clusters (RAC), which was a successor to Oracle Parallel Server. Oracle Database 10*g* offers several RAC-related improvements, including:

- Portable Clusterware

- Rolling upgrades

- Cluster Ready Services

- Enhancements to the Database Configuration Assistant and the Database Upgrade Assistant

- Enhanced recovery parallelism on multiple CPU systems

- A new parameter, **gcs_server_processes**

Portable Clusterware

First introduced on limited platforms in Oracle9*i* Database, Portable Clusterware is now available on most Oracle Database 10*g* platforms. Clusterware provides clustering services for the Oracle Database 10*g* RAC configuration. Prior to Oracle Database 10*g*, most RAC configurations required that third-party clusterware software be purchased and installed. Now, in Oracle Database 10*g*, Oracle offers clusterware that runs on all platforms, eliminating the need for vendor-offered clusterware. Oracle's Portable Clusterware offers a number of features:

- Infiniband high-speed network support

- Simplified client installs

- Simplified cluster installs

Rolling Upgrades

Oracle Database 10*g* provides for limited rolling upgrades for RAC clusters through the use of the **opatch** utility. These patches must be certified by Oracle to be used within a rolling upgrade scheme. There are a number of restrictions on what patches may be used as rolling upgrade patches, such as the fact that the patch cannot impact the contents of the database data dictionary and the patch cannot impact RAC internode communications. Rolling upgrades are available for one-off patches only as of this writing, thus patch sets cannot be applied in a rolling fashion.

Cluster Ready Services

Oracle Database 10*g* introduces Cluster Ready Services (CRS), which provides additional management services to a database cluster, such as node membership, group services, global resource management, and high availability. CRS also interacts with vendor-supplied software in its node management activities.

The Oracle Universal Installer will install CRS on nodes in an ORACLE_HOME location that is different from that of the RDBMS software's ORACLE_HOME install. As with the normal RDBMS software, you can install CRS on each individual node, or into a common ORACLE_HOME location for all the nodes.

CRS allows you to assign services to specific instances in the cluster, and these services can be configured in such a way as to allow you to manage the workload of the various machines of the cluster. Services are created within the DBCA, the Server Control utility, or the **dbms_services** PL/SQL stored procedure. You can administer services via Oracle Enterprise Manager (OEM) or the Server Control utility.

Oracle Database 10*g* provides statistics related to CRS within the Automatic Workload Repository (AWR). This allows you to manage cluster-related performance issues. Additionally, AWR provides the ability to monitor any specific performance thresholds that might be exceeded and send the DBA notification alerts based on these thresholds. Also, Oracle Database 10*g* provide an interface into CRS through the **dbms_service** and **dbms_monitor** PL/SQL procedures.

Database Assistants

Oracle offers new functionality in two of the database assistant GUI programs, the Oracle Database Configuration Assistant (DBCA) and the Oracle Database Upgrade Assistant (DBUA). These assistants are built to make the DBA's job easier, by simplifying database configuration and migration to Oracle Database 10*g*. The DBCA can also be used to add and remove instances from the cluster.

The DBCA now supports the creation and removal of clustered databases. The DBCA will detect a clustered environment when it is executed and give you the opportunity to create a clustered database if that is your desire. The DBUA allows you to upgrade your previous RAC database to Oracle Database 10*g* with RAC.

NOTE
Oracle recommends that you create your
clustered database with the DBCA in the
Oracle Real Application Clusters Deployment
and Performance Guide.

The gcs_server_processes Parameter

A new parameter, **gcs_server_processes**, is introduced in Oracle Database 10*g*.
This parameter defines the initial number of server processes in Global Cache
Service that are started to serve inter-instance traffic. The default value for this
parameter is 2, and the value can range from 1 to 20. This parameter can also
be set differently for each instance in the cluster.

CHAPTER

2

Server Manageability

- **Statistics Collection**
- **Flushing the Buffer Cache**
- **Database Resource Manager New Features**
- **Scheduler Changes**
- **User-Configurable Default Tablespaces**
- **Tablespace Groups and Multiple Default Temporary Tablespaces**
- **Renaming Tablespaces**
- **Dropping Databases**
- **Larger LOBs**
- **Automatic Undo Retention**
- **Shrinking and Compacting Segments Online**
- **Using New Online Redefinition Features**

Oracle Database 10*g* comes with a wealth of features that make life easier for both the old school and the new school DBAs, as you'll see in this chapter. These new features are designed to reduce the overall cost of managing the database and to make it easier for us to actually use at least three days of our generous two week vacation allotment! In this chapter we will look at these specific topics:

- Using new statistics-collection features
- Flushing the database buffer cache
- Using the Database Resource Manager new features
- Firing up the new job scheduler (known as The Scheduler)
- Learning all about user-configurable default tablespaces
- Using tablespace groups and multiple default temporary tablespaces
- Renaming tablespaces
- Dropping databases
- Taking advantage of new LOB storage limitations
- Using Automatic Undo retention
- Shrinking segments online
- Using new online redefinition features

Statistics Collection

Oracle Database 10*g* offers some new features to help you collect database statistics. These new features include automated collection of statistics, collection of data dictionary statistics, new behaviors associated with the **dbms_stats** package, and new features related to monitoring tables in the database. Let's look at these new features in more detail next.

Automated Statistics Collection

By default Oracle will create a job at database creation time that automatically collects database statistics. This job is scheduled in the database job scheduler and can be seen using the DBA_SCHEDULER_JOBS view. The scheduled job runs the stored program **dbms_stats.gather_database_stats_job_proc**. The statistics collection job runs as a single job scheduler program that is assigned to a window which executes the program within two different job windows. The first job window runs the statistics collection job Monday through Friday at 10 P.M. The second job window causes the statistics-gathering process to execute on Saturday starting at midnight.

There may be certain object statistics that you wish not to be overwritten by the automated statistics-collection process. You can use the new PL/SQL procedure **dbms_stats.lock_schema_stats** to lock statistics for a given table and all of its dependent objects. Additionally, you can use the **dbms_stats.lock_schema_stats** procedure to lock statistics for all objects in a given schema.

You can unlock statistics through the use of the procedures **dbms_stats.unlock_ schema_stats** and **unlock_table_stats**. You can tell if an object is locked via the STATTYPE_LOCKED column in the view DBA_TAB_STATISTICS (with ALL and USER versions available as well). Several procedures in **dbms_stats** include a new parameter, **force**, which allows you to force the overwriting of statistics.

A new view, DBA_OPTSTAT_OPERATIONS, has been added to Oracle Database 10*g* that allows you to see the history of executions of the **dbms_stats** package, both at the schema level and at the database level. Through this view, you can confirm the last successful operation of automated or manual statistics collection.

Oracle Database 10*g* enables you to restore statistics to any point in time, in case the new statistics that were collected cause a suboptimal plan to be generated. You can restore statistics for a table, a schema, fixed database objects, or the entire database.

NOTE
*Statistics collection during index creation and rebuilds is now an automatic process in Oracle Database 10*g* unless the statistics on that index are locked. As a result, the **compute statistics** clause of the **create index** and **alter index** commands is now obsolete.*

Collecting Data Dictionary Statistics

The Rule Based Optimizer (RBO) is desupported with Oracle Database 10*g*. It's still there in Oracle Database 10*g*, but Oracle is moving away from it quickly and you will find no bug fixes associated with it in Oracle Database 10*g* or future versions of the database. With desupport of the RBO, it becomes even more important to address the question of collection of database statistics.

Oracle Database 10*g* includes new statistics-gathering features. These include the ability to collect data dictionary statistics, which is now recommended as a best practice by Oracle. Also, Oracle Database 10*g* includes new features that enhance the generation of object-level statistics within the database. Let's look at these features next.

Data Dictionary Statistics Collection

Oracle Database 10*g* is a big departure from previous releases of Oracle insofar as Oracle recommends that you analyze the data dictionary. You can collect these statistics by using either the **dbms_stats.gather_schema_stats** or **dbms_stats.gather_database_stats** Oracle-supplied procedures, as shown here:

```
Exec dbms_stats.gather_schema_stats('SYS')
```

The **dbms_stats.gather_schema_stats** and **dbms_stats.gather_database_stats** procedures are not new in Oracle Database 10*g*, but using them to collect data dictionary statistics is new, as are some new parameters that are available with these procedures.

Oracle Database 10*g* also offers two new procedures in the **dbms_stats** Oracle-supplied package. First, the **dbms_stats.gather_dictionary_stats** procedure facilitates analysis of the data dictionary. Second, the **dbms_stats.delete_dictionary_stats** procedure allows you to remove data dictionary stats. Here is an example of the use of the **dbms_stats.gather_dictionary_stats** procedure:

```
exec dbms_stats.gather_dictionary_stats;
```

This example gathers statistics from the SYS and SYSTEM schemas as well as any other schemas that are related to RDBMS components (e.g., OUTLN or DBSNMP).

From a security perspective, any user with SYSDBA privileges can analyze the data dictionary. However, non-SYSDBA user accounts must be granted the **analyze any dictionary** system privilege to be able to analyze the data dictionary.

Gathering Fixed Table Statistics

A new parameter to the **dbms_stats.gather_database_stats** and **dbms_stats.gather_schema_stats** Oracle-supplied procedures is **gather_fixed**. This parameter is set to FALSE by default, which disallows statistics collection for fixed, in-memory, data dictionary objects (e.g., x$ tables). Oracle suggests that you analyze fixed tables only once during a typical system workload. You should do this as soon as possible after your upgrade to Oracle Database 10*g*, but again it should be under a normal workload. Here is an example of the use of the **gather_fixed** argument within the **dbms_stats.gather_schema_stats** procedure:

```
Exec dbms_stats.gather_schema_stats('SYS',gather_fixed=>TRUE)
```

Yet another new procedure, **dbms_stats.gather_fixed_objects_stats**, has been provided in Oracle Database 10*g* to collect object statistics on fixed objects. It also has a brother, **dbms_stats.delete_fixed_objects_stats**, which will remove the object statistics. Second cousins and new Oracle Database 10*g*–provided procedures include **dbms_stats.export_fixed_objects_stats** and **dbms_stats.import_fixed_**

objects_stats. These allow you to export and import statistics to user-defined statistics tables, just as you could with normal table statistics previously. This allows your data dictionary fixed statistics to be exported out of and imported into other databases as required. One other note: the **dbms_stats** Oracle-supplied package also supports analyzing specific data dictionary tables.

When to Collect Dictionary Statistics

Oracle recommends the following strategy with regard to analyzing the data dictionary in Oracle Database 10g:

1. Analyze normal data dictionary objects (like the DBA_* tables, but not fixed dictionary objects like x$tables) using the same interval that you currently use when analyzing other objects. Use **gather_database_stats**, **gather_schema_stats**, or **gather_dictionary_stats** to perform this action. Here is an example:

    ```
    Exec dbms_stats.gather_schema_stats('SYS',gather_fixed=>FALSE)
    ```

2. Analyze fixed objects only once, unless the workload footprint changes. Generally, use the **dbms_stats.gather_fixed_objects_stats** Oracle-supplied procedure when connected as SYS or any other SYSDBA privileged user. Here is an example:

    ```
    Exec dbms_stats.gather_fixed_objects_stats;
    ```

New DBMS_STATS Behaviors

Oracle has introduced some new arguments that you can use with the **dbms_stats** package in Oracle Database 10g. The **granularity** parameter is used in several **dbms_stats** subprograms (e.g., **gather_table_stats** and **gather_schema_stats**) to indicate the granularity of the statistics that you want to collect, particularly for partitioned tables. For example, you can opt to gather only global statistics on a partitioned table, or you can opt to gather global and partition-level statistics. The **granularity** parameter comes with an **auto** option. When **auto** is used, Oracle collects global, partition-level, and subpartition-level statistics for a range-list partitioned table. For other partitioned tables, only global and partition-level statistics will be gathered.

A second **granularity** option, **global and partition**, will gather the global and partition-level statistics but no subpartition-level statistics, regardless of the type of partitioning employed on the table. Here are some examples of using these new options:

```
Exec dbms_stats.gather_table_stats('my_user','my_tab', -
granularity=>'AUTO');
Exec dbms_stats.gather_table_stats('my_user','my_tab', -
granularity=>'GLOBAL AND PARTITION');
```

Jonathan Says...
When you start to plan your strategy for gathering statistics, remember this—you probably don't need the same level of statistics collection on every object in the schema. Most (large) objects will give perfectly adequate results from a very small sample size, a few objects will need larger samples, and a handful of columns may need carefully considered histograms.

Although Oracle supplies a **gather_schema_stats** procedure, don't worry if you don't have the time window to use it—you probably don't need to. And remember, if you create loads of unnecessary histograms, you could be creating a performance problem—you pay for histograms through extra memory, CPU, and latch costs during optimization.

New options are also available with the **degree** parameter, which allows you to parallelize the statistics-gathering process. Using the new **auto_degree** option, Oracle will determine the degree of parallelism that should be used when analyzing the table. Simply use the predefined value, **dbms_stats.auto_degree**, in the **degree** parameter. Oracle will then decide the degree of parallelism to use. It may choose to use either no parallelism or a default degree of parallelism, which is dependent on the number of CPUs and the value of various database parameter settings. Here is an example of the use of the new **degree** option:

```
Exec dbms_stats.gather_table_stats -
('my_user','my_tab',degree=>dbms_stats.auto_degree);
```

Finally, the **stattype** parameter is a new parameter that allows you the option of gathering both data and caching statistics (which is the default) or only data statistics or only caching statistics. Valid options are ALL, CACHE, or DATA, depending on the type of statistics you wish to gather. CACHE causes only caching statistics to be gathered and DATA causes only data-related statistics to be gathered. ALL implies that both caching and data-related statistics have been collected. Here is an example of the use of the **stattype** parameter:

```
Exec dbms_stats.gather_table_stats -
('my_user','my_tab',stattype=>'ALL');
```

New Table-Monitoring Behaviors

Prior versions of Oracle Database allowed you to monitor a table's usage. The monitoring process keeps track of differential changes to the table. The **dbms_stats** package can be used to apply those differential statistics to the table's dictionary statistics, allowing the Cost Based Optimizer to generate plans based on more current statistics.

Oracle Database 10*g* enables global table monitoring by default. This feature is controlled via the **statistics_level** parameter (**statistics_level** was available in Oracle9*i* Database). When **statistics_level** is set to TYPICAL (which is the default setting) or ALL, then global monitoring is enabled. When the **statistics_level** parameter is set to BASIC, global monitoring is disabled.

Note that if global monitoring is enabled, you cannot disable it for specific tables. The **nomonitoring** clause of the **alter table** command will appear to complete successfully, but will have no effect in reality. Also, the **monitoring** clause of the **alter table** command no longer has any impact on monitoring of tables. It's kind of an all or nothing deal these days!

Flushing the Buffer Cache

Prior to Oracle Database 10*g*, the only way to flush the database buffer cache was to shut down the database and restart it. This was perhaps not the most graceful way of performing this activity because it required shutting down applications and disconnecting users, creating all sorts of mayhem (not that flushing the buffer cache in and of itself can't cause some short-term mayhem of its own!).

Oracle Database 10*g* now allows you to flush the database buffer cache with the **alter system** command using the **flush buffer_cache** parameter, as shown in this example:

```
Alter system flush buffer_cache;
```

NOTE
There is a huge difference of opinion in the Oracle world if this functionality is really all that worthwhile. I'd be interested in hearing from you if it has made a difference in your life as a DBA.

Database Resource Manager New Features

The Database Resource Manager in Oracle Database 10*g* offers a few new features that enable you to do the following:

■ Revert to the original consumer group at the end of an operation that caused a change of consumer groups

■ Set idle timeout values for consumer groups

■ Create mappings for the automatic assignment of sessions to specific consumer groups

Each of these topics is discussed, in turn, in more detail in the following sections.

Reverting Back to the Original Consumer Group

Prior to Oracle Database 10*g*, if a SQL call caused a session to be put into a different consumer group (for example, because a long-running query exceeded a SWITCH_TIME directive value in the consumer group), then that session would remain assigned to the new resource group until it was ended. The new SWITCH_TIME_IN_CALL directive is much like the SWITCH_TIME directive in that it specifices the number of seconds that a given session should execute before the consumer group is changed. However, when using the SWITCH_TIME_IN_CALL directive, the session will be reverted back to the original consumer group once the top call has completed.

This is very useful for n-tier applications that create a pool of sessions in the database for clients to share. Previously, after the consumer group had been changed, all subsequent connections would be penalized based on the settings of the consumer group resource plan. The new SWITCH_TIME_IN_CALL directive allows the session to be reset, thus eliminating the impact to future sessions. Here is an example of the use of this new feature:

```
EXEC DBMS_RESOURCE_MANAGER.CREATE_PLAN_DIRECTIVE(PLAN => 'main_plan',
GROUP_OR_SUBPLAN => 'goonline', COMMENT => 'Online sessions', CPU_P1 => 80,
SWITCH_GROUP => 'ad-hoc', SWITCH_ESTIMATE => TRUE,
SWITCH_TIME_IN_CALL=>30);
```

In this case, I have created a plan directive that is a part of an overall plan called MAIN_PLAN. This particular plan directive is designed to limit the impact of online ad-hoc users (or perhaps applications that are throwing out a great deal of dynamic

SQL that's hard to tune) if they issue queries that take a long time (in this example, 30 seconds). This directive causes a switch to a consumer group called ad-hoc, which would likely further limit CPU and might also provide for an overall run-time limit on executions in this particular plan/resource group. Since I have included the SWITCH_TIME_IN_CALL directive in this plan directive, the consumer group will revert back to the original plan after the completion of the long-running operation.

NOTE
SWITCH_TIME_IN_CALL and SWITCH_TIME are mutually exclusive parameters.

Setting the Idle Timeout

Oracle Database 10*g* allows you to limit the maximum time that a session is allowed to remain idle. The **max_idle_time** parameter allows you to define a maximum amount of time that a given session can sit idle. PMON will check the session once a minute and kill any session assigned to that resource group that has been idle for the amount of time defined in the plan. So, how is this different from the use of idle times in profiles? Well, it's useful if you sign in to an account that by default you don't want to have idle times assigned to. Perhaps it's only if you switch to a specific group or plan that you want to assign an idle timeout. The **max_idle_time** parameter allows you to do this. Here is an example:

```
EXEC DBMS_RESOURCE_MANAGER.CREATE_PLAN_DIRECTIVE(PLAN => 'main_plan',
GROUP_OR_SUBPLAN => 'online', max_idle_time=>300,
comment=> 'Set max_idle_time');
```

Creating Mappings for Automatic Assignment of Sessions to Consumer Groups

The **dbms_resource_manager.set_consumer_group_mapping** procedure allows you to map a specific consumer group to a given session based on either login or run-time attributes. These attributes include

- The username
- The service name
- The client OS username
- The client program name
- The client machine

- The module name

- The module name action

You then have to determine what session attributes you want to map to a given consumer group. In this example, I have mapped the client machine called *tiger* to the resource consumer group LOW_PRIORITY:

```
Exec dbms_resource_manager.set_consumer_group_mapping
(DBMS_RESOURCE_MANAGER.CLIENT_MACHINE,'tiger','low_priority');
```

Thus, if anyone logs in to the database from the machine named tiger, they will be assigned to the consumer group LOW_PRIORITY, which will have already been created.

Often, a number of mappings apply to a given session, so a priority has to be defined. This is done by using the procedure **dbms_resource_manager.set_ consumer_group_mapping_pri**. This example creates two mappings:

```
Dbms_resource_manager.set_consumer_group_mapping
(DBMS_RESOURCE_MANAGER.CLIENT_MACHINE, 'tiger','low_priority');
Dbms_resource_manager.set_consumer_group_mapping
(DBMS_RESOURCE_MANAGER.ORACLE_USER, 'NUMBER_ONE','high_priority');
```

In this case, anyone signing in from tiger is assigned to the LOW_PRIORITY consumer group, but where will the user NUMBER_ONE be assigned? Well, right now it's hard to tell. So, to make sure that NUMBER_ONE is always set to be assigned to the high-priority resource consumer group, I can use the provided procedure called **dbms_ resource_manager.set_consumer_group_mapping_pri**:

```
Dbms_resource_manager.set_consumer_group_mapping_pri(ORACLE_USER=>1,
CLIENT_MACHINE=>2, EXPLICIT=>3, MODULE_NAME=>4, SERVICE_NAME=>5,
CLIENT_OS_USER=>6, CLIENT_PROGRAM=>7, MODULE_NAME_ACTION=>8,
SERVICE_MODULE=>9, SERVICE_MODULE_ACTION=>10);
```

This code will cause Oracle to prioritize consumer group selection based first on username and then on the client machine name. So, now the user NUMBER_ONE will always get the higher-priority consumer group assignment.

Be aware that regardless of consumer group assignments, a user must still be given switching privileges into a given consumer group. If the user has not been granted such privileges, then sessions will not be switched.

Scheduler Changes

Oracle Database 10*g* offers a brand-new job-scheduling facility, known as The Scheduler. The Scheduler is controlled via the new Oracle Database 10*g*–supplied package **dbms_scheduler**. This package replaces the **dbms_job** package that has been around for some time.

Overview of The Scheduler

The new Scheduler offers much added functionality over the **dbms_job** package. The Scheduler enables you to execute a variety of stored code (such as PL/SQL), a native binary executable, and shell scripts. The object that is being run by The Scheduler is known as the *program*. The program is more than just the name; it includes related metadata about the program, such as the arguments to be passed to it and the type of program that is being run.

Different users can use a program at different times, eliminating the need to have to redefine the program every time you wish to schedule a job. Programs can be stored in *program libraries,* which allows for easy reuse of program code by other users.

Each program, when scheduled, is assigned to a *job.* A job can also just contain an anonymous PL/SQL block instead of a program. The job is a combination of the program (or anonymous PL/SQL block) and the schedule associated with the program, which defines when the job is to run. Also associated with the job is other metadata related to the job, such as the job class and the window or window group.

The *job class* is a category of jobs that share various characteristics, such as resource consumer group assignments and assignments to a common, specific, service name. The job class is related to the job window.

The job *window*, or *window group,* essentially allows the job to take advantage of specific resource plans. For example, if the schedule for a job is for it to run every hour, the job window will allow it to run under one resource group in the morning and a different resource group in the evening. That way, you can control the resources the job can consume at different times throughout the day.

Oracle provides two different interfaces into The Scheduler. The first is the **dbms_scheduler** package and the second is through the Oracle Enterprise Manager (OEM).

Practical Use of The Scheduler

There are a few steps to follow when you want to assign a job to The Scheduler:

- Create the program (optional)
- Create the job

Creating a Program in The Scheduler

Creating a program is the optional first step when creating a scheduled operation. This operation may actually take four steps:

1. Create the program itself.

2. Define the program arguments.

3. Create the job.

4. Define job arguments.

The following sections explain each of these steps in turn.

Creating the Program   To create a program, so that you can schedule it, you use the PL/SQL-supplied procedure **dbms_scheduler.create_program**. To use this package in your own schema, you must have the **create job** privilege. To use it to create jobs in other schemas, you need the **create any job** privilege. By default, a program is created in a disabled state (which can be overridden by setting the **enabled** parameter of the **create_program** procedure to TRUE). First, let's look at the definition of the **dbms_scheduler.create_program** procedure:

```
DBMS_SCHEDULER.CREATE_PROGRAM (
program_name IN VARCHAR2,
program_type IN VARCHAR2,
program_action IN VARCHAR2,
number_of_arguments IN BINARY_INTEGER DEFAULT 0,
enabled IN BOOLEAN DEFAULT FALSE,
comments IN VARCHAR2 DEFAULT NULL);
```

It always helps to know what the various parameters are used for, of course, so let's look at a description of the parameters for the **create_program** procedure:

Parameter Name	Description
program_name	Identifies the name of the program. This is an internally assigned name, which represents the **program_action** that will be executed.
program_type	Identifies the type of executable being scheduled. Currently, the following are valid values: PLSQL_ BLOCK, STORED_PROCEDURE, and EXECUTABLE.
program_action	Indicates the procedure, executable name, or PL/SQL anonymous block associated with the program.

Parameter Name	Description
number_of_arguments	Identifies the number of arguments required for the program (ignored if **program_type** is PLSQL_BLOCK).
enabled	Indicates whether the program should be enabled when created.
comments	Allows freeform comments describing the program or what it does.

Here are some examples of the creation of programs:

```
BEGIN
  dbms_scheduler.create_program(
   program_name => 'delete_records',
   program_action => '/opt/oracle/maint/bin/nightly_delete_records.sh',
   program_type => 'EXECUTABLE', number_of_arguments=>2);
END;
```

In this example, I am creating a program called delete_records. It is an external executable, a shell script in this case. The program is located in /opt/oracle/maint/bin and is called nightly_delete_records.sh. Note that Oracle does not check for the existence of the program when the **create_program** procedure is executed. Thus, you can create your program even if the underlying executable doesn't exist.

You can create a program for an anonymous PL/SQL block as well, as demonstrated in this example:

```
BEGIN
      dbms_scheduler.create_program(
         program_name => 'sp_delete_records',
         program_action => 'DECLARE
                            rec_count    number;
                          BEGIN
                          DELETE FROM old_records
                          WHERE record_date < sysdate - 5;
                          rec_count:=sqlcommand%ROWCOUNT;
                          insert into records_removed
                             (date, table, how_many, job_ran) VALUES
                             (sysdate, ''OLD_RECORDS'', rec_count,
                              scheduler$_job_start);
                          COMMIT;
                          END;',
         program_type => 'EXECUTABLE');
END;
```

In the case of this anonymous block, I used one of several Oracle-supplied special variable names in my code (in this case, scheduler$_job_start). These variables are described briefly in the following table:

Variable Name	Description
scheduler$_job_name	Provides the name of the job being executed
scheduler$_job_owner	Provides the name of the owner of the job
scheduler$_job_start	Provides the start time of the job
scheduler$_window_start	Indicates the start time of the window associated with the job
scheduler$_window_end	Indicates the end time of the window associated with the job

OEM also provides an interface to create programs that you can use, if you prefer that method.

You can drop a program with the **dbms_scheduler.drop_program** procedure, as shown in this example:

```
Exec dbms_scheduler.drop_program('delete_records');
```

Defining the Program Arguments   Many programs have arguments (aka parameters) that need to be included when that program is called. You can associate arguments with a program by using the **dbms_scheduler.define_program_argument** procedure. Using the previous program example, delete_records, I can add some arguments to the program as follows:

```
BEGIN
dbms_scheduler.define_program_argument(
program_name => 'delete_records',
argument_name => 'delete_date',
argument_position=>1, argument_type=>'date',
default_value=> 'to_char(sysdate - 5, ''mm/dd/yyyy'')'  );
end;
/
```

To be able to call this program, you need the **alter any job** or **create any job** privilege. Additionally, calling this program does not change the state of the associated job (enabled or disabled). You can replace an argument by simply calling the **define_program_argument** procedure and replacing an existing argument position.

Creating a Job in The Scheduler

To actually get The Scheduler to do something, which is kind of the idea, you need to create a job. The job can either run a program that you have created (refer to the previous section) or run its own job, which is defined when the job is defined. The job consists of these principle definitions:

- **The schedule**   This is when the job is supposed to do whatever it's supposed to do. The schedule consists of a start time, an end time, and an expression that indicates the frequency of job repetition.

- **The associated job argument**   This is what the job is supposed to do. This can be a pre-created PL/SQL or Java program, anonymous PL/SQL, or even an external executable (for example, a shell script or C program call).

- **Other metadata associated with the job**   This includes such things as the job's class and priority, job-related comments, and the job's restartability.

Creating the Job   Jobs are created with the **dbms_scheduler.create_job** package, as shown in this example:

```
Exec dbms_scheduler.create_job(
      job_name=>'CLEAR_DAILY',
      job_type=>'STORED_PROCEDURE',
      job_action=>'JOBS.SP_CLEAR_DAILY',
      start_date=>NULL,
      repeat_interval=>'TRUNC(SYSDATE) + 1/24',
      comments=>'Hourly Clearout Job');
```

This example creates a scheduled job that executes immediately and then runs every hour thereafter. This job is assigned a name called CLEAR_DAILY. When The Scheduler runs the job, a PL/SQL stored procedure called **sp_clear_daily** is executed.

Perhaps another example is in order. In this case, I will create a scheduled job that fires off an external shell script:

```
Exec dbms_scheduler.create_job(
      job_name=>'RUN_BACKUP',
      job_type=>'EXECUTABLE',
      job_action=>'/opt/oracle/admin/jobs/run_job.sh',
      start_date=>to_date('04-30-2003 20:00:00', 'mm-dd-yyyy hh24:mi:ss'),
      repeat_interval=>'TRUNC(SYSDATE) + 23/24',   -
      comments=>'Daily Backup');
```

The **repeat_interval** attribute defines how often and when the job will repeat. If the **repeat_interval** is NULL (the default), the job executes only one time and then is removed.

When determining the interval, you have two options. First, you can use the older PL/SQL time expressions for defining the program execution intervals. Second, Oracle Database 10*g* offers a new feature, Calendar Expressions, which you can use in lieu of the old PL/SQL time expressions. There are three different types of components: the frequency (which is mandatory), the specifier, and the interval. Frequencies indicate how often the job should run. The following frequencies are available:

Yearly	Monthly	Weekly	Daily
Hourly	Minutely	Secondly	

Additional parameters, the specifier and interval, define in more detail how frequently the job should run.

Here are some examples of the use of Calendar Expressions:

```
"FREQ=YEARLY;BYMONTH=SEP;BYMONTHDAY=30"
```

This will cause your job to execute once a year on September 30th (my birthday!).

```
"FREQ=YEARLY;BYWEEKNO=2"
```

This will cause the job to execute every year, only in week two (for example, around the second week in January).

There are a large number of permutations possible when using Calendar Expressions. More detail on Calendar Expressions can be found in the *PL/SQL Packages and Types Reference for Oracle Database 10*g under the documentation page for the DBMS_SCHEDULER package.

Defining the Job Arguments   If you are scheduling a job that is not associated with a program, then that job may be a program that accepts arguments. If this is the case, you need to use the **dbms_scheduler.set_job_argument_value** procedure. Executing this procedure will not enable or disable any given job. Here is an example of setting some parameters for a job. In this case, I am indicating to the RUN_BACKUP job that it should include an argument of 'TABLESPACE USERS', which might indicate that the backup job should back up the users tablespace.

```
exec dbms_scheduler.set_job_argument_value
( job_name =>'RUN_BACKUP',
  argument_name=>'BACKUP_JOB_ARG1',
  argument_value=>'TABLESPACE USERS');
```

Other Job Scheduler Functionality

The Scheduler also allows you to define *job classes,* which allow you to define a category of jobs that share common resource usage requirements and other characteristics. One job can belong to only one job class, though you can change the job class that a given job is assigned to. Any defined job class can belong to a single resource consumer group, and to a single service at any given time.

Job classes, then, allow you to assign jobs of different priorities. For example, administrative jobs (such as backups) might be assigned to an administrative class that is assigned to a resource group that allows for unconstrained activity. Other jobs, with a lesser priority, may be assigned to job classes that are assigned to resource groups that constrain the overall operational overhead of the job, so that those jobs do not inordinately interfere with other, higher-priority jobs. Thus, job classes help you to manage the amount of resources that a given job can consume.

To create a job class, you use the **dbms_scheduler.create_job_class** procedure. All classes belong to the SYS schema, and to create one requires the **manage scheduler** privilege. Here is an example of defining a job class:

```
exec dbms_scheduler.create_job_class(
job_class_name=>'CLASS_ADMIN',
resource_consumer_group=>'ADMIN_JOBS',
service=>'SERVICE_B');
```

This job class will be called CLASS_ADMIN. It is assigned to a resource consumer group (that will have already been created) called ADMIN_JOBS, which will no doubt give administrative jobs pretty unfettered access to resources. This job class is also assigned to a specific service, SERVICE_B, so the administrator can define which service the job class is associated with.

Once the job class is defined, you can define which jobs are members of that class when you create the jobs. Alternatively, you can use the **dbms_scheduler.set_attribute** procedure to assign an existing job to that class.

User-Configurable Default Tablespaces

Oracle Database 10*g* offers user-configurable default tablespaces. Use the **alter database set default tablespace** command to configure this new feature. Once a new default tablespace is configured, all new users will be assigned to that tablespace rather than the SYSTEM tablespace. Here is an example of configuring a default tablespace with the **alter database** command:

```
Alter database set default tablespace users;
```

Tablespace Groups and Multiple Default Temporary Tablespaces

Oracle Database 10*g* now allows you to define tablespace groups, which are logical groupings of tablespaces. This further allows you to assign temporary tablespaces to those groups, and then assign those tablespace groups as the default temporary tablespace for the database. In essence, tablespace groups allow you to combine temporary tablespaces into one tablespace pool that is available for use to the database.

Assigning Temporary Tablespaces to Tablespace Groups

You can assign a temporary tablespace to a tablespace group in one of two ways. First, you can assign it to a tablespace group when you create the tablespace via the **create tablespace** command. Second, you can add a tablespace to a tablespace group via the **alter tablespace** command. An example of each of these operations is listed next (note that OMF is configured in this example):

```
Create temporary tablespace temp_tbs_01 tablespace group tbs_group_01;
alter tablespace temp_tbs_01 tablespace group tbs_group_02;
```

There is no limit to the number of tablespaces that can be assigned to a tablespace group. The tablespace group shares the same namespace as normal tablespaces, so tablespace names and tablespace group names are mutually exclusive. You can also remove a tablespace from a group by using the **alter tablespace** command and using empty quotes as an argument to the **tablespace group** parameter, as shown in this example:

```
Alter tablespace temp3 tablespace group '';
```

Defining a Tablespace Group as the Default Temporary Tablespace

After you have created the tablespace group and assigned a set of tablespaces to that group, you can assign that group of temporary tablespaces (or that tablespace group) as the default temporary tablespace for the system, or as a temporary tablespace group for specific users.

You can do this in the **create database** statement when you create the database, or you can use the **alter database** statement to modify the temporary tablespace settings. Using either statement, you simply define the tablespace group as the default tablespace, as shown in this example:

```
Alter database default temporary tablespace tbs_group_01;
```

This has the effect of assigning multiple tablespaces as the default temporary tablespace. Once you have assigned a tablespace group as the default temporary tablespace group, you cannot drop any tablespace in that group.

Jonathan Says...
Given the introduction of "bigfile" tablespaces (with a maximum size of 8 exabytes, or roughly 8 million terabytes), you have to wonder if there is something more subtle going on here than the declared intention of making more space available for sorting, etc. So, if having multiple tablespaces is good for temporary space, are there some types of systems whose characteristic activity means they should not use "bigfile" tablespaces?

So, now you can define more than a single tablespace as the database default temporary tablespace; as a result, larger SQL operations can use more than one tablespace for sort operations, thereby reducing the risk of running out of space. This also provides more tablespace space, and potentially better I/O distribution for sort operations and parallel slave operations that use temporary tablespaces. If a tablespace group is defined as the default temporary tablespace, then no tablespaces in that group can be dropped until that assignment has been changed.

You can assign a user to a tablespace group that might not be the default tablespace group either in the **create user** or **alter user** statements, as shown in these examples that assign the TBS_GROUP_01 tablespace to the user NO_PS:

```
Create user no_ps identified by gonesville
default tablespace dflt_ts temporary tablespace tbs_group_01;

alter user no_ps temporary tablespace tbs_group_01;
```

Tablespace Group Data Dictionary View

A new view, DBA_TABLESPACE_GROUPS, is available to associate specific temporary tablespaces with tablespace groups. The TEMPORARY_TABLESPACE column of the ALL, USER, and DBA _USERS views will report either the temporary tablespace name or the temporary tablespace group name that is assigned to the user. Here is an example of a query that joins the DBA_USERS and DBA_TABLESPACE_GROUPS views and gives you a list of users who are assigned a tablespace group as their temporary tablespace name, and all the tablespaces that are associated with that group:

```
Select a.username, a.temporary_tablespace, b.tablespace_name
from dba_users a, dba_tablespace_groups b
Where a.temporary_tablespace in (select distinct group_name from
dba_tablespace_groups);
```

Renaming Tablespaces

You have been asking for it, I have been asking for it, and now it's here! Oracle Database 10g includes the ability to rename tablespaces. You use the **alter tablespace** command with the **rename to** parameter, as shown in this example:

```
Alter tablespace production_tbs rename to prod_tbs;
```

Note that you cannot rename the SYSTEM tablespace or the SYSAUX tablespace (refer to Chapter 1). Another nice feature is that if the tablespace is an UNDO tablespace, and you are using a server parameter file (SPFILE), Oracle will change the UNDO_TABLESPACE parameter in the SPFILE to reflect the new UNDO tablespace name.

The ability to rename tablespaces has some great practical applications with operations such as transportable tablespaces. Now, rather than having to drop the existing tablespace before you can transport it in, you only need rename that tablespace. Way to go Oracle!

Something to be aware of is that renaming a tablespace does not change the name of the datafile in any way. For example, OMF uses the name of the tablespace (or part of it) in the OMF datafile naming scheme, and frequently DBAs do the same when they manually create a tablespace datafile. Renaming the tablespace will result in the datafiles no longer reflecting the true name of the tablespace.

CAUTION
You should back up the control file as soon as possible after renaming tablespaces within the database. If you do not, depending on when the backup of the control file took place, a divergence may exist between the tablespace names in the control file and the actual tablespace names in the database. Refer to the Oracle Database 10g documentation for more details on specific recovery scenario responses.

Dropping Databases

The **drop database** command can be used to drop your database. Oracle will drop the database, deleting all control files and all datafiles listed in the control file. If you are using a SPFILE, then Oracle will remove it as well. Only a user with SYSDBA privileges can issue the statement and the database must be mounted (not open) in exclusive and restricted mode. Here is an example of the use of the **drop database** command:

```
Drop database;
```

NOTE
*RMAN also has a new **drop database** command in Oracle Database 10g!*

Larger LOBs

If you use LOBs in your database (NCLOB, BLOB, or CLOB), then you will be happy to know that the limits on LOBs have been increased in Oracle Database 10*g*. The new maximum limits are calculated at (4GB − 1 byte) * (the database block size). Thus, if the database block size is 8KB, there is essentially a 32GB limitation on LOBs in that database. Note that Bfiles are limited to 4GB in size. Load 'em up folks, it's ready to rumble!

Automatic Undo Retention

Oracle Database 10*g* no longer requires that you configure the UNDO_RETENTION parameter. The database now makes a best effort to configure the retention of Undo based on database usage if UNDO_RETENTION is set to 0, which is the default. When automatic Undo retention is enabled, Oracle will never set UNDO_RETENTION to a value of 15 minutes or less.

Shrinking and Compacting Segments Online

Oracle Database 10*g* now allows you to manually shrink the overall size of a table, removing unused space. This feature, combined with the ability to compact the segment and adjust the high-water mark all at the same time, can result in great space savings. This all can occur online, and the recovered space will be released to the database after the operation is complete. You can optionally compact the segment and then shrink it, in two separate **alter** operations. Most Oracle segment types can be shrunk and/or compacted, including tables (partitioned or not), index-organized tables (IOTs), and indexes. Here is an example of shrinking and compacting a table with the **alter table** clause:

```
Alter table my_table shrink space cascade;
```

Note the use of the **cascade** option, which causes all dependent objects (e.g., indexes) to be shrunk as well.

Another thing to know is that before you can shrink a heap-organized segment, you must enable row movement on that segment with the **alter table enable row**

movement command. The **cascade** option can also extend to overflow segments of nonpartitioned or partitioned IOTs. You cannot shrink the following objects:

- Tables that are in clusters
- Any table with a Long column
- A table with an on-commit materialized view
- Any table with a ROWID-based materialized view
- A LOB index
- IOT mapping tables and IOT overflow segments
- Shared LOB segments
- Temporary and Undo segments

The shrink operation actually takes part in two stages. The first stage is the compaction of the data in the table. The second stage is the dropping of the high-water mark located in the table. You can perform just the compaction of the data if you like by using the **compact** clause of the **alter** command, as shown in this example:

```
Alter table my_table shrink space cascade compact;
```

NOTE
Shrinking/compacting of a table or an IOT is the same as coalescing that object.

Using New Online Redefinition Features

Oracle9*i* introduced the ability to rebuild an Oracle table online, reducing outages associated with rebuild operations. Oracle Database 10*g* improves on this functionality. First, Oracle Database 10*g* allows you to redefine tables with CLOB and BLOB data types (but not BFILE). Also, master-master replicated tables can now be redefined online, within a somewhat restrictive set of limitations. Finally, you can now instruct Oracle on how to order the rows when you perform the initial instantiation of the interim table through the use of the **orderby_col**s parameter when the **dbms_redefinition.start_redef_table** procedure is called.

CHAPTER
3

Performance Tuning

- Improvements to the Wait Interface
- The Database Common Management Infrastructure
- Automatic SGA Tuning
- Self-Tuning Checkpointing
- New Oracle Database 10*g* Trace Functionality
- Sorted Hash Clusters
- Shared Server Changes

racle Database 10*g* comes with a number of new features that are designed to provide enhanced performance of the Oracle RDBMS. In this chapter we will cover these features, which include

- Improvements to the wait interface
- The Database Common Management Infrastructure
- The SQL Access Advisor
- SQL Query tuning enhancements
- Automated SGA tuning
- Object growth trending
- Self-tuning checkpointing
- Sorted hash clusters

Improvements to the Wait Interface

Oracle 10*g* offers a number of new and improved database views to assist you in your performance-tuning efforts. The performance-related database views that have been improved through changes include the following:

- V$EVENT_NAME
- V$SESSION
- V$SESSION_WAIT

New views include

- V$SESSION_WAIT_HISTORY
- V$SESSION_WAIT_CLASS
- V$SYSTEM_WAIT_CLASS

Also new in Oracle Database 10*g* are the histogram views V$EVENT_HISTOGRAM, V$TEMP_HISTOGRAM, and V$FILE_HISTOGRAM. Let's look at each of these in more detail next.

Changes to the V$EVENT_NAME View

The V$EVENT_NAME view has had two new columns added to it that allow you to aggregate wait events based on the type of wait being experienced. The WAIT_CLASS column provides a generalized class type for each event. The WAIT_CLASS# column provides a class number that is associated with the class name in the WAIT_CLASS column. For example, Oracle provides event wait classes such as commit-related waits, idle waits, network waits, and I/O-related waits. Here is an example of a query using the new WAIT_CLASS column:

```
SQL > select a.wait_class, sum(b.time_waited)/1000000 time_waited
  2   from v$event_name a, v$system_event b
  3   where a.name=b.event
  4   group by a.wait_class;

WAIT_CLASS           TIME_WAITED
-------------------- -----------
Application           28.983892
Commit                  .096933
Concurrency             .407526
Configuration          1.334352
Idle                  6121.551
Network                1.087704
Other                  7.124999
System I/O             9.055124
User I/O               5.189134
```

This query indicates that application wait events are causing the largest number of waits (after idle events, which are typically ignored). Thus, after running this query, you could drill down into these wait events and try to determine what the cause of the problem is.

New Wait Information in V$SESSION

V$SESSION contains new information on wait events that eliminates the need to join it and V$SESSION_WAIT to get session-specific wait information. New columns include EVENT#, EVENT, P1TEXT, P1, P1RAW, P2TEXT, P2, P2RAW, P3TEXT, P3, P3RAW, and SECONDS_IN_WAIT. Here is an example of a query against V$SESSION using these new columns:

```
SQL> select sid, serial#, event, (seconds_in_wait/1000000) SIW
  2   from v$session
  3   where sid in (13,14,21,23)
  3   order by sid;
      SID    SERIAL# EVENT                                        SIW
---------- ---------- ------------------------------- ----------
       13      28755 SQL*Net message from client          .000001
       14          7 buffer busy waits                  1.648113
       21      51898 jobq slave wait                      .000049
       23      55125 jobq slave wait                      .000111
```

In this example, you can see that SID 14 seems to be currently waiting on a buffer busy wait event. If this problem continues, you might wish to investigate the problem more closely.

Jonathan Says...
Although this is a nice example of Oracle producing something that will be very useful, it is also a demonstration of how you can, on occasion, do better by digging under the V$ to look at the X$.

V$SESSION and V$SESSION_WAIT are the same internal memory structure—and the new improved V$SESSION in Oracle Database 10*g* simply exposes some of the structure types that were there all the time. But why does V$SESSION now do an internal join to X$KSLED to pick up the event names—every per-existing query against V$SESSION just got more expensive!

I think it would be perfectly legitimate to produce your own version of V$SESSION that skips the join, and reports the wait by number.

Using V$SESSION to Find Blocking Sessions

New columns in V$SESSION allow you to easily identify sessions that are blocking other sessions. V$SESSION has a new column called BLOCKING_SESSION that contains the SID of any session that is blocking the session in the row. Also, the BLOCKING_SESSION_STATUS column provides the status of the blocking status.

The V$SESSION_WAIT_HISTORY View

The waits in V$SESSION_WAIT are fleeting and hard to catch. Oracle Database 10*g* offers a new view, V$SESSION_WAIT_HISTORY, that provides a history of the last ten wait events for each active session. These wait events can be sorted in the order that they have occurred via the SEQ# column.

V$SESSION_WAIT_CLASS and V$SYSTEM_WAIT_CLASS Views

The new V$SESSION_WAIT_CLASS and the V$SYSTEM_WAIT_CLASS views provide wait information about the new Oracle Database 10*g* wait classes. The V$SYSTEM_WAIT_CLASS view provides class waits for the system as a whole, and the V$SESSION_WAIT_CLASS view provides wait class details at the session level.

New Histogram Views

Three new views provide histogram-related data for wait events. These are the V$EVENT_HISTOGRAM, V$FILE_HISTOGRAM, and V$TEMP_HISTOGRAM views. Each contains numerous buckets that provide detailed information. Let's look at each of these views in a bit more detail next.

V$EVENT_HISTOGRAM

The V$EVENT_HISTOGRAM view provides a number of buckets that contain wait events that are summarized into several time-related buckets for each event, based on the time that they occurred. The amount of time that each bucket represents is found in the WAIT_TIME_MILLI column, thus you can order on that column to display the wait events in the order that they occur.

V$FILE_HISTOGRAM

The V$FILE_HISTOGRAM view provides a number of buckets that contain datafile block read times that are summarized into several time-related buckets for each block read and how long that read occurred. The amount of time (in milliseconds) that each bucket represents is found in the SINGLEBLKRDTIME_MILLI column.

V$TEMP_HISTOGRAM

The V$TEMP_HISTOGRAM view provides a number of buckets that contain tempfile block read times that are summarized into several time-related buckets for each block read and how long that read occurred. The amount of time (in milliseconds) that each bucket represents is found in the SINGLEBLKRDTIME_MILLI column.

The Database Common Management Infrastructure

It was a challenge to decide whether the new Oracle Database 10*g* Common Management Infrastructure (CMI) features belong in this chapter or in Chapter 2 on manageability, or even in Chapter 1 with the introduction of the Grid. Since the biggest benefit of these new features ultimately results in performance benefits, I decided to introduce these new features here. The CMI consists of various components, and I will discuss the new architecture first in this section.

CMI Architecture Overview

Oracle Database 10*g* offers assistance in performance tuning (and monitoring) of the database through the new Oracle Database 10*g* Common Management Infrastructure. This infrastructure involves several different architectural components that are brought together to make Oracle Database 10*g* perform better and to make it easier to manage. The following are the main components of the CMI:

- The Automatic Workload Repository (AWR) enables Oracle Database 10*g* to collect and store performance-related statistics. Additionally, the AWR provides services to process and maintain that information.

■ Server-based advisors are used to assist the DBA in identifying various database problems. They are used to automatically detect database problems and then provide recommendations on correcting the problem.

■ Automated administrative tasks are supported through The Scheduler as a part of the CMI framework.

■ Server-generated alerts are a part of the new Oracle Database 10*g* CMI framework. Now, Oracle Database 10*g* can send you alerts when database problems occur.

Let's look at each of these elements of the CMI framework in a bit more detail.

The Automatic Workload Repository

The AWR is more than just a bunch of tables in the database. It is an infrastructure unto itself. In addition to collecting and storing database statistics, it is also used to detect database problems and for database self-tuning.

The main job of the AWR is to help relieve you of having to spend your time capturing historical data and interpreting that database data (assuming, of course, that the AWR is always right!). The AWR does this by providing a permanent repository for historical database performance data. The AWR allows for smoother analysis of performance problems, since the data it stores is historical. It also allows for important database trend analysis operations so that you can manage database performance issues and identify not only current database problems but also potential lurking database problems.

The AWR infrastructure (see Figure 3-1) consists of the following components:

■ The in-memory statistics collection area

■ The workload repository

■ New Oracle processes

■ Clients of the AWR

The In-Memory Statistics Collection Area

The AWR initially collects statistics and stores those statistics in the database SGA. The size of the SGA memory allocation varies by the number of CPUs and the operating system that is being used. Typical memory use is between 1 to 2MB per CPU. The total size of the AWR memory area cannot exceed a value greater than 5 percent of the setting of the parameter SHARED_POOL_SIZE.

The AWR memory structure is also known as the in-memory statistics collection facility, and the statistics resident in this area are known as base statistics. Many of the previous Oracle Database statistics (but not all) have been converted to use the new AWR repository. Some or all of the columns of the dynamic performance views,

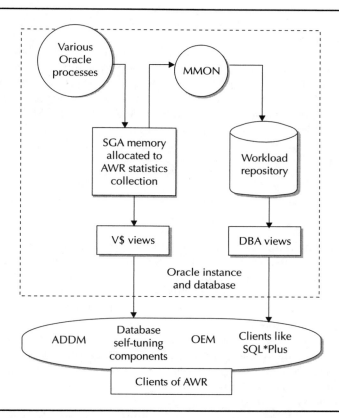

FIGURE 3-1. *AWR infrastructure diagram*

such as V$SYSSTAT, V$SESSTAT, V$SQL, and V$SEGMENT_STATISTICS, provide a view into the memory areas of the AWR. Also, new Oracle Database 10*g* views, such as VSYS_TIME_MODEL, VOSSTAT, V$EVENT_NAME, V$SYSMETRIC_HISTORY, and V$ACTIVE_SESSION_HISTORY, also use the new AWR in-memory statistics facility.

The Workload Repository

The workload repository (WR) component of the AWR provides the persistent statistical data that the AWR requires for analysis of historical data. The SYS user owns the workload repository. The data in this schema is stored in the new Oracle Database 10*g* tablespace called SYSAUX (refer to Chapter 1). The size of the workload repository is related to the number of CPUs on your system as well as the retention period of your snapshots. Typically, for a four-CPU system, you can expect to use 200 to 300MB of disk space for the workload repository.

Jonathan Says...
If at this point you are asking yourself how much of an overhead this might be on your system, you are asking the right question. A dump of the active session history (which may be the most extreme, although the dumps of VSQL, VSQL_PLAN, or V$SQL_BIND are possible contenders for that title) consists of 30 minutes' worth of every tenth row from V$ACTIVE_SESSION_HISTORY—that's 180 rows per session, and the rows aren't small.

The benefits of having this information are enormous if you need it. The cost on a very large system could be more than you could afford unless you adjust the control parameters carefully.

Statistics stored in memory are flushed to the workload repository every 30 minutes (which is configurable and can be turned off) or when the in-memory statistics collection area becomes full. As the statistics are flushed to the WR, an identifier is assigned to that set of collected statistics. Also, manual snapshots (much like those taken with statspack) are supported as well through the use of the **dbms_workload_repository** stored procedure.

Oracle Database 10*g* also takes care of WR housekeeping issues on a nightly basis with an automated cleanup process. By default, all snapshots over seven days old will be removed by this process. This default can be changed easily through the use of the stored procedure **dbms_workload_repository.modify_snapshot_settings**, which is covered later in this section.

Data in the workload repository is visible through several tables. The tables are prefixed with WR{M|H}, where WRM$ tables are used to store metadata information and the WRH$ tables are used to store historical data and snapshots. Also, Oracle Database 10*g* provides several DBA_HIST_* tables that provide historical views into the workload repository.

Baselines in the Workload Repository   You can create a baseline set of snapshots in the workload repository. Baselines are recorded in the database view DBA_HIST_BASELINE, and can be removed with the **dbms_workload_repository.drop_baseline** procedure (which is covered next). Baselines are used to set thresholds for the server alert mechanism in the AWR.

Managing the Workload Repository   Oracle Database 10*g* provides the **dbms_workload_repository** procedure to manage the workload repository. Using this procedure, you can do the following:

■ Create and remove baselines in the workload repository

■ Drop a range of snapshots

- Create a manual snapshot

- Modify settings related to WR population and data retention

Let's look at some examples of the use of this procedure. First, let's use the procedure to manage the interval at which snapshots are moved into the workload repository. As stated earlier in this chapter, by default, a snapshot occurs every 30 minutes. Suppose that you prefer that the snapshot occur every 15 minutes. Using the **dbms_workload_repository.modify_snapshot_settings** procedure, through the use of the **interval** parameter, you can set the interval at which snapshots are taken to 15 minutes, as shown in this example:

```
Exec dbms_workload_repository.modify_snapshot_settings -
(interval=>15);
```

You also can control the cleanout of snapshots in the workload repository through the use of the same procedure, as shown in this example:

```
Exec dbms_workload_repository.modify_snapshot_settings -
(retention=>43200);
```

In this case, retention is set to 30 days (60 minutes * 24 hours * 30 days). You can determine the current settings by using the new DBA_HIST_WR_CONTROL table. Oracle will allow you to retain workload repository records from between 1440 minutes and 52560000 minutes.

You can also opt to drop a range of snapshots, if you choose, using the **dbms_workload_repository.drop_snapshot_range** procedure, as shown in this example:

```
exec dbms_workload_repository.drop_snapshot_range(60, 100);
```

In this case, snapshots 60 through 100 will be removed from the WR.

If you have a baseline established, you can opt to remove it by using the procedure **dbms_workload_repository.drop_baseline**. Note that by default this procedure does not remove the underlying snapshots of the baseline, unless you use the **cascade** parameter of the stored procedure. Here is an example of the use of this procedure:

```
Exec dbms_workload_repository.drop_baseline -
(baseline_name=>'Initial');
```

During testing operations, you may want to create a manual snapshot rather than wait for the database to perform that action for you. The **dbms_workload_repository.create_snapshot** stored procedure allows you to do this, as demonstrated here:

```
Exec Dbms_workload_repository.create_snapshot();
```

Note that once a snapshot is created (manually or automatically), it will be visible in the DBA_HIST_SNAPSHOT table.

NOTE
Oracle Enterprise Manager (OEM) allows you to configure the snapshot and collection intervals also!

Clients of the AWR

The AWR is used by a number of different internal database processes. This includes the ADDM (which will be discussed later in this chapter) as well as the new Oracle Database 10*g* self-tuning components (which will also be described later in this chapter). Additionally, external clients such as SQL*Plus and OEM use the AWR as well.

AWR Active Session History   Previous to Oracle Database 10*g*, it was hard to keep track of historical information on session activity. Oracle Database 10*g* offers a new feature through the AWR called Active Session History (ASH) that tracks the history of recent session activity in the AWR. ASH records information on active sessions from the V$SESSION view every second, and is flushed to the WR as described earlier in this chapter. The collected statistical information that is stored in the AWR memory area is visible via the V$ACTIVE_SESSION_HISTORY fixed view.

Base Statistics and Usage Metrics

Oracle Database 10*g* also stores base statistics and database usage metrics in the AWR. Base statistics are raw database performance and operational data, such as the amount of redo that has been generated. Database usage metrics are derived values based on base statistics. Let's look at each of these in a bit more detail.

Base Statistics   Base statistics are available through the traditional database views, such as V$SYSSTAT. The new database metrics contained in the AWR are available through several views, including:

- DBA_FEATURE_USAGE_STATISTICS

- DBA_HIGH_WATER_MARK_STATISTICS

- V$SERVICE_STATS

Usage Metrics   Oracle Database 10*g* tracks database usage metrics so that you can keep track of how the database is being used. This helps you to determine how often specific database features are being used and also gives you an idea of how hard the database is really being used. These metrics come in two flavors:

- Feature usage statistics with usage information on Oracle features, such as Oracle Streams, Advanced Queuing, database auditing, and more.

■ High-water mark (HWM) statistics provide sample information such as the size of the largest segment in the database, the highest number of users logged in to the database, and the HWM of the size of the database.

These usage metrics are collected once a week by the new MMON process (described later in this section), and are viewable in a number of tables:

■ **V$SYSMETRIC** Displays the current metrics. This view is updated by MMON, and these metrics are stored in memory for about an hour. Examples of metrics included are the buffer cache hit ratio, full index scans per second, and full index scans per transaction.

■ **V$SYSMETRIC_HISTORY** Maintains a historical view of the metrics previously in V$SYSMETRIC. Each metric in the view is based on a begin and end time for that metric, thus you get a history of each metric over a given period of time.

■ **DBA_HIST_SYSMETRIC_HISTORY** Provides a longer-term view of historical system metrics.

■ **V$SESSMETRIC** Provides metrics related to specific sessions.

■ **V$SERVICEMETRIC** Provides metrics for the most recent 60-second interval.

■ **V$FILEMETRIC** Provides file-based metrics that are gathered every ten minutes and are stored in this view for one hour.

■ **V$FILEMETRIC_HISTORY** Provides longer-term storage for metrics that originate in V$FILEMETRIC.

■ **V$EVENTMETRIC** Provides metrics related to waits for the most recent 60-second interval. Join to V$METRICNAME to get the name of the associated metric.

■ **V$WAITCLASSMETRIC** Provides wait-based metrics that are gathered every ten minutes and are stored in this view for one hour.

■ **V$WAITCLASSMETRIC_HISTORY** Provides longer-term storage for metrics that originate in V$WAITCLASSMETRIC.

■ **V$METRICNAME** Provides the metric name and metric ID of each metric that is stored in the AWR.

■ **V$METRICGROUP** Identifies metric groups, and which metric views those groups are assigned to.

NOTE
OEM also provides access to these statistics.

Reporting from the AWR   Oracle Database 10*g* provides reporting from the AWR that looks very similar to statspack in nature. The following reports are available in $ORACLE_HOME/rdbms/admin:

- **awrinfo.sql**   This report provides general AWR information.

- **awrrpt.sql**   This report is much like the statspack report.

- **awrrpti.sql**   This report provides a generated HTML version of the swrfrpt.sql report.

Each report allows you to choose the number of days worth of snapshots to choose from, then the specific snap_id pairs that you wish to report on, and the filename for the resulting output file.

NOTE
While statspack is still available in Oracle Database 10g, Oracle recommends migrating to the AWR.

New Oracle Processes Related to the AWR

Oracle Database 10*g* adds two new processes to the database mix (I think at some point we need to say enough is enough!). The first is called MMON. The MMON process starts automatically when the database starts and is used to transfer the statistics collected by the AWR from memory to disk. MMON flushes the AWR from memory every 30 minutes. The second process, MMML, which also starts at database startup, is responsible for flushing the buffer whenever the buffer is full.

The setting of the **statistics_level** database parameter influences the collection of statistics for the AWR. If **statistics_level** is set to BASIC, then the collection of AWR statistics and related metrics is turned off. If **statistics_level** is set to TYPICAL (which is recommended), then only those statistics typically needed to monitor the database are collected. Finally, if **statistics_level** is set to ALL, Oracle Database 10*g* collects all statistics available for collection.

NOTE
*Setting the **statistics_level** parameter to ALL can have some performance impacts, so change this parameter with care.*

Server-Based Advisors

Oracle Database 10*g* offers a new feature, server-based advisors. These advisors provide information about your database that helps you tune it to maximum performance. The server-based advisor components include the following:

- Automatic Database Diagnostic Monitor (ADDM)
- SQL Tuning Advisor
- SQL Access Advisor
- Shared Pool Advisor
- MTTR Advisor

The server-based advisor architecture fits on top of the AWR, and results of the advisors are stored in the AWR. Advisors can run in either limited or comprehensive mode (though some only support one mode of operation). Comprehensive mode tends to be more detailed, but it also may result in a long run time for the advisor. As you might expect, limited mode is a much less in-depth analysis, which will not take as long.

The dbms_advisor Package

Advisors generally are run via OEM or from the SQL prompt via the **dbms_advisor** stored PL/SQL procedure. Running an advisor from PL/SQL typically involves the following tasks:

1. Create the advisor task with the **dbms_advisor.create_task** procedure.

2. Set task parameters with the **dbms_advisor.set_task_parameter** procedure.

3. Execute the advisor task with the **dbms_advisor.execute_task** procedure.

4. Create a report that contains the results with the stored procedure **dbms_advisor.get_task_report**.

There are a number of other **dbms_advisor** procedures that you can use as well, which are described in Table 3-1 (which includes all procedures).

NOTE
*To run **dbms_advisor** procedures, you must have the **advisor** system privilege.*

The Advisor Data Dictionary Views

Several new data dictionary views have been added to support the advisors. Table 3-2 lists those views and provides some detail about their usage.

The following sections look at each of the advisors in a bit more detail.

Procedure	Purpose
create_task	Create a new advisor task
delete_task	Remove a defined advisor task
execute_task	Execute the specific task
interrupt_task	Suspend a task that is currently running
get_task_report	Produce a text report that contains the recommendations from the advisor
resume_task	Resume a task suspended with the **interrupt_task** procedure
update_task_attributes	Update attributes for a given task
set_task_parameter	Set a task-related parameter
mark_recommendation	Mark a recommendation as accepted, rejected, or ignored
create_task_script	Create a script that contains all the accepted recommendations

TABLE 3-1. *dbms_advisor* Procedures

View Name	Purpose
DBA_ADVISOR_ACTIONS	Provides the actions that are associated with the recommendations in DBA_ADVISOR_RECOMMENDATIONS
DBA_ADVISOR_COMMANDS	Provides information on commands that are associated with actions
DBA_ADVISOR_DEFINITIONS	Provides the definitions associated with the advisors
DBA_ADVISOR_FINDINGS	Provides the findings of the advisor
DBA_ADVISOR_LOG	Provides current information on the status of advisor tasks

TABLE 3-2. *Data Dictionary Views*

View Name	Purpose
DBA_ADVISOR_OBJECTS	Provides information on objects that are referenced by advisor tasks
DBA_ADVISOR_PARAMETERS	Provides information on the parameters of a task
DBA_ADVISOR_RATIONALE	Provides reasoning behind the suggested actions and recommendations
DBA_ADVISOR_RECOMMENDATIONS	Provides the recommendations of the advisor
DBA_ADVISOR_TASKS	Provides information about the advisor task
DBA_ADVISOR_USAGE	Provides usage information for each advisor

TABLE 3-2. *Data Dictionary Views* (continued)

Automatic Database Diagnostic Monitor

A DBA is always interested in how their database is performing. Oracle Database 10*g* offers the Automatic Database Diagnostic Monitor (ADDM) in an effort to assist the DBA in this task. The ADDM is part of the overall Oracle advisor architecture, and it is there to help the DBA be proactive and more efficient in the tuning that they do. The ADDM runs automatically via the MMON process on your database instances, in an effort to detect and report on problems proactively. The data that the ADDM uses for its diagnostic work comes from the WR, and the results of the ADDM operation are stored in the WR as well.

It is the job of the ADDM to analyze the database workload and find bottlenecks that are impacting performance. The ADDM identifies problem areas and then works through a problem-resolution tree to attempt to eliminate areas that are not causing the problem and highlight areas that are causing the problem.

OEM provides a nice interface into the ADDM and its recommendations. Through charting and other visualization methods, OEM makes it easier to interpret ADDM results. If you are an old command-line coot like I am, then you can use the Oracle-supplied views listed in Table 3-2, such as DBA_ADVISOR_FINDINGS, to review the output from the ADDM.

Jonathan Says...
You always have to watch out for activity that is automatic, or semi-automatic, in new releases of Oracle Database 10*g*. Sometimes a default parameter sets a feature running, sometimes the default action of the Database Creation Assistant (DBCA) silently sets up your database with a nondefault value for a parameter that has some special action.

In the case of the advisories, you will find a parameter called **_addm_auto_ enable** that is set to TRUE and causes the ADDM to run immediately after the AWR has completed its 30-minute dump. I'm still looking for the bit that cleans out the DBA_ADVISOR_FINDINGS objects automatically—I'm sure it's there somewhere.

Here is an example of the ADDM in use. First, we need to start the ADDM by creating a task for diagnostic monitoring:

```
DECLARE
    Task_name varchar2(30) := 'test_task';
    Task_desc   varchar2(30) := 'Startup of ADDM';
    Task_id      number;
BEGIN
    dbms_advisor.create_task('ADDM', task_id, task_name,
    task_desc, NULL);
END;
```

We can get the names of the advisors from the DBA_ADVISOR_DEFINITIONS view, as shown in this example:

```
Select advisor_name from dba_advisor_definitions;
```

Once we have started the ADDM, we need to modify some parameters associated with the advisor task we have started. For example, we need to define some required parameters. These parameters are set through the stored procedure **dbms_advisor.set_task_parameter** before we actually execute the advisor. Let's set the parameters we need:

```
-- Start and stop snaps can be found in the
-- the DBA_HIST_SNAPSHOT views
Exec Dbms_advisor.set_task_parameter('test_task',
'START_SNAPSHOT', 1);
Exec Dbms_advisor.set_task_parameter('test_task',
'END_SNAPSHOT',  10);
Exec Dbms_advisor.set_task_parameter('test_task',
'INSTANCE',  1);
```

Now that we have set the required parameters, we instruct Oracle Database 10*g* to perform the analysis with the **execute_task** procedure:

```
Exec dbms_advisor.execute_task('test_task');
```

Having executed the analysis, we will want to look at the results. This is done by using the DBA_ADVISOR_FINDINGS view, a partial example of the output of which is shown here:

```
SQL> select message from dba_advisor_findings where
task_name='task_1';

MESSAGE
----------------------------------------------------------
Wait event "class slave wait" was consuming significant
database time.
Wait class "Other" was consuming significant database time.
Wait class "Administrative" was not consuming significant
database time.
Wait class "Application" was not consuming significant
database time.
```

As with all the advisors, there is a lot more to the ADDM, but I only have so many pages to cover a ton of the Oracle Database 10*g* new features. Hopefully, this was enough to get you interested in the ADDM and encourage you to go seek it out and experiment with it.

SQL Tuning Advisor

The SQL Tuning Advisor provides an interface through OEM or via the PL/SQL stored package **dbms_sqltune** to analyze existing SQL statements and provide tuning recommendations to be implemented. The SQL Tuning Advisor will also provide assistance in the implementation of those suggestions.

The SQL Tuning Advisor can take its input from a number of different sources including SQL statements identified by the ADDM, SQL statements currently in the shared pool, SQL statements stored in the AWR, or a user-created workload. One or multiple SQL statements can be input into the SQL Tuning Advisor for review.

The results from the SQL Tuning Advisor are available from OEM or you can execute the **dbms_sqltune** procedure **report_tuning_task** to produce a report.

Let's put the SQL Tuning Advisor to work in a quick example that I hope will wet your appetite to learn more about the SQL Tuning Advisor. First, just as with the ADDM, we need to create a task for the advisor to chew on. This time, we use the **dbms_sqltune** package and call the **create_tuning_task** procedure:

```
Declare
    ret_val   varchar2(2000);
Begin
```

```
   ret_val:=dbms_sqltune.create_tuning_task(sql_text=>'SELECT *
FROM EMP WHERE EMPNO=7934');
   dbms_output.put_line('Output: '||ret_val);
end;
/
OUTPUT: TASK_00004
```

Now we need to tell the SQL Tuning Advisor to actually get busy and do something. To get this slacker moving along, we use the **execute_tuning_task** procedure in the **dbms_sqltune** package:

```
Exec Dbms_sqltune.execute_tuning_task('TASK_00004');
```

Now, let's display the results. To do this, we need to use the **dbms_sqltune** package again, but this time we call the **report_tuning_task** function, as shown in this example:

```
Declare
   ret_val    varchar2(2000);
PROCEDURE Show_Message(p_Msg_in IN CLOB)
IS
BEGIN
     IF LENGTH(p_Msg_in)   > 255
     THEN
          DBMS_OUTPUT.Put_Line(SUBSTR(p_Msg_in,1,255));
          Show_Message(SUBSTR(p_Msg_in,256,
                       LENGTH(p_Msg_in)));
     ELSE
          DBMS_OUTPUT.Put_Line(p_Msg_in);
     END IF;
END;
begin
   dbms_output.enable(1000000);
   ret_val:=dbms_sqltune.report_tuning_task('TASK_00004');
   show_message(ret_val);
end;
/
```

And here is a partial excerpt from the report:

```
GENERAL INFORMATION SECTION
-------------------------------------------------------
Tuning Task Name    : TASK_00004
Scope               : COMPREHENSIVE
Time Limit(seconds) : 1800
Completion Status   : COMPLETED
Started at          : 11/06/2003 01:47:38
```

```
Completed at        : 11/06/2003 01:47:40
-------------------------------------------------------
SQL ID   : 3z142xs5pc1un
SQL Text: SELECT * FROM EMP WHERE
EMPNO=7934
-------------------------------------------------------
FINDINGS SECTION (1 finding)
--------------------------------------------------------------
Statistics Finding
--------------------
  Table "SCOTT"."EMP" was not analyzed.
  Recommendation
  --------------
    Consider collecting optimizer statistics for this table.
execute dbms_stats.gather_table_stats(ownname => 'SCOTT', tabname =>'EMP',
estimate_percent => DBMS_STATS.AUTO_SAMPLE_SIZE)

  Rationale
  ---------
    The optimizer requires up-to-date statistics for the table
in order to select a good execution plan.
EXPLAIN PLANS SECTION
--------------------------------------------------
1- Original
--------------------------------------------------------
| Id  | Operation          | Name  | Rows  | Bytes | Cost|
--------------------------------------------------------
|  0  | SELECT STATEMENT   |       |       |       |     |
|  1  |  TABLE ACCESS FULL | EMP   |       |       |     |
--------------------------------------------------------
Note: rule based optimization
```

The dbms_advisor.quick_tune Procedure   You can use the **dbms_advisor.quick_tune** procedure to quickly tune a single SQL statement. Here is an example of its use:

```
VARIABLE task_id NUMBER;
VARIABLE task_name VARCHAR2(255);
VARIABLE sql_stmt VARCHAR2(4000);
EXECUTE :sql_stmt := 'SELECT COUNT(*) FROM emp
                    WHERE empno=1122';
EXECUTE :task_name  := 'QUICKTUNE';
EXECUTE DBMS_ADVISOR.QUICK_TUNE('SQL Access Advisor', -
:task_id, :task_name, :sql_stmt);
```

Once this has been completed, call the **report_tuning_task** function to get the results of the run.

Jonathan Says...
Even if you think that a SQL statement can't be tuned, it's worth running the tuning task, for two reasons. First, sometimes Oracle Database 10*g* will find a "profile" (essentially a list of improved statistical information about the data) that allows a better execution path to appear. Second, and more interestingly, the Rationale section of the report may tell you some things about the way the optimizer works that you weren't previously aware of, with text like: "The following statement could be improved if you did XXX because then the optimizer could do YYY." It's a feature that could put me out of business.

SQL Access Advisor

You can use the **dbms_advisor** stored procedure to help you with materialized view tuning. The SQL Access Advisor will show you how to optimize your materialized views, and it will also help guide you in meeting requirements for fast refresh and query rewrite. Use the **dbms_advisor.tune_mview** procedure to tune your materialized view creation statement. You must include either the **refresh fast** clause or the **enable query rewrite** clause in the **create materialized view** statement that you wish to analyze.

The procedure will output the statements that are required to create the associated materialized view. This includes statements to create the correct materialized view logs, alter existing materialized view logs, and output a corrected materialized view statement that will take advantage of the newest query rewrite and fast refresh statements.

The output results can be found in the USER_TUNE_MVIEW or DBA_TUNE_MVIEW view. You can also use the **dbms_advisor** procedures **get_task_script** and **create_script** to generate the SQL scripts.

Shared Pool Advisor

The Shared Pool Advisor comes in the form of advisory statistics that are available from a number of views in Oracle Database 10*g*. These views include the following:

■ **V$SHARED_POOL_ADVICE**   Allows you to estimate how much time you will save on parsing if you change the size of the shared pool. This view was available in Oracle9*i* Database.

■ **V$LIBRARY_CACHE_MEMORY**   Provides information about library cache memory usage. This view was available in Oracle9*i*.

- **V$JAVA_POOL_ADVICE**   Provides information on the Java pool and how changing the size of the pool might impact performance. This is a new view in Oracle Database 10g.

- **V$JAVA_LIBRARY_CACHE_MEMORY**   Provides information on the Java pool library cache and how changing the size of the pool might impact performance. This is a new view in Oracle Database 10g.

MTTR Advisor

Yet another advisor is the Mean Time to Recover (MTTR) Advisor. This advisor, present in the form of the V$MTTR_TARGET_ADVICE view, allows you to properly calibrate the setting of the **fast_start_mttr_target** parameter. The MTTR Advisor is only turned on when the **statistics_level** parameter is set to TYPICAL or ALL and when **fast_start_mttr_target** is set to a non-zero value.

Server-Generated Alerts

Recall that the CMI and the AWR were introduced earlier in this chapter. One of the things that this infrastructure facilitates is the ability of the database to generate alerts in critical situations. In response to these alerts, the database will send an alert to the DBA along with a suggested response.

The MMON process is central to monitoring of the database, the processing of database alerts, and the responses that are triggered by these actions. Other database processes also can detect problems and send messages to MMON to cause specific actions to occur (for example, sending off an alert message).

Database status monitoring criteria can be determined by criteria internal to the database, or externally defined criteria. When these criteria are met and an alert is to be issued, the Oracle database will create the alert and forward it to a predefined queue (as a part of Oracle Database 10g Advanced Queueing) called ALERT_QUE, which is owned by SYS. Alerts with varying severity levels can be defined, and as these different level thresholds are reached, additional alerts can be messaged. You can use Oracle Enterprise Manager to set up alerts and notifications. The primary benefit in Oracle Database 10g is that the server alerts are now server based rather than OEM based. This makes the processing of alerts and messaging much more efficient. Also, with the WR, Oracle Database 10g stores a history of the metrics relating to these alerts, providing a repository of data for later analysis.

Kinds of Server-Generated Alerts

Oracle Database 10g provides two types of server-generated alerts: threshold and nonthreshold alerts. These can generally be configured via either OEM or PL/SQL procedures. Let's look at each of these types of alerts in more detail.

Threshold Alerts   For threshold alerts, you can configure both warning and critical threshold levels on a number of different metrics, such as SQL service response times. Threshold alerts are also known as stateful alerts. When a monitored metric is in alert state, it can be seen in the DBA_OUTSTANDING_ALERTS view. Here is an example of an alert that indicates that the flash recovery area has violated a critical threshold:

```
SQL> select reason, suggested_action
2* from dba_outstanding_alerts;
REASON
--------------------------------------------------------------
SUGGESTED_ACTION
db_recovery_file_dest_size of 2147483648 bytes is 96.25% used
and has 80545280 remaining bytes available.
Add disk space, backup files to tertiary device, delete files
from recovery area using RMAN or consider changing RMAN retention policy.
```

Once the alert is cleared, the alert is moved to the DBA_ALERT_HISTORY view. Out of the box, Oracle Database 10*g* configures one threshold alert. This is based on tablespace space usage. By default, this alert triggers a warning alert level when the tablespace is 85 percent full. A critical alert state is triggered at 97 percent full.

Thresholds can be changed via the OEM interface or through the PL/SQL stored procedure **dbms_server_alerts.set_threshold**. The **dbms_server_alerts.get_threshold** PL/SQL stored procedure enables you to query the database for existing threshold information for a specific alert.

Nonthreshold Alerts   Nonthreshold alerts (or stateless alerts) are event based, such as the occurrence of a Snapshot Too Old error message or if resumable space management suspends a session. Stateless alerts are stored in the DBA_ALERT_ HISTORY view. Nonthreshold alerts that are provided out of the box include the following:

- Any snapshot-too-old conditions

- Any case where the Flashback Recovery area is low on free space

- Any case where a session using resumable space management is suspended

Server-Generated Alert Views
As you probably guessed, new views have been added to support server-generated alerts. These views include

- **V$SYSMETRIC**   Displays the current metrics associated with server-generated alerts. This view is updated by MMON, and these metrics are stored in memory for about an hour.

■ **V$SYSMETRIC_HISTORY**   Maintains a historical view of the metrics previously in V$SYSMETRIC. This view is time limited.

■ **DBA_HIST_SYSMETRIC_HISTORY**   Provides a longer-term view of historical system metrics.

■ **DBA_OUTSTANDING_ALERTS**   Contains current database alerts (this view was introduced earlier in this section).

■ **DBA_ALERT_HISTORY**   Provides a history of threshold alerts that have been resolved, and provides a history of nonthreshold alerts.

■ **DBA_THRESHOLDS**   Defines the threshold settings for the given instance.

■ **V$ALERT_TYPES**   Provides information on various alert types.

Automatic SGA Tuning

If you have ever asked yourself, "How much memory should I allocate to the database buffer cache?" then Automatic Shared Memory Management (ASMM) might just be the thing for you. Of course, if you are a control freak, then you might just not like it at all. Oracle 10*g* allows you to define the size of a new parameter, **sga_target**, and it will allocate that memory as it thinks best to the default buffer cache, the shared pool, the large pool, and the java pool. Setting **sga_target** to 0 disables ASMM, which is the default setting.

Regardless of the setting of **sga_target**, you still need to manually set the following parameters:

■ The log buffer

■ The keep buffer pool

■ The recycle buffer pool

■ The new streams pool

■ Nondefault block-sized buffer cache pools

Also, you must set **statistics_level** to TYPICAL or ALL to use ASMM. Also, if one of the ASMM parameters (e.g., **shared_pool_size**) is set to a non-zero value, then the value that the parameter is set to will be considered a minimum size for that memory area.

The **sga_target** parameter is a dynamic parameter, so if you find that you need additional memory allocated to your database while it's up and running, all you need to do is issue an **alter system** command and allocate more memory to the database (assuming the memory is available).

The new MMAN (Memory Manager) process controls the automatic allocation of the memory within the SGA. Its job (among other things) is to keep track of the sizes of the memory areas, monitor the database and its workload to ensure that memory distribution is optimal, and redistribute memory allocations as required. This is very useful for hybrid databases that have fluctuating demands on memory areas.

Self-Tuning Checkpointing

Oracle Database 10*g* will now self-tune checkpoint operations so that Oracle Database 10*g* can make the best use of the I/O bandwidth that is available to the system. To enable self-tuned checkpointing, you should set the **fast_start_mttr_target** parameter to a non-zero value. Note that this parameter defaults to 0, which disables self-tuning checkpointing.

New Oracle Database 10*g* Trace Functionality

Oracle Database 10*g* offers new trace functionality that makes tracing of user sessions much easier. Now, you can enable tracing of all sessions of a specific user by using the **dbms_monitor** stored PL/SQL package. The **client_id_trace_enable** procedure allows you to enable tracing for all sessions started by a specific client. Here is an example of a call to this procedure:

```
Exec -
dbms_monitor.client_id_trace_enable(client_id=>'PROD_USER');
```

This command will result in the generation of a number of trace files. Oracle Database 10*g* comes with the new **trcsess** utility that allows you to scan through all trace files and combine those produced by the user into a single trace file. Here is an example of the **trcsess** command in action:

```
Trcsess output=prod_user.trc clientid='PROD_USER' *.trc
```

Note that if you have old trace files, they will be included when the **trcsess** utility is run. So, if you do not wish to include these files, you need to either move them or rename them with a different extension. You can use the optional **waits** procedure to generate wait-related information, and the optional **binds** parameter instructs Oracle Database 10*g* to include bind variable values in the trace files.

When you enable tracing of a session via the **dbms_monitor** PL/SQL package, the tracing will appear in the DBA_ENABLED_TRACES view. For example, when we enabled tracing for PROD_USER, the following showed up in the DBA_ENABLED_TRACES view:

```
SQL> select trace_type, primary_id, waits, binds
from dba_enabled_traces;
```

```
TRACE_TYPE              PRIMARY_ID WAITS BINDS
-------------------- ---------- ----- -----
CLIENT_ID               PROD_USER  TRUE  FALSE
```

You can disable session-level monitoring by using the procedure **dbms_monitor.client_id_trace_disable**, as shown here:

```
Exec -
dbms_monitor.client_id_trace_disable(client_id=>'PROD_USER');
```

Also, the **dbms_monitor** package allows you to enable tracing based on a combination of service name, module name (optional), instance name (optional), and action name (optional) via the **serv_mod_act_trace_enable** procedure.

For any specific session that is actively tracing, you can use the procedure **dbms_monitor.serv_mod_act_trace_disable** to turn off tracing for that session. You provide the session ID and serial number of that session to the procedure as shown in this example:

```
Exec dbms_monitor.session_trace_disable(22,2044);
```

Sorted Hash Clusters

If your application is a high-velocity OLTP application and it tends to access data in the same order consistently, you might want to look at sorted hash clusters. Previous to Oracle Database 10*g*, there was no way to control the order in which data within a heap table was stored. As a result, unless your SQL statement included the **order by** clause, you would find your rows returned in an unordered fashion. Oracle Database 10*g* offers a sorted hash cluster, which ensures rows will be stored within the hash cluster in the order defined when you created the hash cluster. This can eliminate the overhead associated with sort operations that might otherwise be required, because data will be returned in a guaranteed order.

If your SQL statements against the sorted hash cluster should contain an **order by** clause that defines a sort operation that requires a different ordering of the rows than the cluster is configured for, you will lose the benefit of the sorted hash cluster, because the **order by** clause will force a sort operation. Therefore, take care when deciding how to order the columns of a sorted hash cluster. As with normal hash clusters, performance of a sorted hash cluster is very dependent on correctly configuring the cluster table. The hash function, number and size of hash keys, and the sort columns that the cluster is built on all require careful consideration.

When deciding on using a sorted hash cluster, you should make sure that the data lends itself to the creation of a hash key that will lead to few collisions (that is, more than one row sharing the same key), and that there are a fixed number of hash keys.

Example of Using a Sorted Hash Cluster

Let's look at an example of the use of a sorted hash cluster. In this example, we have a customer support center that is receiving calls from customers. Within the support center is a fixed number of call center booths with phones for our help desk representatives.

For billing purposes, our customer needs to track all calls coming into our call center by the customer ID, date, and the duration of the call. At the end of the month, a report by customer ID is produced detailing each support call, the date of the call, and the duration of the call.

First, we have to consider what value we wish to use for the hash key. We can use either the CUSTOMER_ID or the BOOTH_ID. Since BOOTH_ID is probably a bit more finite (hopefully we will add more customers but need to add fewer booths in the future!), we will make BOOTH_ID our hash key. There are 50 booths, so let's create 70 hash keys, one for each booth and a bit to grow on as well. Given this information, we will first create the cluster and then create the tables of the cluster, as described in the following sections.

Creating the Sorted Hash Cluster

First, we are going to create the cluster for the sorted hash cluster:

```
CREATE CLUSTER call_center_cluster (
Booth_number NUMBER,
Customer_id   NUMBER SORT,
Call_date     DATE SORT )
HASHKEYS 70
HASH IS booth_number;
```

In this example, we establish BOOTH_NUMBER as the column that the hash key values are built on. We then define the column CUSTOMER_ID as the primary sort column within the hash key. We also defined a secondary sort key column, CALL_DATE. Finally, we assigned 70 hash keys to the table to allow for some additional booths to be added if that were ever required.

Creating the Tables of the Cluster

Now, we need to create the table that will be assigned to this cluster:

```
CREATE TABLE call_center_detail (
    booth_number      NUMBER,
    Customer_id       NUMBER SORT,
    call_date         DATE SORT,
    emp_id            NUMBER,
    call_duration     NUMBER)
    CLUSTER call_center_cluster (booth_number, customer_id, call_date);
```

The table creation SQL is much like the creation of a regular clustered table except for the use of the SORT keyword in the columns that are defined as SORT columns in the earlier **create cluster** command.

Once you have created the table, you access it just as you normally would with a DML command (e.g., **insert**, **select**, etc.). Oracle Database 10*g* will determine if the

SQL statement being executed can take advantage of the fact that the data stored in the sorted hash cluster is in the order of CUSTOMER_ID and CALL_DATE and will sort, or not sort, as required. For example, this query will not require a sort operation:

```
Select booth_number, customer_id, emp_id, call_duration
from call_center_detail
order by customer_id;
```

But the following query will require a sort operation:

```
Select booth_number, customer_id, emp_id, call_duration
from call_center_detail
order by emp_id;
```

> **NOTE**
> *Statistics are, of course, critical to the successful use of a sorted hash cluster.*

Shared Server Changes

Oracle Database 10*g* includes some changes to Oracle shared server architecture. These include

- Changes to shared server configuration

- MTS parameters become obsolete

- Addition of a new V$DISPATCHER_CONFIG view

- Capability to trace shared server sessions

Let's look at each of these features in more detail next.

Changes to Shared Server Configuration

In prior versions of Oracle Database, you had to configure at least one dispatcher in order to use Oracle's shared server features. Now, Oracle 10*g* is shared server "aware" by default and all you need to do is set the **shared_servers** parameter to a value greater than 0 to enable this feature. While other shared server parameters are still available to be used (and ultimately tune the shared server architecture), none needs to be set in order to use the shared server architecture.

As with Oracle9*i*, the **shared_servers** parameter is dynamic in nature, so you can choose to enable or disable the feature at will via the **alter system** command. Since the database requires no other parameters to be set to use shared server features, you can easily enable this architecture without recycling the database, should you determine that your database will benefit from it.

MTS Parameters Obsoleted

The Database 10g Shared Server feature used to be called Multi-Threaded Server (MTS) in Oracle Database versions prior to Oracle9i. Oracle9i replaced MTS with Shared Server in Oracle9i. With that introduction, new parameters for Oracle Shared Server functionality were introduced, and the old MTS parameters were deprecated (but still available for use). In Oracle Database 10g these MTS parameters are now obsolete. You need to remove these parameters from your database parameter file, or your database will not start under Oracle Database 10g. The following table lists the obsolete parameters and the names of the parameters that replace them:

Obsolete MTS Parameter (Must Be Removed in 10g)	New (9i) Shared Server Parameters (Must Be Used in 10g to Use Shared Server Features)
mts_servers	shared_servers
mts_max_servers	max_shared_servers
mts_dispatchers	dispatchers
mts_max_dispatchers	max_dispatchers
mts_circuits	circuits
mts_sessions	shared_server_sessions
mts_service	service_names
mts_listener_address mts_multiple_listeners	local_listener

Each of the replacement parameters is dynamic; however, in the case of the **dispatchers** parameter, some changes to attributes of that parameter will not impact existing dispatcher sessions.

The V$DISPATCHER_CONFIG View

Oracle has added a new view, V$DISPATCHER_CONFIG, to provide information on existing dispatchers. This view provides dispatcher configuration information and can be joined to the V$DISPATCHER view (using the CONF_INDX column of both views) for more complete dispatcher-related information.

Tracing Shared Server Sessions

The **trcsess** utility, introduced earlier, allows you to trace shared server sessions more easily. You simply supply the names of the trace files you would like consolidated (or use wild carding) and **trcsess** will collect them together in one trace file. You can then use **tkprof** to format the trace files and provide output for you to review.

CHAPTER
4

Security

- Virtual Private Database New Features
- Oracle Database 10g Auditing New Features
- Directory (LDAP) Based New Features

racle Database 10*g* comes with a number of new features designed to provide enhanced security within the Oracle database. In this chapter we will cover these new features, which include

■ Virtual Private Database new features

■ Auditing enhancements

■ New directory features

Virtual Private Database New Features

Oracle Database 10*g* includes improvements to Oracle's Virtual Private Database (VPD). New features include the following:

■ Column-level privacy

■ New VPD policies

■ Support for parallel query

Column-Level Privacy

The benefit of VPD is that it provides for row-level security in your Oracle database. Oracle Database 10*g* offers a new feature that allows you to indicate that a VPD policy should only be enforced if specific columns are accessed or referenced. One or more columns can be defined within a policy, though you do not need to specify any columns. In this case VPD will operate just as in Oracle9*i*.

As a result, you can now provide varying levels of security for database tables. For example, you may not need to secure queries against certain columns, such as the name of an employee, but you may require some level of access control for queries against the social security number, because of privacy issues. In this case, you would create a VPD policy that references the column containing the social security number. The policy would be effective for any query that includes the SSN column. This allows you to define privacy policies for certain types of data, such as personal data, while making other data available.

This new feature is supported with the addition of the **sec_relevant_cols** parameter in the **dbms_rls.add_policy** PL/SQL package supplied by Oracle. Here is an example of the use of **dbms_rls.add_policy** to create a policy on a table called RET_SCHEMA .RETIREE:

```
BEGIN
Dbms_rls.add_policy(object_schema=>'ret_schema',
Object_name=>'retiree',
Policy_name=>'retiree_policy',
Function_schema=>'retiree',
Policy_function=>'f_retiree_01',
Statement_types=>'select',
Sec_relevant_cols=>'ssn, sal');
END;
/
```

Note that the steps to implement a VPD policy using this new feature are basically the same as in Oracle9*i*, with the exception of the new **sec_relevant_cols** parameter in **dbms_rls.add_policy** (which is optional). If you do not include the **sec_relevant_cols** parameter, then the policy will apply to all columns, just as it did previous to Oracle Database 10*g*.

New VPD Policies

Prior to Oracle Database 10*g*, Oracle offered just one type of database policy, a dynamic one. Oracle Database 10*g* offers five VPD policy types to choose from, which are listed and described in Table 4-1.

Policy Type	Description
Static	With a static policy, VPD will always use the same predicate for access control. The static policy only applies to a single object.
Shared_static	A shared_static policy is a static policy that is shared by multiple database objects.
Context_sensitive	This is a nonstatic (or dynamic) policy that executes each time the session context changes, such as when the username changes and you want your policy to be different for each user.
Shared_context_sensitive	This policy is dynamic just like a context_sensitive policy, but it can be shared across multiple objects.
Dynamic	This policy is the default type of policy in Oracle Database 10*g*. The policy function is executed each time the command accesses the object and the columns relevant to the access policy.

TABLE 4-1. *Oracle Database 10*g *VPD Policy Types*

Static policy predicates are stored in the SGA, so they execute quickly. Static policies also have the same predicate that is applied to all SQL statements accessing the objects assigned to the policy. Dynamic policies are re-created via the policy function each time the defined columns are accessed, and thus dynamic policy execution can be slower than static policy execution.

Note that some policy types can be shared between different objects. This allows a single policy to scale better, and keeps business rules more consistent. To define the policy type, use the **policy_type** argument to the **dbms_rls.add_policy** procedure for the correct policy type, as shown in this example:

```
BEGIN
Dbms_rls.add_policy(object_schema=>'ret_schema',
Object_name=>'retiree',
Policy_name=>'retiree_policy',
Function_schema=>'retiree',
Policy_function=>'f_retiree_01',
Statement_types=>'select',
Sec_relevant_cols=>'ssn',
Policy_type=>DBMS_RLE.STATIC);
END;
/
```

VPD Support for Oracle Parallel Query

Oracle Database 10*g* now supports the use of parallel query within the VPD framework. This makes VPD much more scalable.

Oracle Database 10*g* Auditing New Features

New features for auditing are also present in Oracle Database 10*g*. These changes include

- New columns in DBA_AUDIT_TRAIL
- Changes to Fine-grained Auditing

New Columns in DBA_AUDIT_TRAIL

Oracle Database 10*g* adds new columns to the DBA_AUDIT_TRAIL view to allow for more synergy between standard auditing and find-grained auditing. New columns include SCN, which contains the system change number; SQL_TEXT, which contains the text of the SQL executed by the user; and SQL_BIND, which contains the values of the bind variables for the SQL being executed.

Jonathan Says...

It's strange, but when the SYSAUX tablespace appeared, I thought that the FGA_LOG$ table and the AUD$ table would probably be pushed into it, especially since they now both contain CLOBs, but they are still in the SYSTEM tablespace. I hope there is an officially approved mechanism for moving them, because I like to isolate special types of activity to their own datafiles, and I'd rather not see the SYSTEM tablespace being hammered without being able to discount auditing as a reason.

Fine-Grained Auditing New Features

Introduced in Oracle9*i*, Fine-grained Auditing in Oracle Database 10*g* becomes even more powerful. First, new view changes have been added that provide even more detail than before. Then, Oracle has added the ability to audit all DML statements (**insert**, **update**, etc...) with Fine-grained Auditing.

View Changes

Oracle Database 10*g* also adds several new columns to the view DBA_FGA_ AUDIT_TRAIL, including:

- **STATEMENT_TYPE**   The type of query that was executed.

- **EXTENDED_TIMESTAMP**   The timestamp of the query.

- **PROXY_SESSIONID**   Proxy session serial number if the session is logged in via a proxy mechanism.

- **GLOBAL_UID**   Global user identifier of the user.

- **INSTANCE_NUMBER**   Instance number that the action occurred on.

- **OS_PROCESS**   OS process identifier.

- **TRANSACTIONID**   Transaction identifier of the transaction.

- **STATEMENTID**   A unique identifier for each statement run (each statement may generate multiple audit records).

- **ENTRYID**   Numeric ID that identifies each statement. This plus the STATEMENTID makes each entry unique.

Note in particular the STATEMENTID and ENTRYID columns. For a given audited database action, one or more audit records may be created. Each audited statement is assigned a unique ENTRYID. However, a given statement execution can result in multiple audit records. If this is the case, then each audit record will have the same ENTRYID. To keep them unique and ordered, each individual audit record for that

ENTRYID will be given a unique value in the STATEMENTID column of the DBA_
FGA_AUDIT_TRAIL view.

Auditing DML Statements
Fine-grained Auditing was introduced in Oracle9*i*, and only **select** statements could
be audited. In Oracle Database 10*g*, you can audit **update**, **insert**, and **delete**
statements. This allows for better auditing of database activities, and more user
accountability. Also, Fine-grained Auditing allows you to audit activity based on
one or more specific columns, though this is not required. You can define which
statement types cause the audit trigger to be fired via the **statements_type** parameter
of the **dbms_fga.add_policy** PL/SQL procedure.

Also, in Oracle9*i*, Oracle auditing was based on an audit condition being true
(though there were ways around this). Oracle Database 10*g* removes this requirement
and allows auditing of all statements, based on specific columns accessed in that
statement. Here is an example of setting an audit policy in Oracle Database 10*g*:

```
Begin
Dbms_fga.add_policy(
Object_schema=>'retiree',
Object_name=>'personal_info',
Policy_name=>'retiree_policy',
Audit_condition=>NULL,
Audit_column=>'SSN',
Enable=>TRUE,
Statement_types=>'update, delete');
END;
/
```

Note that no **audit_condition** is configured, so a record for all **update** and **delete**
operations will be recorded. This statement will configure an audit policy for the
RETIREE.PERSONAL_INFO table. It will only fire if the SSN column is used in any
update or **delete** statement.

Directory (LDAP) Based New Features
One of the benefits of the Grid is that it provided centralized user management and
privilege management. These remotely authenticated users are called *directory users.*
Directory users are authenticated by a source outside of the database (generally
LDAP). When an enterprise user is connected to the database, the user is then
authenticated through the Oracle Internet Directory (OID), and not through the
database.

Oracle Database 10*g* offers additional methods of authenticating directory users.
This includes password-based authentication, Kerberos-based authentication, and
X.509v3 certificate-based authentication. Also, the Oracle Database 10*g* database
can now communicate with the OID via Simple Authentication and Security Layer
(SASL) in addition to Secure Sockets Layer (SSL).

CHAPTER
5

Availability and Recoverability

- **General Database Recovery Improvements**
- **RMAN Improvements**
- **New Flashback Features**
- **New Transaction Recovery Monitoring Features**
- **New Data Guard Features**

racle Database 10*g* comes with a number of new features that are designed to provide enhanced availability and recoverability within the Oracle database. This chapter covers the following topics:

- General database recovery improvements

- RMAN improvements

- New flashback features

- New transaction recovery monitoring features

- New Data Guard features

General Database Recovery Improvements

Several changes have been made in Oracle Database 10*g* that relate to backup and recovery:

- Easier recovery through the **resetlogs** command

- Changes to the **alter database archivelog** command

- New and changed Oracle Database 10g backup commands

Easier Recovery Through the resetlogs Command

One of the downsides to incomplete recovery of an Oracle database in Oracle Database versions prior to Oracle Database 10*g* was the requirement to use the **resetlogs** command when opening the database. Because recovery through **resetlogs** was not supported in Oracle9*i*, you needed to perform a backup of the database in order for it to be recoverable, though there were some goofy and complex (and altogether unreliable) means to recover the database through **resetlogs** prior to Oracle Database 10*g*. Now, Oracle Database 10*g* makes recovery through the **resetlogs** command easier than ever.

The nice thing about being able to recover through the **resetlogs** command is that there is really nothing new that you have to do, it's all internal to Oracle Database 10*g*. You can use the **recover database**, **recover tablespace**, or **recover datafile** commands, just as you always have. The RMAN **restore** and **recover database** commands are also unchanged, and support the ability to recover beyond the point of the last **resetlogs** command.

Supporting Changes to the log_archive_format Parameter

Also associated with the ability to recover through the **resetlogs** command, is a change in the **log_archive_format** parameter. Oracle Database 10*g* now requires that a new format specification be used when the **compatible** parameter is set to 10.0 or greater. This format specification, **%r**, identifies the logical incarnation of the database and changes each time the **resetlogs** command is issued. The default format for **log_archive_format** in Oracle Database 10*g* is %t_%s_%r.dbf. You could modify the **log_archive_format** parameter setting in Oracle Database 10*g* so that it might look something like this:

```
Log_archive_format="mydb_%t_%s_%r.arc"
```

And the resulting physical file might look something like this:

```
/u01/oracle/arch/mydb/mydb_01_01_2035.arc
```

Supporting Changes to Oracle Dynamic Views

To support the ability to recover through the use of the **resetlogs** command, the dynamic views V$LOG_HISTORY and V$OFFLINE_RANGE have been modified. First, the data in these views is not cleared out after a successful **resetlogs** operation. Second, two new columns have been added to each of these views:

- **RESETLOGS_CHANGE#**   Indicates the system change number (SCN) associated with the execution of the **resetlogs** command

- **RESETLOGS_TIME**   Indicates the time associated with the execution of the **resetlogs** command

Also, the V$DATABASE_INCARNATION and V$ARCHIVED_LOG views have been changed such that they will not be cleared after the execution of the **resetlogs** command.

Supporting Changes to Oracle Standby Databases

One other bit of functionality that you might want to be aware of is in regard to Oracle standby databases. When a **resetlogs** operation is detected on a standby database, the managed recovery process will be canceled. At this point, you have two options:

- Maintain recovery following the new logical database branch created by the use of the **resetlogs** command.

- Maintain the same logical database branch, through the use of the **resetlogs** command.

Either way, you can continue to apply all redo generated after the use of the **resetlogs** command on the primary database server.

Changes to the alter database archivelog Command

When you issue the **alter database archivelog** command in Oracle Database 10*g*, archiving will be started by default. Thus, you don't need to use the **log archive start** command. The V$DATABASE view column LOG_MODE indicates AUTOMATIC if archiving is enabled in this fashion and indicates MANUAL if you have decided to use the new **manual** parameter to override the default behavior.

New and Changed Oracle Database 10*g* Database Backup Commands

Oracle Database 10*g* offers a new way to start database backups, with the **alter database begin backup** command. Also, Oracle Database 10*g* offers new functionality with the **alter database end backup** command. Let's look at each of these features in a bit more detail next.

The New alter database begin backup Command

Are you tired of issuing **alter tablespace begin backup** over and over? Now, putting the entire set of database tablespaces in hot backup mode is as simple as issuing the **alter database begin backup** command, as shown in this example:

```
SQL> alter database begin backup;
```

Jonathan Says...
Of course, the traditional advice is to never put your entire database into hot backup mode at once—so you have to ask yourself why Oracle has now made it very easy to do exactly that. Moreover, why do you need this command at all, when RMAN doesn't require the database to be in hot backup mode at all? As ever, Oracle is giving you lots of options, and you have to decide which one is relevant to your system. If your backup strategy ignores Oracle features and uses a simple "split mirror" approach, you are the one customer who should really be pleased with this new command.

If there are already tablespaces in hot backup mode, then the Oracle database will raise an error (ORA-01146). Also, the following conditions cause an error to be returned by the **alter database begin backup** command:

- One or more datafiles are offline or missing

- An RMAN backup is ongoing

Once you have issued the **alter database begin backup** command successfully, you can proceed to back up your Oracle database. As is the case when you put individual tablespaces in hot backup mode, you will be unable to perform a normal or immediate shutdown on the database after issuing this command. However, you can issue **shutdown abort** to terminate the instance if that is required (although one would hope this would never be required).

If the instance crashes or you use the **shutdown abort** command, you need to take the database out of hot backup mode by using the **alter database end backup** command ... and that is a nice segue to the next topic!

Changes to the alter database end backup Command

The **alter database end backup** command has been around since Oracle9i Database, and its functionality is enhanced in Oracle Database 10g. Previously, the **alter database end backup** command could be used only when the database was mounted. In Oracle Database 10g, you can use this command to end backups with the database mounted or the database open—your choice! Here is an example of the use of this command:

```
SQL> alter database end backup;
```

NOTE
A warning will be issued if any datafiles/tablespaces are not in hot backup mode, but the command will complete successfully.

RMAN Improvements

Oracle Database 10g comes with a plethora of improvements (I like that word, plethora!) for RMAN. These include the following:

- Using flash recovery area

- Using backup copies and fast recovery

- Using the **catalog** and **uncatalog** commands

- Dropping a database in RMAN

- Unregistering a database in RMAN

- Making and using RMAN backup copies

- Configuring default disk backup types

- Changes to incremental backups

- Recovering datafiles not backed up

- Changes in error reporting

- Compressing RMAN backups

- Using RMAN-related tablespace point-in-time related recovery changes

Using the Flash Recovery Area

Oracle Database 10g offers the flash recovery area, which allows you to centralize storage of all recovery-related files. The flash recovery area is an area of disk that is defined for use for recovery-related files. The flash recovery area can use locally attached storage, Clustered File Systems, or Oracle Database 10g's new Automatic Storage Management (ASM) features.

Table 5-1 lists the file types that are backed up within the flash recovery area.

Why Use the Flash Recovery Area?

The flash recovery area helps with the management of overall disk space allocation and provides a centralized storage area for all related recovery files. It provides for much faster backup and restore operations as well. The flash recovery area is created in a specific location (defined by a file system, or use of ASM). You define the maximum size of the flash recovery area via database parameters. As files are added or removed from the flash recovery area, records of these events are logged in the database alert log. You can check the new DBA view, DBA_ OUTSTANDING_ALERTS, for information on outstanding issues with the flash recovery area, as shown in this example:

```
Select * from dba_outstanding_alerts;
```

File Type	Notes
Control file	One copy of the control file is created in the flash recovery area when the database is created.
Archived redo logs	When you configure the flash recovery area (as described later in this section), the parameter **log_archive_dest_10** is automatically configured, and archived redo logs are archived to that destination, as well as any other archive log destinations.
Flashback logs	Flashback logs (discussed later in this chapter) are stored in the flash recovery area, if it is defined.
Control file autobackups	The default location for the RMAN control file autobackups is the flash recovery area, if it is defined.
RMAN datafile copies	The default location for the RMAN datafile copies is the flash recovery area, if it is defined.
RMAN backup and other related files	The default location for the RMAN files in general (backup-set pieces, etc.) is the flash recovery area, if it is defined.

TABLE 5-1. *File Types Backed Up Within the Flash Recovery Area*

Jonathan Says...
I really like the basic concept of the flash recovery area. Disks are much too big these days, and the most important thing you can do with big disks is find a good excuse for not using more than about 10GB per disk as "active space." In the past I have advised people to take a couple of generations of backup to disk (then copy to tape) as one way of restricting the amount of "real" data stored per disk. Now it's legal! (Of course, I did have other, more official-sounding arguments in favor of this strategy.)

Retention for files in the flash recovery area is determined by the RMAN retention policy. This is set via the RMAN **configure retention policy** command, a feature which is in and of itself not new in Oracle Database 10*g*. If a file does not have a retention policy associated with it, or it's a permanent file, then it will never be deleted. If a file is not yet obsolete under the RMAN retention policy, then it will not be deleted. Finally, archived logs are eligible for deletion once they are obsolete.

Once the amount of space in the flash recovery area starts to reduce to unsafe levels, Oracle Database 10*g* issues a warning to the alert log (at 90 percent used and at 95 percent used). Also, when there is less than 10 percent free space available in the flash recovery area, Oracle Databse 10*g* removes files that are on the obsolete file list.

NOTE
Running out of space in the flash recovery area can be troublesome if that area is your only archive log destination, as this can cause your database to eventually halt. If the flash recovery area is to be your only archive log destination, monitor space availability carefully.

Setting Up the Flash Recovery Area
To set up the flash recovery area, you need to configure the following parameters (which are new in Oracle Database 10*g*):

db_recovery_file_dest_size
Example:

```
Alter system set db_recovery_file_dest_size=20G scope=both;
```

Purpose:
This parameter sets the allocated size of the flash recovery area, and must be defined in order to enable the flash recovery area. This allows you to control how much disk space will be allocated to the flash recovery area.

You should not set this value to a size that is greater than the total amount of available disk space that is available to you. Otherwise, backups will fail.

db_recovery_file_dest
Example:

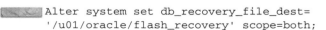
```
Alter system set db_recovery_file_dest=
'/u01/oracle/flash_recovery' scope=both;
```

Purpose:
This is the location of the flash recovery area. The parameter can be set to any valid file system, or you can use Oracle Database 10g Automatic Storage Management (ASM) disk group.

Note that you must specify the **db_recovery_file_dest_size** parameter before you specify the **db_recovery_file_dest** parameter. Failure to do so will result in an ORA-32001 error message. In a similar fashion, you must disable the **db_recovery_file_dest** parameter before you reset the **db_recovery_file_dest_size** parameter. Leaving **db_recovery_file_dest** empty disables the flash recovery area. Here is an example of disabling the flash recovery area by resetting the **db_recovery_file_dest** parameter:

```
Alter system set db_recovery_file_dest=' ' scope=both;
```

Finally, in an Oracle Real Application Clusters environment, you cannot specify these settings for a specific instance; they must be consistent throughout the whole cluster.

Flash Recovery Area Views
The V$RECOVERY_FILE_DEST view, new in Oracle Database 10g, provides an overview of the recovery area that is defined in your database. It provides the size that the flash recovery area is configured for, the amount of space used, how much space can be reclaimed, and the number of files in the flash recovery area.

A new column, IS_RECOVERY_DEST_FILE, can be found in a number of Oracle Database 10g's V$ views, such as V$CONTROLFILE, V$LOGFILE, V$ARCHIVED_LOG, V$DATAFILE_COPY, and V$BACKUP_PIECE. This column is a Boolean that indicates whether or not the file is in a flash recovery area.

Another new column, BYTES, can be found in the views V$BACKUP_PIECE and RC_BACKUP_PIECE (an RMAN recovery catalog view). This column indicates the size, in bytes, of the backup-set piece. This can be used to help you determine how much of the flash recovery area your backups are already consuming.

NOTE
*Manually removing fixed files from the flash recovery area can have unexpected consequences. Oracle Database 10g does not immediately detect the removal of these files, and thus the space is not reclaimed. If you end up manually removing files (or lose a disk perhaps), use the RMAN **crosscheck** command along with the **delete** command to cause Oracle Database 10g to update the current control file information on the flash recovery area.*

RMAN Commands Related to Flash Recovery Areas

RMAN has been enhanced with new commands that allow you to back up and restore the flash recovery area. The RMAN command **backup recovery area** allows you to back up all files required to restore the database via RMAN from a recovery area to an sbt (tape) device. The following types of files are backed up with this command:

- Full and incremental backup sets
- Control file autobackups
- Archive logs
- Datafile copies

Note that this command does not back up the following:

- Flashback logs
- Incremental bitmaps
- The current control file
- Online redo logs

As you have seen, the RMAN command **backup recovery area** backs up all files needed for recovery in the flash recovery area. There is a second command, **backup recovery files**, that backs up all recovery files that are on the disk, wherever they may be (in flash recovery areas or otherwise). The **backup recovery files** command must also go to an sbt device and cannot go to disk.

NOTE
*The **backup recovery area** and **backup recovery files** commands are nice commands to have available when you do your primary backups to disk but want to later back up those backup sets to tape!*

RMAN Backup and Restore to a Flash Recovery Area

When a flash recovery area is defined (via the **db_recovery_file_dest** parameter), RMAN sends backups directly to the flash recovery area. If you are using a local or CFS file system, you will find that RMAN creates a directory structure for the flash recovery area. Typically, the structure includes a directory for the database being backed up and, underneath that directory, another directory for the type of backup.

Recoveries also use the flash recovery area if the appropriate backup set is within the flash recovery area. Also, you can specify a recovery area to use when restoring a control file or SPFILE from an autobackup by using the new **recovery area** clause, as shown in this example:

```
RMAN> Restore controlfile from autobackup using
recovery area 'c:\recovery';
```

Other Flash Recovery Area Features

The **alter database add logfile** and **alter database add standby logfile** commands, by default, now create an online redo log member in the flash recovery area if the OMF-related parameter **db_create_online_log_dest_n** is not set. The **alter database drop logfile** and **alter database rename file** commands also support files in the flash recovery area.

During database creation, Oracle Database 10g can use the flashback recovery area to store the database control file and online redo logs. If the OMF-related parameter **db_create_online_log_dest_n** is defined, then the control file and redo logs will be created in those locations, but will not be created in the flash recovery area, even if the flash recovery area is defined. If **db_create_online_log_dest_n** is not defined but **create_file_dest** is defined, then the control file and online redo logs will be created in the location defined by **create_file_dest**. If the parameter **db_recovery_file_dest** is also defined, then a copy of the control file and online redo logs will get created there as well. Finally, if only **db_recovery_file_dest** is defined, then the control file will get created in that location. If none of these parameters is defined, then the control file and online redo logs will be created to a default location, which is OS specific.

Using Backup Copies and Fast Recovery

RMAN allows you to back up the entire database now as a copy image via the **backup as copy** command. In addition, RMAN allows you to easily switch over to these copy images during a recovery situation, speeding up your recoveries significantly. Let's look at these new features in a bit more detail.

Using the RMAN backup as copy Command

RMAN introduces the **backup as copy** command, which allows you to create file image copies of the database datafiles, rather than creating backup sets (which is the default). You can use this command for the following kinds of backups:

- Database
- Tablespace
- Datafile

Examples of the use of these commands are shown here:

```
RMAN> backup as copy database plus archivelog;
RMAN> backup as copy datafile 1;
RMAN> backup as copy tablespace users;
```

The file backup copies are exact duplicates of the database datafiles, thus they are larger than normal RMAN backup sets. Backup copies can be made to any disk location (and only to disk) via the **format** parameter. You can also configure a default device for disk copies with the **configure** command (discussed in more detail shortly) or, if you have configured a flash recovery area (also covered shortly), RMAN will create your backup copies in that area.

NOTE
An error will be generated if the datafiles are in backup mode during a backup copy.

RMAN Backup File Image Copies: The Up Side and the Down Side

So, what are the benefits of RMAN backup file image copies? As you will see later in this section, RMAN backup copies can reduce your mean time to recover significantly. Use of image copies comes with a price, however, chiefly the requirement for additional disk space to store the copies, as opposed to RMAN backup sets. Since copies are not compressed, each full database copy essentially requires that an amount of space equivalent to the size of your database be allocated.

Another risk with datafile copies is the fact that these copies are stored on disk by RMAN. This leads to a pretty obvious single point of failure that you will want to address in your overall backup and recovery scheme.

Configure the Default Device Type to Copy

Oracle Database 10*g* allows you to configure your default backup type to be a copy backup with the **configure device type** command, as shown here:

```
RMAN> Configure device type disk backup type to copy;
```

Fast Recovery Using RMAN Copies

Previously, if you wanted to restore a database from an RMAN backup, you had a couple of options. The first was to restore the backup-set pieces via RMAN and then recover the database. Even if the backup-set pieces were on disk, this could take a significant amount of time. The second option was to make RMAN copies of each individual datafile and then manually restore from those copies, or locate those copies on a different set of disks and then rename the datafiles from within Oracle Database 10*g*. This was time- and labor-intensive.

Oracle Database 10g allows you to create a backup copy of the database to a different disk location and then quickly switch over to that disk location via the **switch database to copy** RMAN command. When the **switch database** command is issued, RMAN resets the location of the datafiles in the control file to the location of the datafile backup copies previously made via RMAN. After this switch is complete, you then recover the database, using those copies. This method of recovering the database can significantly reduce the overall mean time to recover your database.

Note also that when you switch your database to your datafile copies, you effectively lose one backup of your database. Also, the entire database is then located in one file system, such as the flash recovery area, which can be problematic.

Use RMAN to Back Up the Current Control File

In Oracle Database 10g, RMAN offers a new command, **backup current controlfile**, which is effectively the same as the **alter database backup controlfile** command that you would issue from the SQL prompt. The result is a copy of the control file, stored in the location defined (e.g., a location defined via the **format** command, the default copy value, or the flash recovery area). RMAN also allows you to create a standby control file with the **backup current controlfile for standby** command. The **backup controlfilecopy** command allows you to create backups of previous control file copies.

Using the catalog and uncatalog Commands

Oracle Database 10g offers additional commands that allow you to manipulate the catalog entries of backup sets. The **catalog** command allows you to enter new backup set–related information into the catalog. RMAN will overwrite any pre-existing catalog information that conflicts with the information being cataloged. This command can be handy if you need to move the location of your backup-set pieces. Here is an example of the use of this command:

```
RMAN> catalog backuppiece
'/opt/oracle/oracle-10.0.0/dbs/backup';
```

The **change backuppiece uncatalog** command will remove backup-set pieces from the catalog. If the **change backuppiece uncatalog** command removes the last remaining backup-set piece, then it will also remove the backup-set record. Here is an example of using the change **backuppiece uncatalog** command:

```
RMAN> Change backuppiece
'/u01/oracle/RMAN/mydb/mydb_user01_01.bak' uncatalog;
```

One of the nice uses of the **catalog** command is to allow you to catalog moved backup-set pieces. If you have moved a large number of backup-set pieces, then it can be a great deal of work to generate a bunch of **catalog** statements to catalog the moved pieces. Instead, you can use the **catalog** command with the **start with** option. The **start with** option allows you to define the directory that contains the RMAN backup-set pieces to be cataloged. RMAN will then catalog all backup-set pieces in that directory. Here is an example of using the **catalog** command this way:

```
RMAN> catalog start with '/u01/oracle/RMAN/mydb';
```

Once you press ENTER, this command prompts you with a list of files to catalog, and asks if you wish to catalog the files listed. If you respond in the affirmative, RMAN catalogs all the backup-set pieces listed (which will be contained in the `/u01/oracle/RMAN/mydb directory`). This command also allows you to catalog several like-named backup-set pieces. For example, if you want to catalog several backup-set pieces that start with the name backup (e.g., backupset01, backupset02, etc.), then you could issue the following command:

```
RMAN> catalog start with '/u01/oracle/RMAN/mydb/backup';
```

When you use the **catalog start with** command, it is indiscriminate about the files it tries to catalog; it will try to catalog everything that matches the argument list. However, as the catalog process proceeds, files that are not backup-set pieces will fail the catalog process and an error will occur. Files that are backup-set pieces will be cataloged successfully, in spite of other errors.

Dropping a Database in RMAN

In Oracle Database 10*g*, RMAN provides the capability to drop a database to remove all physical database files, by using the **drop database** command. To drop the database, first log in to the database to be dropped. Then, make sure the database is mounted in exclusive mode, but is not open. Finally, issue the **drop database** command. If you also want to remove all RMAN database-related backups (but not recovery catalog information), you can include the **including backups** option when you issue the **drop database** command. Here is an example call:

```
RMAN> shutdown
RMAN> startup mount
RMAN> drop database;
```

Unregistering a Database in RMAN

Prior to Oracle Database 10*g*, unregistering a database from the recovery catalog was a manual process. Now, Oracle Database 10*g* makes removing a database from the recovery catalog as easy as issuing the command **unregister database**. Here is an example:

```
RMAN> Unregister database mydb;
```

Note that the backup files for this database, and any associated control file records, are not deleted by this command; only the recovery catalog references to those backup files are deleted. Also note that you only need to be connected to the recovery catalog to issue this command.

Changes to Incremental Backups

Oracle Database 10*g* offers some new improvements to incremental backups in RMAN. First, the block change tracking file is introduced to allow for better and faster incremental backups. Also, new features allow you to apply incremental backups to file image copies (another Oracle Database 10*g* new feature introduced earlier in this chapter) for recovery purposes. Let's look at each of these new features in more detail.

The Block Change Tracking File

Oracle Database 10*g* improves incremental backups through the introduction of block change tracking. With block change tracking, a block change tracking file is created and used to track all changed blocks. The block change tracking file is updated on a regular basis as redo is generated in the database. The file is then used by RMAN during incremental backups so that, rather than having to read through each datafile to determine whether a block has changed, Oracle Database 10*g* only needs to read the block change tracking file to know which blocks within a datafile need to be backed up. So, now the time required to back up an Oracle Database 10*g* database with an incremental backup is more a factor of how much data has changed than a factor of how big the datafiles are. Also, the use of block change tracking has the benefit of reducing the overall size of your incremental backup sets.

By default, Oracle Database 10*g* does not record block change information in the database. Using the **alter database enable block change tracking** command, you can enable recording of block change information. Once this command is executed, Oracle Database 10*g* creates the block change tracking file and keeps it current. To disable block change tracking, you can use the **alter database disable block change tracking** command.

The block change tracking file is maintained in the directory defined by the **db_ create_file_dest** parameter, if it is configured. You can also define the location of the block change tracking file via the **using file** clause of the **alter database enable block change tracking** command. You can rename the block change tracking file with the **alter database rename file** command, just as you would with any normal database file. Here is an example of turning on block change tracking, using the **using file** clause to define where the block change tracking file should be

```
Alter database enable block change tacking
using file '/u01/oracle/RMAN/blocktrack/my_db_tracking.chg';
```

Jonathan Says...

In Chapter 6 we will introduce you to a new feature in Oracle Database 10*g*, *bigfile* tablespaces. These tablespaces allow you to store up to 8 exabytes, a rather large amount of data to back up. You probably wondered how you (or RMAN) were going to handle a hot backup of a file that is 8 exabytes—after all, earlier versions of RMAN have to scan the entire file to find out which blocks have changed since the last RMAN backup. Using the block change tracking file is the answer—but it does suggest that if you start thinking about bigfiles, you really ought to be looking at RMAN as your strategic backup mechanism. By the way, this is yet another I/O load on your system—do you have the bandwidth to handle it? Better check the impact carefully.

The block change tacking file size is a factor of a number of things, including the number of enabled redo threads, the size of the database, and the number of RMAN backups for which change data needs to be stored. The formula looks like this:

$$R=((T * 2)+ B) * (S/250000)$$

where the following are the values:

- ■ **R** The size of the block change tracking file, in bytes
- ■ **T** The number of enabled redo threads
- ■ **S** The size of the database, in bytes
- ■ **B** The number of incremental backups for which RMAN needs to store change tracking data

In a test 800MB database, the tracking file (with one backup) was about 10MB. Note that Oracle Database 10*g* will only track change tracking data required for a maximum of eight incremental backups.

If you want to see the status of the block change tracking file, you can use the V$BLOCK_CHANGE_TRACKING view, which gives you the name and location of the block change tracking file, its size, and its status.

The V$BACKUP_DATAFILE view can be used to determine how effective the use of the block change tracking file is. This view can tell you what percentage of blocks in the tablespace that RMAN will be reading (via the BLOCKS_READ column). If the percentage is high, then RMAN will take longer to back up the database. If this is the case, you may want to schedule your incremental backups more frequently.

Applying Incremental Backups to Restore Datafile Image Copies

Earlier, this chapter introduced datafile image copies, a new feature in Oracle Database 10*g*. If you perform incremental backups in Oracle Database 10*g*, another new feature that might interest you is that you can restore your database using a combination of datafile image copies and incremental backups. To apply incremental backups to datafile copies, you restore the datafile copies (using the RMAN **restore** command), and then use the **recover copy of datafile** command to finish the recovery process. Here is an example:

```
RMAN> Recover copy of datafile 6;
RMAN> recover copy of database;
RMAN> recover copy of tablespace users;
```

Note that RMAN will return a warning, not an error, if it cannot restore the database forward to the specified or current time with incremental backups.

Recovering Datafiles Not Backed Up

Previous to Oracle Database 10*g*, a datafile had to have been backed up for RMAN to restore and recover it. In Oracle Database 10*g*, RMAN allows you to perform recovery of a datafile without it having first been backed up. If the datafile is not available in a backup set, RMAN uses the control file to create an empty copy of that datafile. RMAN can then use archived redo logs to recover the datafile. This implies that, to successfully complete the recovery, Oracle Database 10*g* requires all archived redo to be available since the datafile was created. RMAN performs this type of recovery automatically if required.

NOTE
You can only restore missing datafiles with the **restore datafile** *command. The* **restore database** *and* **restore tablespace** *commands do not support this functionality.*

Automatic Channel Failover

In Oracle Database 10*g*, the behavior of RMAN changes with regard to the failure of a channel during an RMAN backup. In Oracle Database 10*g*, if a channel fails, the backup process on that channel fails and will not be restarted. However, backups on other remaining channels will continue to run. Once the backup process is complete, RMAN will report errors that occurred during the backup process. This feature ensures that as many datafiles get backed up as possible, in spite of the error condition.

Compressing RMAN Backups

Prior to Oracle Database 10*g*, RMAN reduced the size of backup images by backing up only the blocks that had been used. That was great if you had a database that was way oversized, but it was of little use for larger databases or databases that had little free space available in the tablespaces.

Oracle Database 10*g* offers real-life compression (Yea!) of RMAN backup sets through the use of the **compressed** parameter when issuing the **backup** command. Here is an example:

```
RMAN> Backup as compressed backupset database;
```

Note that only backup sets can be compressed (e.g., database, tablespace, and datafile backups). Specifically, image copies cannot be compressed. Also, by default, compression is disabled. You can use the **configure** command to define the default disk device to use compression, as shown in this example:

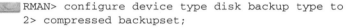
```
RMAN> configure device type disk backup type to
2> compressed backupset;
```

NOTE
I found that backup sets were compressed by about 80 percent when compared to a regular backup set of a rather empty database.

Jonathan Says...
The trade-off between bottlenecks can be tricky. In general, you probably want to reduce the I/O load, so compression sounds like a good idea. But if the compression factor is poor and the CPU cost is relatively high, then you may want to switch the compression off to save CPU.

Controlling Backup Rates and Duration

RMAN allows you to control the rate and duration of RMAN backups. This allows you to back up the database with some control over the impact that that backup has on the operating system. The **duration** parameter of the **backup** command causes RMAN to back up the database files in question at a rate that allows the backup to complete in the time stated. This allows you to spread the backup over a longer period of time, reducing CPU and disk I/O workloads. By default, if the backup is not completed in the time required, an error occurs. You can use the **partial** parameter to indicate that Oracle Database 10g should not return an error at the end of the time duration, but rather should execute normally. In any event, a partial backup will be marked as unusable. The **minimize load** parameter allows you to control the rate of the backup even further. The **minimize load** parameter indicates that RMAN should monitor the speed of the backup process and adjust the throughput rate as required if the backup appears it will consume less time than the stated duration. Here is an example of the use of these commands:

```
RMAN> backup as copy duration 5:00 minimize load database;
```

RMAN-Related TSPITR Changes

Oracle Database 10g removes some of the manual work associated with the use of tablespace point-in-time recovery. You no longer need to create the Oracle auxiliary instance manually; rather, RMAN creates the auxiliary instance for you, performs the TSPITR, and then removes the auxiliary instance.

RMAN Enhanced Scripts

RMAN in Oracle Database 10g allows you to store text-based scripts in the RMAN catalog repository, and these scripts can be used by any database that connects to the RMAN catalog repository. With the enhanced script features, you can load scripts into the recovery catalog with either the **create script** command (for a local script that is only visible to the database that loaded it) or the **create global script** command (for a global RMAN script that is accessible to all databases). Here is an example of creating an enhanced global script:

```
Create global script full_db_backup from file
'/u01/admin/RMAN/backup/backup.rman';
```

You can replace scripts with the **replace script** or **replace global script** command, and you can remove scripts with the **delete script** command. You can also reverse the process, saving a stored script to a file via the **print script** or **print global script** command. The **list script names** and **list global script names** commands provide a listing of all global scripts. Also, the **list all script names** command provides a listing of all scripts in the recovery catalog.

To execute the stored scripts, use the **execute script** or **execute global script** command. It is possible for a private and a global script with the same name to exist. In this case, the **execute script** command executes the private script first; if a private script does not exist, then it executes the global script. A global script is the only script executed when the **execute global script** command is used.

New Flashback Features

Oracle Database 10*g* offers some new features associated with flashback query. The first is Flashback Database, which allows you to flash back the entire database to a specific point in time. The second feature is Flashback Drop, which allows you to undrop an object in the Oracle Database 10*g* database. We will also look at flashback version query, which allows you to look at a set of changes that have occurred in the database between two sets of times. Also, Oracle Database 10*g* allows you to configure a tablespace for guaranteed retention, ensuring that the undo in the tablespace will be retained. The following sections discuss these features in more detail.

Flashback Database

Flashback query is a very powerful feature in Oracle Database that was introduced in Oracle9*i* and enhanced in Oracle9*i* Release 2. Now, Oracle Database 10*g* offers even more functionality in the form of Flashback Database. Flashback Database allows you to flash back the entire database to a specific point in time. This can be useful to resolve problems such as logical data corruption that might be caused by wayward application code. Also, Flashback Database can help in the resolution of user errors that might cause the loss or unintentional change in data (we all know that never happens!).

NOTE
Flashback Database is not a means of recovering the database in the event of some physical loss, or recovering from some form of physical corruption.

One of the principle benefits of Flashback Database is that it can be a much faster method of recovering data than other recovery methods (e.g., via tablespace point-in-time recovery or logical backups or Log Miner). Let's look in a bit more detail at the architecture associated with Flashback Database, and then look at how to use Oracle Database 10*g*'s Flashback Database.

Flashback Database Architecture

Flashback Database involves some new Oracle Database 10*g* architectural components that you will want to be aware of: Flashback Database logs, and RVWR, one of the new Oracle Database 10*g* background processes.

Flashback Database Logs   A Flashback Database log is a new kind of log file that contains the before image of Oracle database blocks. The Flashback Database logs must be created in the database recovery area (and thus a flashback recovery area must be configured). Flashback logs are not archived, as are database redo logs, and they are not used for physical database recovery.

The RVWR Background Process   When Flashback Database is enabled, a new background process, RVWR, is started. This process is responsible to write Flashback Database data to the Flashback Database logs.

Using Flashback Database

You can use Oracle Database 10*g*'s Flashback Database features from three different tools: SQL*Plus, RMAN, and OEM. Let's look at some basic requirements for using Oracle Flashback Database.

Basic Flashback Database Use Requirements   To use Flashback Database, the database must first be in archivelog mode. Also, you must have any Real Application Clusters databases mounted in exclusive mode. You must also have a flashback recovery area configured, as described earlier in this chapter (done by setting the **db_recovery_file_dest** and **db_recovery_file_dest_size** database parameters). The **compatible** parameter should be set to 10.0 or higher.

Jonathan Says...
Oh dear, another Oracle process generating yet more I/O. You had better have a good reason for wanting flashback logging switched on. You should always be very reluctant about introducing expensive run-time features without some very solid justification.

Flashback Database from SQL*Plus   To use Flashback Database from the SQL*Plus prompt, you must connect to the database by using the AS SYSDBA login. To enable Flashback Database from SQL*Plus, follow these steps:

1. Shut down the database.

2. Mount the database (if it is a Real Application Clusters database, mount it in exclusive mode).

3. Via the **alter system** command, set the database parameter **db_flashback_retention_target** to a value that defines how far you want to flash back the database. Although this indicates to Oracle Database 10*g* how far you wish to flash back your database, the availability of undo back to that point in time is critical. Here is an example:

```
alter system set
db_flashback_retention_target=2880;
```

4. Enable Flashback Database with the **alter database** command using the new Oracle Database 10*g* syntax, **flashback on**:

```
alter database flashback on;
```

5. Now, open the database with the **alter database open command**. You are now prepared to use flashback database! Make some changes to your database at this point. Once you have made some changes, record the current SCN (from the CURRENT_SCN column in the V$DATABASE view if you like!).

6. **Shutdown** and then **mount** the database again.

7. Use the **Flashback Database to timestamp** or the **Flashback Database to scn** command to enable Database Flashback:

```
SQL> Flashback Database to timestamp (sysdate-2);
SQL> Flashback Database to scn 2034455;
```

8. Open the database in read-only mode with the **alter database open read only** command, and make sure that you have flashed back the database to the point in time you are interested in.

9. Once you are sure the database is at the point in time that you wish to restore it to, open the database using the **alter database open resetlogs** command.

10. You can flash forward or backwards via the **flashback database** command as much as you like until you have opened the database with the **alter**

database open resetlogs command. Once the **alter database open resetlogs** command has been issued, the database changes cannot be altered.

NOTE
It's always a good idea to record the SCN of the database before you perform a flashback operation. That way you can recover to that SCN if need be.

You can disable database flashback through the use of the **alter database flashback off** command (the database must be mounted and in exclusive mode). If you wish to disable flashback logging for a specific tablespace, use the **alter tablespace flashback off** command; you can re-enable flashback logging with the **alter tablespace flashback on** command. If you disable flashback for a specific tablespace, you must also take its associated datafiles offline.

Flashback Database from RMAN   In Oracle Database 10*g* RMAN supports the use of Flashback Database to restore the database back to a specific point in time, using the database SCN or log sequence number. Using the RMAN **Flashback Database** command allows you to restore the database as it looked at a specific point in time, as long as the undo is available to flash back to that point in time. This makes for much quicker restores. Here is an example of using RMAN to restore the database using Flashback Database (note that the database must be mounted, and not open, to execute these RMAN operations)

```
-- Flashback to a specific date and time
RMAN> Flashback Database to_time =
to_date('2003-12-01 01:05:00','YYYY-MM-DD HH24:MI:SS');

-- Flashback up to but not including a specific SCN
RMAN> Flashback Database to scn = 302223;

-- flashback up to but not including a specific sequence
-- number.
RMAN> Flashback database until sequence=1022 thread=1;
```

Once RMAN has completed its Flashback Database operation, you can open the database in read-only mode and make sure it's recovered to the point you want it recovered to. If it is, simply open the database using the **alter database open resetlogs** command to open the database for write operations.

Flashback Database Views

Oracle Database 10*g* offers several views that are associated with database flashback:

- V$DATABASE

- V$FLASHBACK_DATABASE_LOG

- V$FLASHBACK_DATABASE_STAT

V$DATABASE View   The V$DATABASE view has a new column associated with it for Flashback Database called FLASHBACK_ON. This column is a Boolean value that indicates whether or not Flashback Database is enabled.

V$FLASHBACK_DATABASE_LOG View   The V$FLASHBACK_DATABASE_LOG view is a new view in Oracle Database 10*g* that allows you to monitor the Flashback Database retention target. This view can help you to estimate the amount of space in the recovery area that will be required for the flashback workload. This view contains columns that allow you to query the following:

- The lowest Flashback Database SCN or time (OLDEST_FLASHBACK_SCN and OLDEST_FLASHBACK_TIME columns)

- The retention target time (RETENTION_TARGET column)

- The current size of the flashback data, in bytes (FLASHBACK_SIZE column)

- The estimated size of flashback data that you need for your current target retention (ESTIMATED_FLASHBACK_SIZE column)

V$FLASHBACK_DATABASE_STAT View   The V$FLASHBACK_DATABASE_STAT view can be used to monitor the overhead of maintaining the flashback data in the Flashback Database logs. From this view, you can estimate the total amount of space that will be required for future Flashback Database operations.

Flashback Database Limitations

Some limitations to Flashback Database exist. You cannot use Flashback Database to flash back a database to a point in time before the following operations occurred:

- The database control file has been restored or re-created

- The object that you need to query belongs in a tablespace that has been dropped

- The database datafile that contains the object to be queried has been shrunk

- A recovery through the **resetlogs** command has occurred

As an example, suppose that you drop the TOOLS tablespace and re-create it and the objects within it. You cannot flash back the database to a point before you dropped the TOOLS tablespace and successfully query objects in that tablespace (though you can query objects in other tablespaces at that time). You can, however, flash back the database to a point-in-time after you re-created the TOOLS tablespace, and perform a query against any changes that occurred in that tablespace after it was re-created.

Flashback Drop

Oracle Database 10*g* offers Flashback Drop. This feature allows you to undo the effects of a **drop table** command via the new **flashback table** SQL command using the **to before drop** syntax. This section looks at the Flashback Drop of a table via the **flashback table** command. First, it introduces you to the recycle bin. Then, it shows how to undrop tables with the **flashback table** command. Finally, it describes the data dictionary views associated with Flashback Drop.

NOTE
You do not need to enable Flashback Database in order to use this feature.

Recycle Bin

To support Flashback Drop, Oracle Database 10*g* introduces the concept of a recycle bin. So, now when a table is removed, it is moved to the recycle bin and remains there until the recycle bin is purged. Thus, a statement like **drop table parts** causes the parts table to be moved to the recycle bin. If you want to drop the parts table and not have it get moved into the recycle bin, use the new **purge** parameter of the **drop table** command:

```
SQL> Drop table parts purge;
```

Note that objects that are dropped and moved into the recycle bin do not have their extents deallocated, so they will continue to take up space in your database until you purge them from the recycle bin or free space is consumed, in which case Oracle Database 10*g* will purge older objects from the recycle bin automatically. Use the **purge table** command to purge objects from the recycle bin, as shown in this example:

```
Purge table rb$$44022$table$0;
```

You can also use the **purge tablespace** command to purge all objects in the recycle bin associated with a specific tablespace, as shown in this example:

```
Purge tablespace all_users;
```

Note that this command will not remove objects in the tablespace (not already in the recycle bin) or drop the tablespace itself.

You might have noticed in the **purge table** command example that the command referenced a rather odd-looking object name, rb$$44022$table$0. The reason for this odd name is that Oracle Database 10g renames objects when they are moved to the recycle bin, to avoid naming conflicts. The naming convention takes the form

rb$$*OBJ#*$$*ObjectType*$*Version*

where:

- *OBJ#* is the dictionary object number of the object

- *ObjectType* is the type of the object. This might be table, normal index, or bitmap index.

- *Version* makes sure the object name is unique.

Flashback Drop Data Dictionary Views

You can find a list of objects in the recycle bin, and their associated object names, through a query against the USER_RECYCLEBIN view. Here is an example of a query against this view that demonstrates the relationship between the object name of the objects in the recycle bin and the old database objects:

```
SELECT object_name, original_name, type
from user_recyclebin;
```

What's really cool about the recycle bin is that you can continue to query an object after you have dropped it! You simply query the object based on its new object name, as shown in this example:

```
Select * from rb$$44022$table$0;
```

The flashback table to before drop Command

The benefit of the recycle bin is that it enables you to recover a table that you have dropped. To do this, you issue the **flashback table** command using the **to before drop** parameter:

```
SQL> flashback table mytab to before drop;
```

This is a very easy way to recover your table from the recycle bin. If you have created and dropped the same object multiple times, then the one most recently dropped will be recovered. You can use the recycle bin name for the table if you prefer, which allows you to restore the specific version of the table that you wish to restore. Also, you can use the **rename to** clause to rename the table that is being recovered as seen in this example:

```
SQL> flashback table mytab to before drop rename to test;
```

Once the table is recovered by the **flashback table** command, it is removed out of the recycle bin (though other, older versions of that object may still exist in the recycle bin).

When you retrieve a table from the recycle bin, all associated indexes will be retrieved as well, except bitmap join indexes, which are not saved in the recycle bin after a **drop table** operation. If the recycle bin starts running out of space, Oracle Database 10g will remove index entries before it removes table entries. Thus, **flashback table** operations might not restore all indexes.

Triggers and constraints are restored as well except foreign key constraints. Note that all restored, table-related objects will be restored with their recycle bin names, rather than their original names. So, you might want to make a note of the original names before you do the restore. Also, materialized views (Mviews) that are dependent on the tables being dropped are dropped and are not saved in the recycle bin, so they are lost forever.

Flashback Versions Query

Can you conceive of a case where you would like to see all the versions of data for a given row over a given point in time? Perhaps you would like to see how much a specific employee's salary has changed over the last month for auditing purposes. Oracle Database 10g offers Flashback Versions Query for just such an occasion. With this feature, you can define a minimum and maximum time (using the **versions between timestamp** clause of the **select** statement) or scn range (using the **versions between scn** clause of the **select** statement), and then query a specific row or set of rows in a table to see a list of all values assigned to those rows.

Jonathan Says...

Don't forget to ask your application suppliers, the ones who create and drop temporary tables all over the place, how they plan to handle the side effects of this feature. It's a good thing that items in the recycle bin will be purged automatically on an "out of space" condition.

Here is an example of using Flashback Versions Query. In this example, we want to look at a list of employee salary values and how they have changed between 30 minutes ago and 1 minute ago.

```
SELECT ename, sal FROM emp
   VERSIONS BETWEEN TIMESTAMP
     SYSTIMESTAMP - INTERVAL '30' MINUTE AND
     SYSTIMESTAMP - INTERVAL '1' MINUTE
     WHERE empno=22;
```

Note that the changes that are shown are only committed changes (changes committed or rolled back). Also note that you cannot use the **versions between** clause of the **select** statement when querying a view, but this clause can be used within the definition of a view. Also, the ability to use Flashback Versions Query is dependent on the availability of undo records, which also implies that it's dependent on the setting of the **undo_retention** parameter. If the time or SCN listed in the BETWEEN clause represents a point in time beyond the **undo_retention** parameter setting, then an error will be returned.

Flashback version query requires that the **flashback** and **select** privileges be granted to any nonprivileged user who you wish to allow to use flashback version queries. Also, if you will be using Flashback Versions Query or other Oracle flashback features frequently on specific objects, you might want to consider another new feature, Guaranteed Undo Retention, which is the next topic.

Configuring Guaranteed Undo Retention

With Oracle Flashback Query and all the new derivatives of Flashback Query in Oracle Database 10*g*, dependency on the presence of undo can be critical. If you have a database that you will be performing frequent flashback operations on, then you might want to consider setting the UNDO Tablespace to guarantee the retention of all undo information until it has expired (as defined by the **undo_ retention** parameter). Note that if the UNDO Tablespace is set to guarantee retention of undo, then operations that need to generate undo will fail if sufficient undo area is not available, because Oracle Database 10*g* will not expire undo before its time when undo retention is specified.

You can use the **retention guarantee** parameter of the **create UNDO Tablespace** or **alter UNDO Tablespace** command, as shown in these examples:

```
-- Assumes OMF is configured.
Create UNDO Tablespace undotbs01
size 200m autoextend on
retention guarantee;
alter tablespace undotbs01 retention guarantee;
```

To reset an UNDO Tablespace so that undo retention is no longer guaranteed, use the **alter tablespace retention noguarantee** command.

The **create database** command also supports the **retention guarantee** clause. You can tell if you have put the UNDO Tablespace in retention mode through a query against the RETENTION column of the DBA_TABLESPACES view. Here is an example:

```
Select tablespace_name, retention from dba_tablespaces;
```

Flashback Transaction Query

Oracle Database 10*g* provides the ability to easily reconstruct SQL statements that have been previously executed by the database. Previously, you would need to use Log Miner to generate SQL redo statements that could be used to replicate SQL statements executed in the database. Now, Flashback Transaction Query can be used to reconstruct the SQL statements used to make changes in the database, and those that can be used to undo the change.

Flashback Transaction Query is supported through the new Oracle Database 10*g* view FLASHBACK_TRANSACTION_QUERY. The use of this view is dependent on the presence of undo, so the **undo_retention** parameter needs to be set in such a way as to preserve the undo that you will need. Likewise, you may want to configure guaranteed undo retention (as described earlier in this chapter) as well.

The following is an example of using the FLASHBACK_TRANSACTION_QUERY view. In this case, suppose that records got inserted into the mytab table in the last hour, and we want to remove all of those records. We can query the FLASHBACK_TRANSACTION_QUERY view for all SCNs between 21553 and 44933 (we could use a timestamp as well) and, using the UNDO_SQL column, extract the SQL that will be required to undo those operations:

```
SELECT undo_sql FROM flashback_transaction_query
WHERE table_owner='ROBERT' and table_name='MYTAB'
AND start_scn between 21553 and 44933;
```

NOTE
The indexing on the FLASHBACK_TRANSACTION_ QUERY view seems to be lacking, and some queries (like the one in the example) can take some time to return.

Flashback Table

Restoring a table to a point in time different than that of the rest of the database can be a messy operation. If you are lucky, you will have an export from the point in time right before the data change. The other possibility is to use tablespace point in time recovery, but that is time consuming and messy. What if, instead, we could just flash back our table to the point in time we are interested in. Well, with Oracle Database 10*g* we can! Now, with the **flashback table** command, you can flash back an Oracle Database 10*g* table based on timestamp or database SCN. All flashback table operations must be at the beginning of any transaction, and flashback table operations are not supported for the SYS user. Here is an example:

```
SQL> Commit;
SQL> Flashback table emp to SCN 220360;
SQL> flashback table emp to TIMESTAMP
to_timestamp('2003-09-30 09:00:00',
             'YYYY-MM-DD HH:MI:SS');
```

To be able to flash back a table, the table must have row movement enabled via the **alter table enable row movement** command (row movement is disabled by default). Enabling row movement is something that can be done just before you issue the **flashback table** command, so you don't need it enabled all the time. The **flashback table** command allows you to flash back or flash forward; thus, you can undo the effects of a previous **flashback table** command. You cannot flash back to a time prior to most DDL operations on the table being flashed back, or before the last time that the database was opened with the **resetlogs** command. Also, when you execute a **flashback table** statement, the execution of that statement is recorded in the alert log.

> **NOTE**
> *Since you can flash forward, it is a good idea to record the current SCN of the database before you flash back a table. The current SCN is available in the CURRENT_SCN column in the V$DATABASE view. Record the SCN before you issue the **flashback table** command, not after.*

New Transaction Recovery Monitoring Features

Oracle Database 10*g* offers enhancements to monitoring the rollback of transactions by SMON, and offers historical information about transaction recovery and rollback operations. This allows you to determine how much work remains during recovery operations. This monitoring is supported via the V$FAST_START_TRANSACTIONS view, which provides information about transactions that Oracle Database 10*g* is recovering as well as transactions that have been recovered. Also, the V$FAST_START_SERVERS view provides information about recovery operations that the database server is performing.

The following SQL provides a report that allows you to track transaction recovery during instance recovery:

```
Select state, undoblocksdone, undoblockstotal, cputime
FROM v$fast_start_transactions;
```

Transactions that are recovered will have a state of RECOVERED, thus these views provide historical information on rollbacks and recoveries. This information is available until the next time the instance is cycled.

NOTE
Smaller recovery operations do not show up in the views V$FAST_START_TRANSACTIONS and V$FAST_START_SERVERS.

The V$SESSION_LONGOPS view can now be used to monitor transaction rollback operations. This can assist you in determining how long a given rollback operation will take to complete.

New Data Guard Features

In Oracle Database 10g, Data Guard comes with a number of new features that you will want to be aware of. These include

- The ability to apply redo in real time on both physical and logical standby databases

- A new attribute, **valid_for**

- New features related to transmission of database generated redo

- New parameters associated with Oracle Database 10g standby databases

- Changes to the way that Oracle Database 10g will start a standby database

- The ability of the ARCH process to write directly to the standby redo logs

- The ability to assign threads to standby redo log groups

- Enhancements to Oracle Database 10g logical standby database

Apply Redo in Real Time

Prior to Oracle Database 10g, at best, redo could be shipped to a physical standby database, in real time, and it would be stored in standby redo logs. Unfortunately, that redo would still not be applied to the physical standby database until a log switch occurred on the primary database. Thus, the data in the primary and standby databases was always physically divergent. Logical standby databases were even worse, since they only supported application of redo from archived redo logs on the remote database after a log switch. As a result, not only was the logical standby database data divergent from that of the primary, but the redo data was really at risk too. This lag in applying the redo also has implications with mean time to recover, since the standby has to apply the remaining redo in the standby redo log before it can come up. This can delay the opening of the standby database as the new primary database.

Oracle Database 10g solves both of these problems! Now the log apply services can be configured to apply redo data almost in real time from the standby redo logs. When configured for real-time application, redo will be written to the standby database itself at nearly the same time (by the Managed Recovery Process [MRP] or Logical Standby Process [LSP]) that the primary database LGWR and Remote File System (RFS) processes write the redo to the standby redo log files. Let's look in a bit more detail at the use of real-time log apply and how it works on both physical and logical standby databases.

NOTE
The Dataguard Broker also supports real-time apply.

Real-Time Log Apply: Physical Standby Database

If the standby database is a physical standby database, real-time log apply can only occur while the physical database is in log apply mode. If the physical standby database is in read-only mode, then no application of redo data will occur. Once the physical standby database is put back into application mode, the log apply service will catch up and return to real-time apply as quickly as possible.

For a physical standby database, the MRP is responsible for application of the redo log files. The application of the redo log file data occurs once the RFS process has actually written the redo. To start the real-time application process on the standby database, use the **alter database recover managed standby database** command along with the new **using current logfile** parameter, as shown in this example:

```
Alter database recover managed standby database
using current logfile;
```

Real-Time Log Apply: Logical Standby Database

The LSP is responsible for the application of redo on the standby database. Again, once the RFS process has finished writing the redo from the primary database, the LSP will pick up that redo and apply it. To start the real-time application of redo, use the **alter database start logical standby** command with the new **apply immediate** clause, as shown in this example:

```
Alter database start logical standby apply immediate;
```

Monitoring Real-Time Log Apply

You can determine if the logical standby database is running in real-time apply mode by querying the V$ARCHIVE_DEST_STATUS view on the standby database. The column RECOVERY_MODE will indicate MANAGED REAL TIME APPLY if the standby database is in real-time apply mode.

NOTE
*It is not possible to configure a delay if you are using real-time apply mode. Oracle Database 10*g *will simply ignore the **delay** attribute if it is used.*

The valid_for Attribute

The **valid_for** attribute is a new attribute that can be associated with the **log_archive_dest_n** parameter in Oracle Database 10*g*. This attribute allows you to define when an archive log destination will be used and the role of the archived redo at that destination.

The **valid_for** attribute takes two parameters, the **archival_source** parameter and the **database_role** parameter. The **archival_source** parameter defines when the destination is used. Valid settings for this parameter are as follows:

- **ONLINE_LOGFILE**   This destination is used only when archiving online redo log files. This destination is not used when archiving standby redo log files, or if log files are being received from another database.

- **STANDBY_LOGFILE**   This destination is used only when standby redo log files are being archived or if archived redo logs are being received from another database.

- **ALL_LOGFILES**   This destination can be used in either role, archiving online or standby redo log files.

The **database_role** parameter is the second parameter of the **valid_for** attribute. As the name implies, this parameter defines the role of the database that the parameter is associated with and, thus, when the archive log destination will be used. Valid settings for this parameter are as follows:

- **PRIMARY_ROLE** This destination is used only when the database is in the primary database role.

- **STANDBY_ROLE** This destination is used only when the database is in a standby role. This applies to both physical and logical standby databases.

- **ALL_ROLES** Open the barn doors Bessie! This destination is used if the database is in primary or standby mode.

The parameters for the **valid_for** attribute can be specified in any order, but only specific combinations are valid for the attribute. For example, the combination of STANDBY_LOGFILE and PRIMARY_ROLE is invalid and will generate an error at database startup.

Here is an example of an archivelog destination having been set, using the **valid_for** attribute of the **log_archive_dest_1** parameter:

```
LOG_ARCHIVE_DEST_1= service=STANDBY_DB
VALID_FOR = (STANDBY_LOGFILE, STANDBY_ROLE)
```

Data Dictionary Views and valid_for

The V$ARCHIVE_DEST data dictionary view has a new column, VALID_NOW, that indicates if the archivelog destination will be used. Valid values include

- **YES** The destination is properly defined and will be used.

- **WRONG VALID_TYPE** The archivelog destination is properly defined, but in the current role it cannot be used. This might occur if the archive log destination was defined for a standby database, and the database was currently configured as a primary database.

- **WRONG VALID_ROLE** The archivelog destination is not defined correctly for the current database role (primary or standby).

- **UNKNOWN** Indicates that the archivelog destination is not defined.

Also, the V$ARCHIVE_DEST view provides two additional new columns, VALID_TYPE and VALID_ROLE, that allow you to see how the **valid_for** parameter for each archivelog destination is configured.

Redo Transmission Enhancements

Oracle Database 10*g* provides two new enhancements with regard to redo transmission. First of all, database authentication must now be set up for all databases. This means that the **remote_login_passwordfile** parameter must be set to either SHARED or EXCLUSIVE at both the primary and all standby sites. Also, a password file must be generated, and all SYS passwords must be set the same at all sites. If you change the SYS password, it will be automatically changed at all sites.

Oracle Database 10*g* now also supports encryption of the redo stream to the standby databases as an optional feature. You must have the Oracle Advanced Security option installed at all database sites, and have configured Oracle Net for encryption and integrity checksumming.

New Standby Database Parameters

Oracle Database 10*g* depreciates the **lock_name_space** parameter in favor of a new parameter, **db_unique_name**. Going forward, you should use the **db_unique_name** parameter to assign unique names to each of your standby databases. The name can be up to 30 characters long, and each Real Application Clusters instance should use the same name.

> **NOTE**
> *Deprecation of a parameter indicates that it is still available for use. If a parameter is obsolete, then it is no longer available for use in the database.*

The **remote_archive_enable** parameter is replaced with the **log_archive_config** parameter (Oracle recommends replacing **remote_archive_enable** with **log_archive_config** in Oracle Database 10*g*). The **log_archive_config** parameter allows you to define the standby database configuration currently in use, and update it dynamically. The **db_unique_name** parameter contains the name of each database in the standby database configuration, and then defines the role in the configuration as one of these four values:

- **send** Indicates that the database, when in primary database mode, can send redo logs to the standby database (default).

- **nosend** Opposite of **send**, the database cannot send redo logs to the standby.

- **receive**   Indicates that when running in standby mode, the database can receive redo logs from the primary database (default).

- **noreceive**   Opposite of **receive**, the database cannot receive redo logs from the primary database.

The **log_archive_config** parameter should be the same for each Real Application Clusters instance. Also, the **log_archive_config** parameter has an attribute, **db_config**, that lists all databases in the standby database configuration. You can dynamically add databases to the configuration by changing this setting dynamically. This eliminates the need to shut down the database when running in maximum availability or maximum protection mode.

Here is an example of the configuration of the **log_archive_config** parameter, using the **db_config** parameter:

```
LOG_ARCHIVE_CONFIG=('SEND,RECEIVE,
DB_CONFIG=('MAIN_DB_DFW','STBY_NY','STBY_LAX')')
```

Changes to Standby Database Startups

Prior to Oracle Database 10*g*, you would first need to start the database instances (**startup nomount**) and then either mount it as a standby database and start managed recovery, or open the database in read-only mode.

In Oracle Database 10*g*, if you issue the **startup mount** command, Oracle Database 10*g* reads the database control file and, if the database is a standby database, mounts the database as a standby database in preparation for managed recovery to be started. You still need to start managed recovery. Also, if you have issued the **startup** command and the database is a standby database, it will open the standby database in read-only mode.

ARCH Process Writes to Standby Redo Logs

In Oracle Database 10*g*, the ARCH process now has the ability to write to standby redo logs. This helps with the registration of partially archived redo logs and allows for the configuration of an almost unlimited number of cascaded redo log destinations.

Assign Threads to Standby Redo Log Groups

Oracle Database 10*g* allows you to assign standby redo logs to specific redo threads if you are running a Real Application Clusters configuration. This is supported with the new thread parameter of the **alter database add standby logfile** command. The assignment of a thread is optional, however, and Oracle Database 10*g* will assign the standby redo log to a thread as required.

Logical Standby Database Enhancements

Oracle Database 10*g* offers a number of improvements in logical standby databases. These include the following:

- The ability to instantiate your logical standby database with zero downtime

- The ability of logical standby databases to support maximum protection mode

- New SQL Apply support for data types

- Optimized switchover operations on logical standby databases

- New data dictionary views to manage standby databases

- The ability to bypass the SQL Apply services to make changes to the logical standby database

- The ability to skip a failed transaction

Instantiate a Logical Standby Database with Zero Downtime

Prior to Oracle Database 10*g*, instantiation of a logical standby database would likely require an outage of the primary database, because the primary database would need to be quiesced, an operation that required that Resource Manager be enabled at database startup. Since many production databases operate without Resource Manager enabled, this would require a cycle of the database. Also, a quiesce of a database could take a long time, particularly in databases with a great deal of activity. Oracle Database 10*g* removes the requirement to quiesce the database before making the online backup that is the source of the logical standby database. This makes the creation of the logical standby database possible without any downtime at all. This change is supported by changes to the standby control file in Oracle Database 10*g*.

The following is a quick highlight of the steps needed to create a logical standby database, to demonstrate the changes in the procedure. I recommend that you look at the Oracle documentation ("Oracle Data Guard Concepts and Administration") for more detail on this procedure (as it may change in interim releases of the database). The general steps are as follows:

1. Take an online backup of the primary database (no quiesce is required; also note there is no need to record the SCN at the end of the backup).

2. After the backup is complete, create a logical standby database control file on the primary by using the **alter database create standby logical control file** command:

```
Alter database Create standby logical control file AS
'/tmp/control_logical.fil';
```

3. Copy the backed-up datafiles, archived redo logs, and the logical standby control file to the location where you will create the logical standby database.

4. Restore the database at the standby site with the logical standby control file. Do not open the database.

5. Configure log transport services on the primary and standby database sites so that redo can be shipped from the primary site to the standby sites as it's generated.

6. Start managed recovery on the standby database with the **alter database** command:

```
Alter database recover managed standby database;
```

Note that this is the same method of recovering a physical standby database.

7. Activate the standby database with the **alter database** command:

```
Alter database activate standby database;
```

8. Using the DBNEWID program, change the DBNAME and DBID of the standby database. Follow the instructions in the *Oracle Database 10*g *Database Utilities* guide on how to do this.

9. Start the logical standby database log application services:

```
Alter database start logical standby apply;
```

Once these steps are complete, you have created an Oracle Database 10*g* logical standby database!

Logical Standby Database Support for Maximum Protection Mode

Previously, logical standby databases did not support maximum protection mode. This implied that there was always some level of data divergence between the primary and the logical standby database, which meant that there was a risk of data loss during an unplanned switchover operation.

Oracle Database 10*g* allows you to configure a logical standby database in maximum protection mode. You can now create standby redo logs for a logical standby database, which is required for maximum protection mode, and you can configure the primary database to send redo to the logical standby database in maximum protection mode.

New SQL Apply Support for Data Types

SQL Apply now supports a number of new data types. These include CLOB, NCLOB, LONG, and LONG_RAW. Also, two new Oracle Database 10*g* data types,

BINARY_FLOAT and BINARY_DOUBLE, are supported by SQL Apply. SQL Apply also supports tables with columns set to UNUSED. Note that index organized tables with overflow segments or BLOB columns are still not supported.

Optimized Switchover Operations on Logical Standby Databases

Switchover operations to logical standby databases are optimized with the new **prepare to switchover to** command. With the **alter database prepare to switchover to primary** command, the logical standby database will proceed to build the Log Miner dictionary before the actual switchover operation occurs from a standby to a primary configuration. The **alter database prepare to switchover to standby** command notifies the primary database that it will soon find itself converted to a standby role. After the **alter database prepare to switchover** command is executed, it should be followed by the **alter database commit to switchover** command.

As a result of these new commands, the process to switch over between primary and standby mode has changed. I recommend that you look at the Oracle documentation ("Oracle Data Guard Concepts and Administration") for more detail on this procedure (as it may change in interim releases of the database). However, in summary, the new steps are as follows:

1. Issue the **alter database prepare switchover to standby** command on the primary database.

2. Issue the **alter database prepare to switchover to primary** command on the logical standby database. Watch for any errors that might be raised by Oracle Database 10*g* during the execution of this command.

3. On the primary database, start the switchover operation via the **alter database commit to switchover to logical standby** command.

4. On the logical standby database, after the apply commits, finish the switchover operation with the **alter database commit to switchover** command.

5. On the new logical standby database, start the SQL Apply service using the **alter database start logical standby apply** command.

NOTE
*After you have used the **prepare switchover** commands, you should complete the **commit to switchover** operations as soon as possible. The longer you wait, the longer the actual switchover will take.*

New Data Dictionary Views to Manage Standby Databases

Oracle Database 10*g* offers new and updated data dictionary views to assist you in managing your standby database. These include

- **DBA_LOGSTDBY_UNSUPPORTED** This view defines unsupported object storage attributes.

- **DBA_LOGSTDBY_LOG** This view allows you to determine which archived redo logs have been applied to the standby database.

- **DBA_LOGSTDBY_PROGRESS** This view has new columns that provide more detail on the progress of the SQL Apply service. These columns include

  - **APPLIED_SEQUENCE#** Sequence number of the log that contains the APPLIED_SCN column, which existed prior to Oracle Database 10*g*

  - **APPLIED_THREAD#** Thread number for the log associated with the APPLIED_SCN column

  - **READ_SEQUENCE#** Sequence number of the log associated with the READ_SCN column

  - **READ_THREAD#** Thread number of the log that is associated with the READ_SCN column

  - **NEWEST_SEQUENCE#** Sequence number of the log associated with the NEWEST_SCN column

  - **NEWEST_THREAD#** Thread number of the log that is associated with the NEWEST_SCN column

Bypassing the SQL Apply Services to Make Changes to the Logical Standby Database

If you need to make changes to your logical standby database (adding indexes, etc.), you need to bypass the Data Guard process. New commands that supercede the use of the Oracle-supplied procedures **dbms_logstdby.guard_bypass_on** and **guard_bypass_off** are available in Oracle Database 10*g*. The new commands are **alter session enable guard** and **alter session disable guard**.

Skipping a Failed Transaction

In many cases, if the SQL Apply operation halts, all you really want to do is skip the transaction that failed and continue on with the next transaction. Oracle Database 10*g* makes this easy with the **skip failed transaction** option of the **alter database start standby apply** command. This command is identical to the **dbms_logstby.skip_transaction** stored procedure, but will find the transaction automatically and then restart the SQL Apply operation.

CHAPTER
6

Business Intelligence

- Oracle Data Pump
- Bigfile Tablespaces
- Cross-Platform Transportable Tablespaces
- Enhanced Merge Functionality
- Enhanced External Table Functionality
- New Materialized View, Query Rewrite, and Summary Management DDL Features
- Partitioning New Features

racle Database 10*g* comes with a number of new features that are designed to improve data warehouses, data marts, and operational data stores. Also, several features that existed in earlier versions of Oracle Database have new features added to them. This chapter discusses several new and enhanced features, including:

- Oracle Data Pump (previously **exp** and **imp**)
- Bigfile tablespaces
- Cross-platform transportable tablespaces
- External table unload
- Enhanced table functions
- Enhanced merge functionality
- Materialized view and query rewrite changes
- Partitioning new features

Oracle Data Pump

Oracle Database 10*g* offers new and improved support for logical extracts of data in the form of Oracle Data Pump. This section introduces several topics related to Oracle Data Pump:

- The Oracle Data Pump architecture
- The data dictionary views associated with Oracle Data Pump
- The new interactive mode available with Oracle Data Pump
- The Oracle Data Pump API
- Oracle Data Pump Export and Import

Oracle Data Pump Architecture

Oracle Database 10*g* introduces the new Data Pump infrastructure. A major part of this infrastructure replaces the **imp** (import) and **exp** (export) programs in previous versions of Oracle Database. The new Data Pump architecture is designed to provide significant performance increases over the previous **imp** and **exp** utilities. Data Pump provides new methods of moving data between databases, including the use of specially formatted files (as was the case with **imp/exp**) as well as a new network mode of data transport. This section describes the overall architecture of Oracle Data Pump.

NOTE
*The Oracle **exp** and **imp** utilities are still available in Oracle Database 10g. Also the Oracle Data Pump can read export files created by the **exp** process.*

The Oracle Data Pump architecture contains a number of components, as listed and described in Table 6-1.

Component Name	Purpose
Direct Path API (DPAPI)	DPAPI supports a direct interface between the database and Oracle Data Pump.
External Table Services	A new access driver, ORACLE_DATAPUMP, is available in Oracle Database 10g to allow Oracle to both read and write to external files. This API uses an Oracle proprietary format when writing to the external file.
dbms_metadata package	This package is used to provide object definitions to Oracle Data Pump for use when an object needs to be re-created.
dbms_datapump package	This package provides the interface for the Oracle Data Pump utilities to call. The new utilities, **impdp** and **expdp**, are really just thin clients that call this package.
SQL*Loader	SQL*Loader has been fully integrated with external tables in Oracle Database 10g. This allows for automatic migration of SQL*Loader control files with external table access parameters.
impdp and **expdp** clients	These two new programs make calls to the **dbms_datapump** package for all database-related Data Pump operations.

TABLE 6-1. *Oracle Data Pump Architecture Components*

Component Name	Purpose
Other external clients	Other Oracle clients that take advantage of the Oracle Data Pump infrastructure include Oracle Enterprise Manager, replication, transportable tablespaces, and so on. Additionally, you can interface with the procedure **dbms_datapump** from a client like SQL*Plus.
The dump file set	This is the formatted flat file(s) that gets created by the **expdp** client. Note that unlike the exp utility, the dump file set is always created on the server, never on the client.

TABLE 6-1.   *Oracle Data Pump Architecture Components* (continued)

Figure 6-1 provides a general architectural overview of the Oracle Data Pump infrastructure.

NOTE
*Oracle recommends that you not log in using **sysdba** privileges when using the Data Pump utilities, because the **sysdba** login grants special privileges that you will generally not need with Data Pump.*

Internally, Oracle Data Pump processes takes place in two different stages: the preparation stage and the execute stage. In the preparation stage, the client starts the Master Control Process (MCP). Most of the Data Pump operation centers around the MCP. At the same time queues are established for communication between the MCP (Wow...I'm having flashbacks to the movie *Tron*!) and the client and other processes that will be started.

Once everything is set up on the client side, the execute stage begins. At this point, if the process is an export process, the initial dump file set is created and worker processes are started. If the process is an import process, the dump file set is opened. The MCP then controls the export/import processes, directing the worker processes to write or extract the required information. During processing, worker processes spawn off parallel server slaves to provide the degree of parallelism that is required.

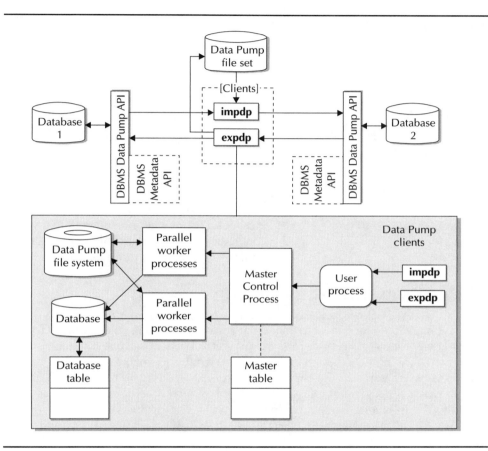

FIGURE 6-1.   *Oracle Data Pump infrastructure*

During this process, Oracle Database 10*g* creates a master table to keep track of the status of the process. This master table is critical and allows for restartable operations. The master table is also loaded into the dump file set being created during an export. Note that this master table is critical to recovering your database from the export dump file set. Once the export or import has completed, the processes then shuts down. Also, Oracle Database 10*g* removes the master table once the Data Pump process has completed if the job is successful or it is terminated with the **kill_job** command from the **impdp** or **expdp** client. If a job is aborted for unknown reasons (for example, an error) or if the **stop_job** command is used from the **impdp** or **expdp** client, the master table will be retained to allow the Data Pump job to be restarted.

Data Pump Data Dictionary Views

Oracle provides several data dictionary views that you can use to manage and monitor Data Pump operations. These views are listed and described in the following table:

View Name	Purpose/Description
DBA_DATAPUMP_JOBS	Displays information on running Data Pump jobs. Also comes in the USER_DATAPUMP_JOBS variety.
DBA_DATAPUMP_SESSIONS	Provides session-level information on Data Pump jobs.
DATAPUMP_PATHS	Provides a list of valid object types that you can associate with the **include** or **exclude** parameters of **expdp** or **impdp**.

Data Pump Interactive Mode

One of the nice new features available with Oracle Data Pump is that you can detach from a job and then reconnect to that job at a later time. When you reconnect to the job, you enter interactive mode. When you reattach via interactive mode, you need to know the job name to attach to. You can assign this job name via the **job_name** parameter when you start the export job (I strongly recommend this method) or the system will assign a default job name to the job (which is perhaps not quite as user friendly. The job name for any **expdp** job can be found by querying the DBA_DATAPUMP_JOBS view or the USER_DATAPUMP_JOBS view and is displayed at the beginning and the end of the export job.

To detach from the job, simply press CTRL-C after the job has initialized (you should wait for the assigned job name to appear on the console before you disconnect because there is some delay between the time you start the export or import process and the time the job is actually assigned). After you press CTRL-C, a prompt appears. The job continues running in the background, even though you are at a prompt. From this prompt you can execute any of the utility-appropriate interactive job commands (which are listed later in this chapter for both **expdp** and **impdp**).

CAUTION
Pressing CTRL-C *more than once may exit you out of the interface completely and you will need to reconnect!*

If you have exited to the command-line prompt, you can reconnect to the job by simply using the **attach** parameter of either the **impdp** or **expdp** commands, which puts you into interactive mode. Here is an example of exiting the client and then reentering interactive mode using **expdp**. A couple of things to note. First, some interactive commands are different between **expdp** and **impdp**. Second, note that the output that you will see has been reformatted slightly to fit on the page. Also, we will talk in much more detail about both **expdp** and **impdp** later in this section, so if you try this example and it doesn't work (which out of the box it probably won't), don't worry, we will get to how to use the Data Pump in detail shortly.

```
C:\Oracle\Oracle Database 10g-beta2\BIN>expdp scott/tiger
dumpfile=pump_dir:myd_%U.dat filesize=100m
nologfile=y job_name=robert full=y
<snip some of the banner for brevity>
Connected to: Oracle10i Enterprise Edition Release 10.1.0.1.0
Starting "SCOTT"."ROBERT":  scott/********
dumpfile=pump_dir:myd_%U.dat filesize=100m nologfile=y
job_name=robert full=y
Estimate in progress using BLOCKS method...
<ctrl-c>
Export> exit
```

At this point, you are returned to the command prompt. Now, to reattach to the session, you would use the following:

```
C:\Oracle\Oracle Database 10g-beta2\BIN>expdp scott/tiger attach=Robert
<snip some of the banner for brevity>
Connected to: Oracle10i Enterprise Edition Release 10.1.0.1.0
Job: ROBERT  Owner: SCOTT  Operation: EXPORT
Creator Privs: FALSE
GUID: 28DAC493131A4F77BB6363F2877414E9
Start Time: Saturday, 29 November, 2003 13:27  Mode: FULL
Instance: beta2  MaxDegree: 1
EXPORT Job Parameters:
   Parameter Name      Parameter Value:
      CLIENT_COMMAND       scott/********
      Dumpfile=pump_dir:myd_%U.dat filesize=100m
nologfile=y job_name=robert full=y
<snip some output for brevity>
Worker 1 Status:  State: EXECUTING
   Object Schema: SYSMAN  Object Name: MGMT_USER_TARGETS
   Object Type: DATABASE_EXPORT/SCHEMA/TABLE/TABLE_DATA
   Completed Objects: 586  Total Objects: 586
Export> status
Job: ROBERT  Operation: EXPORT  Mode: FULL
State: EXECUTING  Degree: 1  Job Error Count: 0
Dump file:  c:\oracle\admin\beta2\pump_dir\myd_%u.dat
size =  104857600
Dump file:  C:\ORACLE\ADMIN\BETA2\PUMP_DIR\MYD_01.DAT
size =  104857600 bytes written =  2048
```

```
Worker 1 Status:
State: EXECUTING Object Schema: SYSMAN
Object Name: MMT_USER_TARGETS
Object Type: DATABASE_EXPORT/SCHEMA/TABLE/TABLE_DATA
Completed Objects: 586   Total Objects: 586
Export> continue_client
Total estimation using BLOCKS method: 39.87 MB
Processing object type DATABASE_EXPORT/TABLESPACE
Processing object type DATABASE_EXPORT/DE_SYS_USER/USER
Processing object type DATABASE_EXPORT/SCHEMA/USER
<snip remaining output for brevity>
```

In this example, we did a couple of things. First, we entered interactive mode and prompted for the status of the job. Second, we re-entered client mode, which provides us with a real-time status of the job. We could have pressed CTRL-C again to exit out of client mode.

Data Pump API

Oracle Database 10*g* also provides an interface into Oracle Data Pump through the **dbms_datapump** procedure. The **dbms_datapump** procedure allows you to write custom code that interfaces with the Oracle Data Pump driver. This allows you to write code that can import or export data using Data Pump, and suspend, resume, or monitor Data Pump jobs and other Data Pump–related activities.

Data Pump Export

The Data Pump Export utility (**expdp**) works much like the **exp** utility does from a look and feel point of view. However, **expdp** comes with a number of new features and is much more efficient than **exp**. In this section, we will first review Data Pump architectural specifics for the Data Pump Export program. Then, we will look at new features of **expdp** (compared to **exp** in Oracle9*i* Database). Finally, I demonstrate the use of **expdp**, concentrating on these new features.

New Features of Data Pump Export

The new Data Pump Export client, **expdp**, has much the same functionality as the Oracle Database 10*g* **exp** program, plus a number of new features, including:

- The ability to estimate the size of the files that will result from the **expdp** operation, without actually having to write those files.

- The ability to suspend and resume an export job at will.

- The ability to attach or detach from a running export job at will.

- The ability to restart many failed jobs from the point of failure.

- The ability to do fine-grained object selection when exporting. Thus, you can choose to only export procedures and functions.

- The ability to control the number of threads that will be used during the export operation.

- The availability of two data access methods: external tables (taking advantage of the new features associated with external tables in Oracle Database 10g, which are discussed later in this chapter) or the direct path access method. The method used is selected automatically during the export process.

- Support for network mode operations, which allow you to load from another database, through a database link, directly.

- Control over the version of the object that is exported. This allows you to export data from one version of Oracle Database and ensure that it is compatible with a lower-level version of Oracle Database. Note that this applies to versions of Oracle Database after 10g and that this feature is not available for any version earlier than Oracle Database 10g.

- The ability to choose between three methods of database extraction: extract only database metadata (e.g., table and index creation statements); extract only data from the database; extract both database metadata and data at the same time.

Using Data Pump Export

This section discusses the practical application of Oracle Database 10g Data Pump Export. First, there is some initial setup that we have to deal with, after which we will look at the parameters available.

Preparing to Use Data Pump Export   Before you use **expdp**, you will want to create a directory object in the database that you will be exporting from. This is done with the **create directory** and **grant** commands, as shown in this example:

```
SQL> CREATE DIRECTORY pump_dir AS
'c:\oracle\admin\beta2\pump_dir';
Directory created.

SQL> GRANT READ ON DIRECTORY pump_dir TO scott;
Grant succeeded.
```

The reason we create the directory PUMP_DIR (which you can call whatever you want) is that all Data Pump–related files are stored on the server, and not on the client. It is from this location that Oracle Data Pump will write/read all files. This provides a layer of security on the server, in that you can only read or write to specific locations. This prevents users from placing files where they do not belong and from reading files that they do not have a right to read.

When using **expdp**, the following order of operations is used to determine where the file will be written:

1. Oracle writes to a directory specifically listed as a part of the **dumpfile** specification in the **expdp** command line.

2. Oracle writes to the directory specified in the **directory** parameter setting in the **expdp** command line.

3. Oracle writes to a location defined by the value of an environment variable (which is OS specific) on the client running the export that defines the default directory location.

Also, if a user other than a SYSDBA user is going to use **expdp** to export anything other than the schema that is associated with their login, that user must be granted the privilege **exp_full_database**.

Data Pump Export Parameters   A number of parameters are available when using Data Pump Export. Table 6-2 lists and describes each parameter. Examples of using many of these parameters are provided later in this chapter.

Parameter	Description
attach	Indicates that Data Pump Export should attach to an existing job that is already running.
content	Allows you to control if data or just database-related metadata is exported. Options: ALL, DATA_ONLY, and METADATA_ONLY.
directory	Defines the directory object to be used for the export dump files and log files. A directory of the same name must be created in the database that you are exporting or an error will occur.
dumpfile	Provides a list of destination dump files. Multiple dump files can be comma delimited. Also, a directory name can be included, separated from the filenames with a colon (:). Additionally, a substitution variable (%U) is available, which is a two-digit number from 01 to 99. This allows for the creation of multiple dump files. Note that **expdp** will not overwrite an existing file.

TABLE 6-2.   *Data Pump Export Parameters*

Parameter	Description
estimate	Tells the **expdp** process how to calculate the size of the resulting dump file. Options include BLOCKS Calculates the dump file size based on the number of blocks of data times the database block size (default method). SAMPLING Calculates the size based on a sample of the number of rows per table. STATISTICS Bases the size of the export on the current object statistics.
estimate_only	Causes **expdp** to determine the estimated size of the job, without actually doing the export.
exclude	Excludes certain metadata from the export operation. Note that for any object excluded, any dependent objects also are excluded. For example, exclusion of a table also excludes any indexes, triggers, constraints and the related table data. You can also use wildcard characters and SQL statements to exclude specific ranges of objects.
filesize	Limits the size of the dump files being created. This parameter can be specified in bytes, or you can follow the size with the letter B (bytes), K (kilobytes), M (megabytes), or G (gigabytes).
flashback_scn	Allows you to use the Oracle database flashback features when exporting the database. In this case, **expdp** will use the stated SCN to flashback to.
flashback_time	Allows you to use the Oracle Database flashback features when exporting the database. In this case, **expdp** will use the stated time to flashback to.
full	If set to Y, this parameter indicates that **expdp** should export the entire database. The default value for this parameter is N, which does not do a full export.
help	Allows you to display help messages and the syntax of **expdp**.
include	Allows you to define specific objects that you want exported. Only those objects, and dependent objects, are exported.
job_name	Defines the name of the export job. This name is used to manage the job (for example, via the **attach** command). By default, this name is system generated using the naming convention sys_*operation_mode_nn*. For example, a full export might take the job name sys_export_full_01.

TABLE 6-2. *Data Pump Export Parameters* (continued)

Parameter	Description
logfile	Identifies the log file that is generated during the export operation. By default, it's called export.log and stored in the location defined by the **directory** parameter.
network_link	Allows for a network export through a remote database link to a predefined source system.
nologfile	Suppresses the writing of the **expdp** log file. Set to N by default.
parallel	Defines the maximum number of threads that can operate on behalf of the export job. This parameter allows you to adjust the level of parallelism, to provide a balance between system resource usage and time to create the export. This can be set when the export is started, and can also be changed via interactive mode (described elsewhere in this chapter). If the system resources allow, the number of parallel processes should be set to the number of dump files being created. The default for this setting is 1.
parfile	Allows you to define an external parameter file for the **expdp** process. The parameter file is local to the client and does not use a database directory as do the export dump files or log files.
query	Allows for the application of a SQL predicate to filter the database being exported. For example, this allows you to export from the STORE_SALES table the sales from store 100.
schemas	Defines the schemas you wish to export data from. The user must have the **exp_full_database** privilege to export any schema other than the schema that they have logged **expdp** into. Any table in the SYS.NOEXP$ table will not be exported in schema export mode.
status	Defines how frequently the job status should be updated, in seconds. Defaults to 0 seconds.
tables	Allows you to export specific tables only. Dependent objects are exported also.
tablespaces	Allows you to export objects listed in the specified tablespaces. All dependent objects in other tablespaces (e.g., indexes) also are exported.
transport_full_check	During transportable tablespace operation, verifies that there are no dependencies between objects inside the transportable set and objects outside the transportable set.
transport_tablespaces	Allows for the export of transportable tablespace metadata.

TABLE 6-2. *Data Pump Export Parameters* (continued)

Parameter	Description
version	Restricts objects being exported to a specific version level of the database. This is designed to help with compatibility issues when moving database objects from a higher version of the database to a lower version of the database.

TABLE 6-2. *Data Pump Export Parameters* (continued)

Date Pump Export interactive mode, discussed earlier in the chapter, has several commands available when called by **expdp**, as described in Table 6-3.

Data Pump Export Quirks

There are a few quirks to be aware of with regard to Oracle Data Pump. When you run a Data Pump job, a temporary table is created in the schema that you log in to. This table is supposed to be cleaned up after the job ends. If the job ends abnormally (e.g., database crash in the middle of the job), then you may need to clean up the table. You will find the table in the same schema that you logged in to, and it will be named the same as the **job_name** parameter setting. Therefore, if you logged in using the SCOTT account and your **job_name** was set to FULL_EXPORT, the table will be in the SCOTT schema and the name of it will be FULL_EXPORT.

Command	Description
add_file	Allows you to add a file to the list of dump files
continue_client	Returns you to client logging mode
exit_client	Exits client logging mode without killing the job
help	Provides help on all commands
kill_job	Allows you to detach from and delete an existing job
parallel	Changes the number of active workers for current job
start_job	Allows you to start or resume the current job
status	Defines the refresh frequency for monitoring a job in seconds (default is 0 seconds)
stop_job	Stops job execution and exits the client

TABLE 6-3. *Data Pump Interactive Mode Commands*

This leads to another little quirk: if you have in the schema that you are logging in to a table that is named the same as the JOB_NAME, the job will fail because the table already exists.

Data Pump Export Examples

This section provides you with several examples of the use of Oracle Data Pump Export. I have not included the output from most of these commands, but rather only the text of the commands. This is done for brevity's sake, so that I can provide a number of examples in the space available.

This section including examples of the following:

- A full database export

- A tablespace export

- Exporting only data

- Exporting only specific database object types

- Estimating the size of a database export

Example: A Full Database Export This first example is pretty basic. It's simply a dump of the entire database.

```
C:\Oracle\Oracle Database 10g-beta2\BIN>expdp scott/tiger
dumpfile=pump_dir:mydb_%U.dat filesize=100m
nologfile=y job_name=robert full=y
```

You saw this example earlier in this chapter when the interactive interface was presented. This example creates a full database export. Each file will be no more than 100MB in size, and all dump files and the log file will be stored in the PUMP_DIR library. The job is assigned a job name of Robert and will not create a log file.

Example: Export Tablespace Data In this example, we want to just export data from a single tablespace, named USERS. So, we use the following command:

```
C:\Oracle\Oracle Database 10g-beta2\BIN>expdp scott/tiger
dumpfile=pump_dir:mydb_tbs_users_%U.dat
nologfile=y job_name=tablespace tablespaces=users
```

Example: Exporting Just Database Data In this case, we want to just export database data for the entire database. We have also decided to create a log file, so we have included the **logfile** parameter. You might be asking why we didn't just allow **expdp** to create the default log file. The reason is that we did not define the default directory entry that **expdp** would be looking for, which is called DPUMP_DIR in the database. Thus, the **expdp** process would have failed when trying to create the directory.

```
C:\Oracle\Oracle Database 10g-beta2\BIN>expdp scott/tiger
dumpfile=pump_dir:mydb_%U_data.dat filesize=100m
content=data_only job_name=data_extract full=y
logfile=pump_log:mydb_exp.log
```

Example: Exporting Specific Database Object Types   In this example, we create
a parameter file that has individual **include** statements. This export will export all
database functions, procedures, and any table that has a name that starts with EMP.

```
-- Parameter file
INCLUDE=FUNCTION
INCLUDE=PROCEDURE
INCLUDE=TABLE:"LIKE 'EMP%'"
DUMPFILE=pump_dir:mydb_%U_objects.dat
NOLOGFILE=Y
JOB_NAME=specific_objects
FULL=y
```

Along with the preceding parameter file, we use the following command line to
get just what we asked for:

```
C:\Oracle\Oracle Database 10g-beta2\BIN>expdp scott/tiger
parfile=c:\oracle\admin\mydb\exp\mypar.fil
```

Example: Estimating the Size of the Export   It would be nice to know if we have
enough space to do our export. Fortunately, Data Pump provides the capability to
make that determination. Simply use the **estimate_only** clause and you will get the
estimate of how big the dump file will be without the actual creation of the dump
file. Here is an example:

```
C:\Oracle\Oracle Database 10g-beta2\BIN>expdp scott/tiger
full=y estimate_only=Y estimate=statistics nologfile=y
```

In this example, we also chose to use the database statistics as the base for our
estimate. We could have also used the sampling method, which samples a fixed
number of rows in each table and extrapolates from that number the total size of the
backup. The default value for this parameter, BLOCKS, is the most accurate but also
the most time consuming.

NOTE
*In tests that I performed, the default method of
calculating the size of the resulting dump file took
a great deal longer to complete than using either of
the alternative methods. This resulted in significantly
longer export run times.*

Data Pump Import

The counterpart to the Data Pump Export utility is the Data Pump Import (**impdp**) utility. The **impdp** utility works much like the **imp** utility does from a look-and-feel perspective. However, **impdp** comes with a number of new features and is much more efficient than **imp**. In this section, we first review Data Pump architectural specifics for the Data Pump Import program. Then, we look at new features of **impdp** (compared to imp in Oracle9*i* Database). Finally, we demonstrate the use of **impdp**, concentrating on these new features.

New Features of Data Pump Import

Data Pump Import has a number of new features over its predecessor, **imp**. These include the following:

- Support for the use of metadata filters that allow you to control which object types (e.g., indexes, functions, or procedures) you import.

- The ability to suspend and resume an import job at will.

- The ability to attach or detach from a running import job at will.

- The ability to restart many failed jobs from the point of failure.

- The ability to control the number of threads that will be used during the import operation.

- Support for network mode operations, which allows you to load from another database directly.

- Support for direct mode import operations. (Everyone say, "Yeaaaa!")

- Control over the version of the object that is imported. This allows you to import data from one version of Oracle Database and ensure that it is compatible with a lower-level version of Oracle Database. Note that this applies to versions of Oracle Database after 10*g* and that this feature is not available for any version earlier than Oracle Database 10*g*.

To use **impdp**, you need to be aware of the privileges that are required. If creation of the export dump files you are using required **exp_full_database** rights, or if the import is done using the **full** parameter, then the user doing the import must have the **imp_full_database** privilege.

Using Data Pump Import

These next sections provide some details regarding use of the Data Pump Import program, starting with a look at the parameters that are used with it. Following that,

Jonathan Says...

I can't get very excited about Data Pump Export—although the parallel option may allow you to eliminate messy (hence risky) hand-written code to speed up exports.

However, the ability to do selective "imports" across a database link may be something of a boon for pulling production extracts efficiently into development systems.

I will clue you into a few quirks that I discovered while experimenting with this new feature. Finally, I will provide you with some examples of using **impdp**.

Data Pump Import Parameters   A number of parameters are available when using Data Pump Import. Table 6-4 lists and describes each parameter. Examples of using most of these parameters are provided later in this chapter.

Parameter	Description
attach	Indicates that Data Pump Import should attach to an existing job that is already running.
content	Allows you to control if data or just database-related metadata is imported. Options: ALL, DATA_ONLY, and METADATA_ONLY.
directory	Defines the directory object to be used as the source of the dump files and log files. A directory of the same name must be created in the database that you are importing or an error will occur.
dumpfile	Provides a list of the dump files to source the import from. Multiple dump files can be comma delimited. Also, a directory name can be included, separated from the filenames with a colon (:). Additionally, a substitution variable (%U) is available, which is a two-digit number from 01 to 99. This allows for the use of multiple dump files.
estimate	Tells the **impdp** process how to calculate the amount of data that will be generated and provides information for percent complete operations. If a dump file is being used, no estimate is needed.

TABLE 6-4.   *Data Pump Import Parameters*

Parameter	Description
exclude	Excludes certain metadata from the import operation. Note that for any object excluded, any dependent objects also are excluded. For example, exclusion of a table also excludes any indexes, triggers, constraints, and the related table data. You can also use wildcard characters and SQL statements to exclude specific ranges of objects.
flashback_scn	Allows you to use the Oracle Database flashback features when doing a network import directly from another source database. Used only in conjunction with the **network_link** parameter.
flashback_time	Allows you to use the Oracle Database flashback features when exporting the database. Used only in conjunction with the **network_link** parameter.
full	Indicates that **impdp** should import the entire database. The default for this parameter is N. If the **network_link** parameter is being used, or the creation of the source dump file set required the use of the **exp_full_database** privilege, then the user account used to load the dump file must have the **imp_full_database** privileges.
help	Allows you to display help messages and the syntax of **impdp**.
include	Allows you to define specific objects that you want imported. Only those objects, and dependent objects, are imported.
job_name	Creates an import job. This name is used to manage the job (for example, via the **attach** command). By default, this name is system generated using the naming convention sys_*operation_mode_nn*. For example, a full import might take the job name sys_import_full_01.
logfile	Identifies the log file that is generated during the import operation. By default, it's called import.log and stored in the location defined by the **directory** parameter.
network_link	Allows for a network import through a remote database link to a predefined source system.
nologfile	Suppresses the writing of the **impdp** log file. This is set to N by default.
parallel	Defines the maximum number of threads that can operate on behalf of the import job. The default for this setting is 1.

TABLE 6-4. *Data Pump Import Parameters* (continued)

Parameter	Description
parfile	Allows you to define an external parameter file for the **impdp** process. The parameter file is local to the client and does not use a database directory as do the import dump files or log files.
query	Allows for the application of a SQL predicate to filter the data being imported.
remap_datafile	Allows you to redefine the datafile names and directories during the import.
remap_schema	Allows you to map objects destined for one schema to another schema.
remap_tablespace	Allows you to map objects to tablespaces other than the ones the objects were originally assigned to.
reuse_datafiles	Allows for re-creation of the tablespace datafiles.
schemas	Defines the schemas you wish to import. Oracle Database 10*g* creates the schemas, and then the schemas are imported. The user must have the **exp_full_database** privilege to use this command, or only the objects within the schema will be restored (no schema definition is imported).
skip_unusable_indexes	Indicates the indexes that have an UNUSABLE status should not be created.
sqlfile	Extracts all SQL DDL that is imported to an output file.
status	Defines how frequently the job status should be updated, in seconds. Defaults to 0 seconds.
streams_configuration	Indicates if any general Streams metadata in the export dump file should be imported.
table_exists_action	Determines the action to take if the table already exists. Options include SKIP Do not load the data (default) and move on to the next object. APPEND Append to existing data already in the table. REPLACE Drop the table, if it exists. Re-creates the table and loads the data. TRUNCATE Remove all rows before the load.
tables	Allows you to import specific tables only. Dependent objects are imported also.

TABLE 6-4.   *Data Pump Import Parameters* (continued)

Parameter	Description
tablespaces	Allows you to import objects listed in the specified tablespaces. All dependent objects in other tablespaces (e.g., indexes) also are imported.
transform	Allows you to alter the object creation DDL for either specific objects or all objects. This allows you to manipulate storage or physical attributes of objects.
transport_datafiles	Defines the list of datafiles in the source database that are to be imported into the target system by the transportable mode import. Used with the **network_link** parameter.
transport_full_check	During transportable tablespace operation, verifies that there are no dependencies between those objects inside the transportable set and those objects outside the transportable set. This is only valid when the **network_link** parameter is used.
transport_tablespaces	Allows for the import of transportable tablespace metadata.
version	Restricts objects being imported to a specific version level of the database. This is designed to help with compatibility issues when moving database objects from a higher version of the database to a lower version of the database.

TABLE 6-4. *Data Pump Import Parameters* (continued)

Interactive mode, discussed earlier in the chapter, has several commands available when called by **impdp**, as described in Table 6-5.

Command	Description
continue_client	Returns you to client logging mode
exit_client	Exits client logging mode without killing the job
help	Provides help on all commands
kill_job	Allows you to detach from and delete an existing job
parallel	Changes the number of active workers for current job
start_job	Allows you to start or resume the current job
status	Defines the refresh frequency for monitoring a job, in seconds (the default is 0 seconds)
stop_job	Stops job execution and exits the client

TABLE 6-5. *Data Pump Import Interactive Parameters*

NOTE
The quirks mentioned earlier with regard to Oracle Data Pump Export (in the section "Data Pump Export Quirks") also apply to Oracle Data Pump Import.

Data Pump Import Examples

This section provides you with several examples of the use of Oracle Data Pump Import. I have not included the output from most of these commands, but rather only the text of the commands itself. This is done for brevity's sake, so that I can provide a number of examples in the space available.

This section includes examples of the following:

- A full database import

- A tablespace import

- Importing only data

- Importing only specific database object types

Example: A Full Database Import   This first example demonstrates using Data Pump Import to do a full database import:

```
C:\Oracle\Oracle Database 10g-beta2\BIN>impdp scott/tiger
dumpfile=pump_dir:mydb_%U.dat
nologfile=y job_name=robert full=y
```

Example: A Tablespace Import   This example imports objects contained in the USERS tablespace that is contained in the dump file `mydb_tbs_users.dat`:

```
C:\Oracle\Oracle Database 10g-beta2\BIN>impdp scott/tiger
dumpfile=pump_dir:mydb_tbs_users_%U.dat
nologfile=y job_name=tablespace tablespaces=users
table_exists_action=truncate
```

Example: Importing Only Specific Table Data   This is an example of importing data for a specific table from a dump file that was previously created. In this case, we import data only into the SCOTT.EMP table.

```
C:\Oracle\Oracle Database 10g-beta2\BIN>impdp scott/tiger
dumpfile=pump_dir:mydb_%U_data.dat
content=data_only job_name=data_import full=y
logfile=pump_log:mydb_imp.log tables=scott.emp
```

Example: Importing Specific Database Object Types   In this example, we create a parameter file that has individual **include** statements. This export will export all database functions, procedures, and any table that has a name that starts with EMP.

```
-- Parameter file
INCLUDE=FUNCTION
INCLUDE=PROCEDURE
INCLUDE=TABLE:"LIKE 'EMP%'"
DUMPFILE=pump_dir:mydb_%U_objects.dat
NOLOGFILE=Y
JOB_NAME=specific_objects
FULL=y
```

Along with the preceding parameter file above, we use the following command line to get just what we asked for:

```
C:\Oracle\Oracle Database 10g-beta2\BIN>impdp scott/tiger
parfile=c:\oracle\admin\mydb\exp\mypar.fil
```

Bigfile Tablespaces

Another new feature in Oracle Database 10*g* are bigfile tablespaces (BFTs). This section begins by describing what BFTs are and what they can be used for. It then looks at BFT management issues, such as how to create BFTs, how to migrate an existing tablespace to a BFT, and the changes to the ROWID format associated with BFTs.

What Are Bigfile Tablespaces?

A BFT contains only one datafile, as opposed to a normal tablespace, which might consist of one or more datafiles. The maximum size of a BFT varies based on the database block size. It can range anywhere from 8 terabytes to 128 terabytes. A BFT is always a locally managed tablespace, an undo tablespace, or a temporary tablespace.

Why Bigfile Tablespaces?

BFTs can simplify the management of your database. With a BFT, you need to manage only one datafile per tablespace, as opposed to multiple datafiles. BFTs are also compatible with OMF datafiles, so there is no need to manage datafiles, or even to be aware of the existence of datafiles.

The biggest benefit of BFTs is that they increase the overall storage capacity of your Oracle database significantly. Oracle Database 10*g*, with BFTs, can now handle 8 exabytes of storage (dependent on the block size), all with fewer (but larger) datafiles. Another nice benefit of BFTs is datafile transparency, since there is a direct one-to-one relationship between the datafile and the BFT.

When should you not use BFTs? When disk space is limited or separated onto smaller file systems, you should not use BFTs. Also, if you are not using some form of disk redundancy (e.g., RAID-5 or ASM), BFTs and large datafiles are probably not a good idea. Also, if the OS and/or file system that your database is using does not support large datafiles, then using BFTs will probably reduce, rather than increase, the overall capacity of the database.

Bigfile Tablespace Management

With the addition of BFTs come new management issues. This section looks at these issues. First, we look at actually creating, altering, and dropping BFTs. Then, we look at migrating existing tablespaces to BFTs. We then address the new and changed views associated with BFTs.

Using DDL on Bigfile Tablespaces

In this section we first look at database defaults with regards to BFTs. Then we look at the various DDLs used to create, alter, and remove BFTs.

Database Defaults   By default, Oracle Database 10*g* creates all datafiles as smallfile datafiles. You can define BFTs as the database default when issuing

Jonathan Says...
You might also ask yourself how you back up a 128TB file in anything like a realistic time. The only option is probably going to be RMAN with the database block change tracking feature enabled (refer to Chapter 5).

And I don't think I'd be too happy on any file system with file sizes of this magnitude—some file systems have an inode locking issue, and the larger the files you use, the more likely you are to need highly concurrent access to any one file, so the more blocking on inodes you will suffer. If you want to adopt bigfiles, you should check the layer of software under Oracle Database 10*g* very carefully.

Make sure that you test any maintenance scripts you use before you switch to bigfiles. There may be odd little traps waiting for you. For example, the **dbms_metadata.get_ddl** procedure hasn't been updated for bigfiles yet—the space management section at the start of the file is 128K instead of the 64K that you get from smallfiles, and so on.

the **create database** command. Also, you can define the temporary and undo tablespace as bigfile or smallfile. Here is an example:

```
Create database mydb set default bigfile tablespace
Datafile '/db01/data/mydb/mydb_system_01.dbf' size 200m
sysaux datafile '/db01/data/mydb/mydb_sysaux_01.dbf' size 250m
default temporary tablespace temp_tbs
smallfile tempfile '/db02/data/mydb/mydb_temp_tbs_01.dbf'
size 100m
bigfile undo tablespace undo_tbs_01 datafile
'/db03/data/mydb/mydb_undo_tbs_01.dbf' size 150m;
```

The SYSTEM and SYSAUX tablespaces are created using the defined default database tablespace type. For temporary tablespaces and undo tablespaces, the **bigfile** keyword can be used to override the default for these tablespace types. (I included the **bigfile** keyword for the undo tablespace just so that you can see how it's used; by default, the previous example would have created the undo tablespace as a BFT anyway.)

You might want to change the default setting for your database between smallfile and bigfile. The **alter database** command allows you to perform this action:

```
ALTER DATABASE SET DEFAULT BIGFILE TABLESPACE;
ALTER DATABASE SET DEFAULT SMALLFILE TABLESPACE;
```

Creating a Bigfile Tablespace   You can create a BFT by using the **create tablespace** command and including the **bigfile** keyword, as shown in this example:

```
CREATE BIGFILE TABLESPACE DATA_TBS
DATAFILE '/db02/data/mydb/mydb_data_tbs_01.dbf' SIZE 400m;
```

Altering a Bigfile Tablespace   To alter a BFT, just use the **alter tablespace** command as you normally would. For example, this statement resizes the single bigfile datafile in the DATA_TBS bigfile tablespace:

```
ALTER TABLESPACE data_tbs RESIZE 1g;
```

Dropping a Bigfile Tablespace   You can use the **drop tablespace** command to drop a BFT, as shown in this example:

```
Drop tablespace data_tbs;
```

Migrating to Bigfile Tablespaces

You can migrate objects to BFTs using the **alter table move** and **create table...as select** commands or through Oracle Database 10*g*'s Online Redefinition capabilities. The Data Pump utilities can also be used to migrate data between tablespaces. This allows your existing objects to take advantage of the benefits of Bigfile Tablespaces.

Bigfile Tablespaces Data Dictionary Views

Oracle has added columns to three views to help you manage BFTs. The following table lists each view that has been changed and describes the changes:

View Name	Columns or Rows Added or Modified	Description
DATABASE_PROPERTIES	A new row has been added. The property name for this row is DEFAULT_TBS_TYPE.	Defines the default tablespace type for the tablespace (BIGFILE or SMALLFILE)
DBA_TABLESPACES	Bigfile	Indicates whether the tablespace is a bigfile or a smallfile tablespace using the values SNALLFILE or BIGFILE.
V$TABLESPACE	Bigfile	A Boolean (YES/NO) that indicates whether the tablespace is a bigfile or a smallfile tablespace

Bigfile Tablespaces and Extended ROWIDs

To support BFTs, Oracle has made some changes to the ROWID format for objects that exist in BFTs. This section describes those changes. First, we look in detail at the nature of the ROWID changes. Then, we look at changes to the **dbms_rowid** package.

Changes to ROWIDs Associated with BFTs

Rows within tables created in a BFT have a slightly different ROWID format. ROWIDs derived from tables within a BFT's rows do not contain a relative file number but instead contain a block number. Thus, the extended ROWID format now contains the following:

- A data object number for that row.
- A tablespace datafile number (relative to the tablespace) for that row. (Of course, there is only one datafile!)
- The data block for the row. These block numbers are relative to the datafile.
- The slot number that identifies a specific row within a block.

There is no relative file number in the ROWID of a BFT row, because the relative file number is 1024 for all BFTs.

NOTE
The change in the ROWID format for BFTs may impact applications that extract, interpret, and use ROWIDs.

dbms_rowid Changes Related to Bigfile Tablespaces

Because there are now different types of ROWIDs, the functions of the **dbms_rowid** package have a new parameter, **ts_type_in**, that allows you to define the type of ROWID you are processing. The values allowed in this parameter include BIGFILE and SMALLFILE. The procedures that have this parameter included are the following:

- rowid_info
- rowid_block_number
- rowid_relative_fno

If you wish to construct a ROWID string for a row in a BFT, you can use the **rowid_create** function with the **relative_fno** argument set to 1024.

Cross-Platform Transportable Tablespaces

In Oracle Database 10*g*, transportable tablespaces can now be moved across platforms. You can now unplug a tablespace on your Windows NT database and move it to your Sun Solaris database without a hitch. This section introduces cross-platform transportable tablespaces and then discusses the different byte-ordering forms of Oracle datafiles and the conversion requirements related to cross-platform transportable tablespaces.

Introduction to Cross-Platform Transportable Tablespaces

As a DBA, on several occasions I've really wanted to be able to move my tablespaces between my development Windows NT Oracle database and my production Sun Oracle database. I've also had cases where I really wanted to move my tablespaces between a Sun platform and an AIX platform. Until Oracle Database 10*g* this was just a dream.

Now, Oracle Database 10*g* supports transporting tablespaces across almost all platforms of the Oracle Database family. This has a number of benefits, including:

- Efficient publication of data between different content providers

- Easy movement of data between data warehouses, data marts, and OLTP systems

- Easy migration of databases across platforms

NOTE
Not all platforms currently support this functionality. Check your platform-specific documentation to determine if your platform is eligible.

There remain a few other issues to mention. First, to be able to move a tablespace between platforms, **compatible** must be set to 10.0.0 or higher. When this occurs, tablespace datafiles are made platform aware upon the next startup operation. Also, read-only and offline datafiles will become cross-platform compatible only after they have been made read-write or brought online. So, after you have upgraded your database and set **compatible** to 10.0.0 or higher, you may want to quickly make your read-only tablespaces read-write and then reset them to read-only.

Datafile Byte Ordering: Endian Formats

One of the possible hiccups involved in transporting tablespaces between different platforms is the datafile byte-ordering format. This section first introduces you to the concept of byte ordering in Oracle Database datafiles and how this impacts transporting your tablespace between different platforms. Then, we look at how to convert these datafiles in preparation for migration to another platform, if that is required.

Introduction to Datafile Byte Ordering
The OS platforms that the Oracle Database server runs on generally use one of two different byte-ordering schemes (known as the endian formats). The byte ordering schema of a given platform is not an Oracle property, but a property of the OS itself. If the platforms use the same byte-ordering scheme, then you can transport tablespaces as you always have in the past, no problem…. Go ahead and try it—I will wait for you!

If the byte-ordering scheme is different between platforms, then you need to use the **convert** command in RMAN to convert the tablespace to the format that it needs to be in on the target platform. You can determine the endian format via a join of the dynamic view V$DATABASE and the new V$TRANSPORTABLE_PLATFORM view, as shown in this example:

```
SQL> SELECT endian_format
  2  FROM v$transportable_platform tp, v$database d
  3  WHERE tp.platform_name=d.platform_name;

ENDIAN_FORMAT
--------------
Little
```

In this case, the system is using the Little endian format (the other option is Big endian format). Thus, if the query returns the same result on both systems, you have a compatible datafile format; if not, you need to use RMAN and the **compatible** parameter to transport the tablespaces.

Converting the Tablespace Endian Format with RMAN

If you need to convert a tablespace for another platform, RMAN is the tool you use. First, create the directory that the converted file will be copied to. The following example uses the directory path `c:\oracle\oradata\betatwo`. Next, make the tablespace that you wish to convert read-only. Then, simply start RMAN and use the new **convert tablespace** command:

```
Rman target=/
RMAN> CONVERT TABLESPACE users
TO PLATFORM = ' AIX-Based Systems (64-bit)'
DB_FILE_NAME_CONVERT='c:\oracle\oradata\betatwo',
'c:\oracle\admin\transport_aix';
```

You can also convert datafiles at the destination site, as shown in this example:

```
Rman target=/
RMAN> CONVERT DATAFILE =  'c:\oracle\oradata\betatwo\*'
FROM PLATFORM = 'AIX-Based Systems (64-bit)'
DB_FILE_NAME_CONVERT='c:\oracle\oradata\betatwo',
'c:\oracle\admin\transport_aix';
```

The platform name used here comes from the PLATFORM_NAME column of the V$TRANSPORTABLE_PLATFORM view mentioned earlier. Oracle Database 10*g* is very picky about putting the name in just right.

Note that there are cases where CLOB columns may need further conversion after the tablespace has been transported. This conversion is handled automatically by Oracle Database 10*g* as the data is accessed, but the conversion may have performance impacts. You can avoid these impacts by rebuilding these tables after the migration has completed.

> **Jonathan Says...**
> Converting tablespaces with CLOB columns starts to look expensive. Perhaps you should test the relative performance of Data Pump Import before jumping on this option for moving tablespaces across platforms.

Enhanced Merge Functionality

Oracle Database 10g offers new functionality for **merge** statement operation. New conditional clauses and extensions are now available for use with the **merge** statement. Also, a new optional **delete** clause has been added to the **merge** SQL statement. Let's look at each of these in more detail next.

New merge Conditional Clauses and Extensions

Several new options are available with regard to the execution of the **merge** statement:

- The option to omit either the **update** or **insert** clause

- The ability to use conditional **update** and **insert** clauses

- New functionality in the form of the new **on** condition

The Option to Omit Either the update or insert Clause

Oracle Database 10g now allows you to execute a **merge** statement in which you can omit either the **update** or **insert** clause. Here is an example:

```
-- Look at our data first
SQL> SELECT * FROM emp_history;
     EMPNO   TOTAL_PAY UPDATE_DATE
---------- ---------- -----------
         1         100   15-NOV-03
         2         200   15-NOV-03

SQL> SELECT * FROM emp_history_adds;
     EMPNO     NET_PAY
---------- ----------
         1         100
         3         300
-- Now, run our merge statement
SQL> MERGE INTO emp_history eh
```

```
  2  USING emp_history_adds eha
  3  ON (eh.empno =  eha.empno)
  4  WHEN MATCHED THEN
  5  UPDATE SET eh.total_pay=eh.total_pay+eha.net_pay,
  6  eh.update_date=sysdate;

-- And look at the result
SQL> SELECT * FROM emp_history;
     EMPNO   TOTAL_PAY UPDATE_DATE
---------- ---------- -----------
         1        200   15-DEC-03
         2        200   15-NOV-03
```

In this example, the TOTAL_PAY and the UPDATE_DATE columns of the EMP_HISTORY table were updated for record 1. At the same time, record 2 was not touched, and the additional record in the EMP_HISTORY_ADDS table for employee 3 was not inserted. You could do the same processing with an **insert** condition.

Conditional Updates and Inserts
Oracle Database 10*g* now allows you to add a **where** clause to the **update** or **insert** operation of a **merge** statement. This allows you to test for specific conditions, and skip the **update** or **insert** operation if that is your desire. Here is an example:

```
MERGE INTO emp_history eh
USING emp_history_adds eha
ON (eh.empno =  eha.empno)
WHEN MATCHED THEN
UPDATE SET eh.total_pay=eh.total_pay+eha.net_pay,
eh.update_date=sysdate
WHERE eh.pay_code <> 'Retired';
```

In this case, the update will only occur if the PAY_CODE column of the EMP_HISTORY table is not set to a value of Retired. The same logic is possible with **insert** operations as seen in this example:

```
MERGE INTO emp_history eh
USING emp_history_adds eha
ON (eh.empno =  eha.empno)
WHEN MATCHED THEN
UPDATE SET eh.total_pay=eh.total_pay+eha.net_pay,
eh.update_date=sysdate
WHERE eh.pay_code <> 'Retired'
WHEN NOT MATCHED THEN
INSERT (eh.empno, eh.total_pay, eh.update_date)
VALUES (eha.empno, eha.net_pay, sysdate)
WHERE eha.pay_code <> 'Retired';
```

The New on Condition

You can now insert all rows that are in the source table into the destination table without having to join the source and target tables. This is done using the **merge** command together with the new **on** constant filter predicate. Here is an example:

```
MERGE INTO new_sales ns
USING sales s
ON (1=0)
WHEN NOT MATCHED THEN
INSERT (ns.store_id, ns.sale_date, ns.upc, ns.new_sale_amt)
VALUES (ns.store_id, ns.sale_date, ns.upc, ns.sale_amt);
```

In this case, the entire contents of the SALES table will be inserted into the NEW_SALES table.

Optional delete Clause in the merge Statement

During data operations, there may be times when you will want to perform data cleansing. Oracle Database 10*g* allows you to include an optional **delete** clause in the **merge** statement so that you can remove rows that may have become obsolete. Here is an example:

```
MERGE INTO emp_history eh
USING emp_history_adds eha
ON (eh.empno =  eha.empno)
WHEN MATCHED THEN
UPDATE SET eh.total_pay=eh.total_pay+eha.net_pay,
eh.update_date=sysdate
WHERE eh.pay_code <> 'Retired'
DELETE WHERE (eha.pay_code = 'DELETE')
WHEN NOT MATCHED THEN
INSERT (eh.empno, eh.total_pay, eh.update_date)
VALUES (eha.empno, eha.net_pay, SYSDATE)
WHERE eha.pay_code <> 'Retired';
```

Enhanced External Table Functionality

Oracle Database 10*g* offers some new external table functionality. This includes the capability to write to an external table, perform parallel external table operations, and indicate that only referenced columns should be projected, which can eliminate failures during external table **select** operations due to data quality problems. Let's look at these features in a bit more detail next.

Writing to External Tables

Oracle Database 10*g* now allows you to write to an external table, enabling you to move data from within the database to an external flat file outside of the database.

This is made possible by the new Data Pump access driver included with Oracle Database 10*g*. The ability to write to an external table is restricted to the use of the **create table as select** command only; therefore, **insert**, **update**, and **delete** operations are not supported. The resulting flat file is of an Oracle proprietary format that is independent of the OS the file is created on.

NOTE
An external table defined to use the oracle_loader (which is the only driver that was available in Oracle9i Database) access driver is not writable.

The obvious benefit of this new feature is the ability to load and unload tables, enabling you to perform data transforms in either direction. This makes external tables somewhat more flexible than Oracle's Data Pump utilities (**impdp** and **expdp**) because you not only can move data but also can perform transform operations on that data as you load or unload the data. Additionally, you can create joins on the data as you load or unload it, which cannot be done with the Data Pump utilities.

Let's look at an example of the creation of a writable external table:

```
SQL> CREATE DIRECTORY external_directory AS
'c:\oracle\admin\betatwo\directory';

SQL> GRANT READ, WRITE ON DIRECTORY external_directory
TO scott;
SQL> CREATE TABLE emp_history_ext
(ename, retire_date,
last_retirement_pay_date, pay_amount)
ORGANIZATION EXTERNAL
( TYPE oracle_datapump
  DEFAULT DIRECTORY external_directory
LOCATION ('emp_history_01.exp', 'emp_history_02.exp') )
parallel
AS
SELECT a.ename, b.retire_date,
b.last_retirement_pay_date, b.pay_amount
FROM emp a, retire_pay b
WHERE a.empno=b.empno;
```

In this example, there are a few things to notice. First, we had to create a directory entry, and we granted read and write permissions to that directory. This is only required if the user who defined the directory is not the user who will be creating the external table. Next, we define the external table, using the ORACLE_DATAPUMP driver as the access driver and using the **create table as select** command to populate the external table.

Once the external table is created, we can then read from our external table:

```
SQL> SELECT * FROM emp_history_ext;

ENAME       RETIRE_DA LAST_RETI PAY_AMOUNT
---------- --------- --------- ----------
SMITH       25-NOV-03 15-DEC-03      1000
```

This operation also results in the creation of an external file and, by default, a log file, as shown in this directory listing (formatted for your reading enjoyment!):

```
C:\> dir c:\oracle\admin\betatwo\directory
  Volume in drive C has no label.
  Volume Serial Number is 3CE9-7321
  Directory of c:\oracle\admin\betatwo\directory
 12/15/2003  07:52 PM        90    EMP_HISTORY_EXT_2528_1760.log
 12/15/2003  07:52 PM     1,808    emp_history.exp
```

NOTE
Even though the resulting dump file is in a proprietary format, make sure that it is as secure as it can be. It is still a security risk.

When you drop an external table (with the **drop table** command), the files that were created by that external table are not removed. This can be problematic, because if you try to re-create the external table, using the same external filenames, the creation will fail if those files exist with an Oracle error. Therefore, you must manually remove or rename any files with duplicate names (or change the name in the **create table** statement).

Finally, writing to external tables can involve a great deal of data and thus can take a long time to load. Oracle Database 10*g* supports a parallel load process for external tables. This helps to speed up the process significantly. To take advantage of parallel processing, you will want to define multiple output files in the **create table** statement, as we did in the previous example. Oracle Database 10*g* only creates one process for each file that is defined, so the degree of parallelism is limited to the number of files that are defined for the external table to write to.

Projecting Columns in External Tables

Sometimes, external tables are based on external files that contain unclean (or malformed) data. Before you shun all the data in these external files, you should decide whether, in fact, you really want some of the data that resides within and whether you can do without the unclean data.

For example, if your loader process defines a column as a number (3) but the actual number in the dump file is a 9999.99, then this would have killed a query against the external table in Oracle9*i* Database, since the data in the external table violates the format that the data is limited to. Oracle Database 10*g* offers new functionality that allows you to determine how the access driver will validate rows in the external table. You can decide whether to have it error out or to continue processing, skipping the invalid column.

By default, in Oracle Database 10*g*, Oracle will only process and validate columns on the **select** list of the query against the external table. You can also define this action by using the new **project column** clause in the **alter table** command. If you want the access driver to process and validate all column values, use the **project column all** clause of the **alter table** command. If you use the **project column all** clause, any column that is incorrectly defined will generate an error, regardless of whether or not it is selected.

New Materialized View, Query Rewrite, and Summary Management DDL Features

Oracle Database 10*g* offers a number of new features related to materialized views (Mviews) and query rewrite. These improvements include

- Partition change tracking (PCT) enhancements

- Query rewrite enhancements

- Mview fast refresh enhancements

- Summary management DDL enhancements

Partition Change Tracking Enhancements

Oracle9*i* Database introduced PCT, which allows you to track changes in partitions of detail tables related to an Mview. PCT also is used to support fast refresh after partition maintenance operations, such as **partition truncate**. PCT also allows for a wider variety of query rewrites.

In Oracle9*i* Database, PCT was only available on a table partitioned using either range or composite partitioning. Oracle Database 10*g* improves PCT by making it available for list-partitioned tables. The PCT requirements for list-partitioned tables are the same as for range- and composite-partitioned tables.

Another new feature related to PCT is that an Mview now only needs to be based on the pseudocolumn ROWID to support PCT. Previously, the Mview must have been based either on the partition key column or a partition marker or on a join-dependent expression of the detail table.

In Oracle Database 10*g*, PCT updates execute a **truncate** during certain Mview refresh operations, rather than a **delete**, as was the case in Oracle9*i* Database. This makes the refresh operation much more efficient. This operation is subject to some restrictions, such as the fact that the base table and the Mview must be range partitioned and there must be a one-to-one relationship between those partitions. Also, the Mview must be partitioned on a single PCT key column, which must be either the partition key or the partition marker from the detail table.

You can force a PCT refresh via the **dbms_mview.refresh** procedure using the new **method** parameter value, P. If a PCT refresh is not possible, the session will return an error. Here is an example of using **dbms_mview.refresh** to force a PCT refresh:

```
Exec dbms_mview.refresh(my_mview, method=>'P');
```

Query Rewrite Enhancements

Oracle Database 10*g* offers new query rewrite functionality. This section looks at the following features:

- Query rewrite and self-joins
- Using unenforced trusted constraints
- Dependent Mview refresh
- Changes to **dbms_mview.explain_rewrite**
- The new **rewrite_or_error** hint
- Some additional new features

Query Rewrite and Self-Joins

Query rewrite does not support self-joins in either the originating query or the underlying Mviews that the query might be rewritten to use. In order to allow for a rewrite of a self-joined query, you must alias each multiple table instance. There are two methods that Oracle Database 10*g* uses to decide if it can rewrite the query: the alias method and the general method.

Alias Method   With the alias method, Oracle Database 10*g* looks at the table aliases included in the query and compares them to those in the eligible Mviews. If the aliases match, and the view is eligible for query rewrite otherwise, then Oracle Database 10*g* will rewrite the query.

In the following example, we want to look at the differential in pay for employees at the beginning of the current year versus today (perhaps security is looking for a hacker who has increased pay rates for certain employees). Here is an example of a query we might use:

```
SELECT a.ename, c.net_pay - b.net_pay Pay_Diff
FROM emp_hist a, pay_hist b, pay_hist c, pay_dates d
WHERE a.empno=b.empno
AND    a.empno=c.empno
AND    a.empno=d.empno
AND    b.pay_date = d.first_pay_date
AND    c.pay_date = d.last_pay_date;
```

Let's convert this into an Mview:

```
CREATE MATERIALIZED VIEW sal_emp_diff_mv
ENABLE QUERY REWRITE AS
SELECT a.ename, c.net_pay - b.net_pay Pay_Diff
FROM emp_hist a, pay_hist b, pay_hist c, pay_dates d
WHERE a.empno=b.empno
AND    a.empno=c.empno
AND    a.empno=d.empno
AND    b.pay_date = d.first_pay_date
AND    c.pay_date = d.last_pay_date;
```

This Mview would allow the earlier query to be rewritten to use the Mview now, rather than have to scan the PAY_HIST table. Here is an example of the execution of the query, and the associated execution plan where we see the rewrite in action:

```
SQL> SELECT a.ename, c.net_pay - b.net_pay Pay_Diff
   FROM emp_hist a, pay_hist b, pay_hist c, pay_dates d
   WHERE a.empno=b.empno and a.empno=c.empno
   AND    a.empno=d.empno And  b.pay_date = d.first_pay_date
   AND    c.pay_date = d.last_pay_date;
ENAME          PAY_DIFF
---------- ----------
MILLER              300

Execution Plan
-------------------------------------------------------
   0      SELECT STATEMENT Optimizer=CHOOSE
(Cost=4  Card=327 Bytes=6540)
   1    0   MAT_VIEW REWRITE ACCESS (FULL) OF 'SAL_EMP_DIFF_MV'
          (MAT_VIEW REWRITE) (Cost=4 Card=327 Bytes=6540)
```

General Method   The general method of multiple table instance support is used to provide for query rewrite in cases where aliases assigned to objects in the underlying Mview and the potentially rewritable query are not the same. This is probably a fairly likely situation, because you don't want developers to have to spend time tracking down source code for a given Mview just to figure out what aliases it's employing!

The general method compares the query to the query definitions of the various available Mviews. The optimizer examines each of the Mviews and determines if the views contain joins such that the query can be rewritten. Joins within an Mview need not be in the exact same order as the query that is the rewrite candidate, and additional columns can exist in the Mview. Let's reuse the example query we used to demonstrate the alias rewrite method to demonstrate the general method of query rewrite:

```
SELECT a.ename, c.net_pay - b.net_pay Pay_Diff
FROM emp_hist a, pay_hist b, pay_hist c, pay_dates d
WHERE a.empno=b.empno and   a.empno=c.empno
AND   a.empno=d.empno And   b.pay_date = d.first_pay_date
AND   c.pay_date = d.last_pay_date;
```

Next, let's create a new Mview that aliases the joins differently:

```
DROP MATERIALIZED VIEW sal_emp_diff_mv;
CREATE MATERIALIZED VIEW sal_emp_diff_mv
ENABLE QUERY REWRITE AS
SELECT a.ename, z.net_pay - y.net_pay Pay_Diff
FROM emp_hist a, pay_hist y, pay_hist z, pay_dates d
WHERE a.empno=y.empno and a.empno=y.empno
AND   a.empno=d.empno And y.pay_date = d.first_pay_date
AND   z.pay_date = d.last_pay_date;
```

Here is the resulting query plan after the creation of the Mview:

```
SELECT a.ename, z.net_pay - y.net_pay Pay_Diff
From   emp_hist a, pay_hist y, pay_hist z, pay_dates d
WHERE  a.empno=y.empno and a.empno=y.empno
AND    a.empno=d.empno And y.pay_date = d.first_pay_date
AND    z.pay_date = d.last_pay_date;
ENAME          PAY_DIFF
---------- ----------
MILLER              300
Execution Plan
-------------------------------------------------------
    0       SELECT STATEMENT Optimizer=CHOOSE (Cost=4 Card=327
            Bytes=6540)
    1   0   MAT_VIEW REWRITE ACCESS (FULL) OF 'SAL_EMP_DIFF_MV'
            (MAT_VIEW REWRITE) (Cost=4 Card=327 Bytes=6540)
```

NOTE
*The execution plan seen in the previous example indicates that an Mview is being used for the rewrite. This is new in Oracle Database 10*g*! Previously, Oracle Database would just indicate that a table was being used.*

Using Unenforced Trusted Constraints

When designing Mviews for your database, you need to consider whether or not to use unenforced trusted constraints. Examples of unenforced trusted constraints include constraints such as PK/FK relationships created using the **rely** option, or defined dimensions. Because these constraints are not enforced, they can cause unreliable query rewrites, but allowing query rewrite to occur using these trusted constraints can lead to more frequent use of query rewrite, and thus more efficient query responses. So, what to do?

Oracle Database 10*g* now allows you to determine if query rewrite can occur in cases where these unenforced trusted constraints are being used. Now, when creating an Mview, you can use the **using enforced constraints** or **using trusted constraints** parameter of the **create materialized view** command to qualify trusted constraints for query rewrite for that view. You can also use the **alter materialized view** command to allow the use of enforced trusted constraints. Here is a fairly simple example of the creation of an Mview that allows the use of trusted constraints:

```
CREATE MATERIALIZED VIEW sal_emp_mv
REFRESH USING TRUSTED CONSTRAINTS
AS
SELECT b.empno, b.ename, b.deptno, c.dname,
TO_CHAR(a.pay_date, 'yyyy') AS FY, SUM(a.net_pay)
FROM pay_hist a, emp_hist b, dept_hist c
WHERE b.deptno=c.deptno AND a.empno=b.empno
GROUP BY b.empno, b.ename, b.deptno, c.dname,
TO_CHAR(pay_date, 'yyyy');
```

To support trusted refresh, a column, UNKNOWN_TRUSTED_FD, has been added to the DBA_MVIEWS, USER_MVIEWS, and ALL_MVIEWS data dictionary views. This column is used to indicate if the Mview is in an unknown state because trusted dependencies were used during a refresh. If this column is marked Y, it indicates that the Mview is based on a trusted relationship and that query rewrites will only be possible in either TRUSTED or STALE_TOLERATED mode.

Dependent Mview Refresh and Rewrite

Oracle Database 10*g* also can detect if the refresh of a given Mview is dependent on the refresh of other Mviews. In this case, Oracle Database 10*g* detects these dependencies, refreshes the Mview in the proper order, and rewrites dependent Mview refreshes as needed to make the overall refresh process more efficient.

For example, assume we have two Mviews. The first is a summary of flight revenues for our airline by month, and the second is a summary of our flight revenues by year. We can create these Mviews by using the **deferred** option, which causes the Mview metadata to be created but does not populate the Mview itself. Here is an example:

```
CREATE MATERIALIZED VIEW flt_revs_mon
BUILD DEFERRED REFRESH USING TRUSTED CONSTRAINTS
AS
SELECT a.fltno, to_char(b.flt_date, 'mm/yyyy') FD,
SUM(b.net_revenue)
FROM flight_dim a, flight_fact b
WHERE a.fltno=b.fltno
GROUP BY a.fltno, to_char(b.flt_date, 'mm/yyyy');

CREATE MATERIALIZED VIEW flt_revs_year
BUILD DEFERRED REFRESH USING TRUSTED CONSTRAINTS
AS
SELECT a.fltno, to_char(b.flt_date, 'yyyy') FD,
SUM(b.net_revenue)
FROM flight_dim a, flight_fact b
WHERE a.fltno=b.fltno
GROUP BY a.fltno, to_char(b.flt_date, 'yyyy');
```

Once we have created our Mviews, they are not yet populated with data since we used the **build deferred** parameter of the **create materialized view** command. This allows us to use the **dbms_mview.refresh_dependent** procedure to refresh those views. When **dbms_mview.refresh_dependent** is executed, it determines the hierarchical relationships between the views and refreshes them based on those relationships. It then rewrites higher-level views so that they can use the lower-level views of the hierarchy. For example, let's refresh the FLIGHT_REVS_MON and FLIGHT_REVS_YEAR views:

```
DECLARE
v_num_fails     NUMBER;
BEGIN
dbms_mview.refresh_dependent(number_of_failures=>v_num_fails,
list=>'FLIGHT_DIM', method=>'C');
END;
/
```

In this case, the view FLIGHT_REVS_MON is refreshed first, and then the FLIGHT_REVS_YEAR view is refreshed, based on a rewrite of the FLIGHT_REVS_MON view. Note that the **query_rewrite_enabled** parameter must be set to TRUE (which is now the default setting in Oracle Database 10*g*, if the **optimized_features_ enable** parameter is set to 10.0.0 or higher) and all normal query rewrite rules apply. Also, when we executed the **refresh_dependent** procedure, note that we used the FLIGHT_DIM table as the underlying base table to start the refresh with. That is because the FLIGHT_DIM table is the base table in the hierarchy of all these views, and it becomes the table that we want to start our dependent refresh from.

Changes to dbms_mview.explain_rewrite

The **dbms_mview.explain_rewrite** procedure can be used to help determine if a query has been rewritten and, if not, why. The output from **dbms_mview.explain_ rewrite** can be directed to a table called REWRITE_TABLE, which is created via the utlxrw.sql script in $ORACLE_HOME/rdbms/admin. In Oracle Database 10*g*, this table has the following new columns added to it to further assist you in determining why the rewrite failed:

- **MV_IN_MSG**   The Mview name associated with the row

- **MEASURE_IN_MESSAGE**   The measure or aggregate that is required to rewrite the query

- **JOIN_BACK_TBL**   Contains the name of the table in which a join back was required in order to rewrite the query

- **JOIN_BACK_COL**   The column in the table in which a join back was required to rewrite the query

- **ORIGINAL_COST**   The cost of the original query

- **REWRITTEN_COST**   The cost of the rewritten query

Note that a given execution of the **dbms_mview.explain_rewrite** procedure can result in multiple rows in the REWRITE_TABLE.

Also, in Oracle Database 10*g*, the **dbms_mview.explain_rewrite** procedure allows you to specify the input query text as a CLOB, thus circumventing the previous 32K size restriction. This allows rather large queries (up to 4GB!) to be run through the procedure.

The New rewrite_or_error Hint

Sometimes you may want a query to fail if it cannot be rewritten. The new **rewrite_ or_error** hint causes Oracle Database 10*g* to throw an ORA-30393 error if the query cannot be rewritten. This can be handy during the development process to determine if your queries (for example, dynamically generated queries) are being rewritten.

A Few Final New Features

The default sort order when using the **order by** clause in the **rank** function is ascending (asc). In Oracle Database 10*g*, if a calling query does not have the **asc** keyword in it, Oracle Database 10*g* will still be able to rewrite the query. Previous versions of the Oracle database did not support this functionality.

Also, in Oracle Database 10*g*, if the query includes a grouping rollup that is a subset of the grouping of an Mview, that query can be rewritten to use the Mview. For example, if your Mview ends with a grouping statement such as **group by part_bin, sub_part_id** and your query has a grouping statement such as **group by part_bin**, then it would be able to be rewritten (assuming that the statement is otherwise rewritable).

Mview Fast Refresh Enhancements

Previously in Oracle, fast refresh of Mviews that contained joins and aggregates were only supported in the following cases:

- Self-joins
- Flattened views
- If there were remote tables in the FROM clause of the Mview

Oracle Database 10*g* now supports fast refresh for Mviews that only contain joins (known as Mview joins), with no aggregation. There are some requirements associated with fast refresh of Mview joins, including:

- You must include in the select list the ROWID column for each table in the **from** clause.

- The associated Mview log must also contain the ROWID column in it.

- If the Mview join contains an inline or named view in the **from** clause, the view must be able to be merged into the Mview join definition by Oracle Database 10*g*. Also, the merged view must meet the requirements for fast refresh, specifically with regard to the use of the ROWID column for each table in the view. Also, Mview logs must be present on all base tables of any merged view.

- If the Mview join includes the use of remote tables, then those tables must all be from the same site. Mview logs must be created at the remote site for each remote table used in the Mview.

- Compatibility must be set to 10.0.1 or higher.

Also, prior to Oracle Database 10*g*, a refresh of an Mview would not consider multilevel dependency refresh issues. If an Mview was based on another Mview, then the lower-level Mview would not be refreshed. Therefore, if the lower-level Mview were stale, the upper-level Mview would remain stale as well.

In Oracle Database 10*g*, Oracle refresh procedures now support nested refreshes of Mviews. Thus, if an Mview is built on a nested set of Mviews, Oracle Database 10*g* will update the hierarchy of Mviews all at once, guaranteeing the freshness of the Mviews throughout the hierarchy. The Mviews are refreshed in dependency order, from the lower-level nested Mviews to the final top-level Mview.

To facilitate these changes, the Oracle-supplied procedures **dbms_mview.refresh** and **dbms_mview.refresh_dependent** have a new option, **nested**. When set to TRUE, the **nested** option will cause Oracle Database 10*g* to refresh the top-level Mview and all lower-level Mviews that it depends on. Here are examples of the use of the new **nested** option in the **dbms_mview** procedures:

```
EXEC dbms_mview.refresh('FLT_REVS_YEAR', nested=>TRUE);
EXEC dbms_mview.refresh_dependent('FLIGHT_SUB',nested=>TRUE);
```

A nested refresh can walk up a tree of Mviews or down a tree of Mviews, depending on which type of refresh Oracle Database 10*g* requires. Thus, if you refresh an Mview downstream, all Mviews dependent on it upstream will be refreshed. If you refresh an Mview upstream, all Mviews downstream will also be refreshed.

Summary Management DDL Enhancements

Oracle Database 10*g* offers new features when executing DDL operations against Mviews:

- The ability to define column aliases outside of the query itself

- Enhanced Materialized View partition maintenance functionality

- Changes to commenting materialized views

- Enhancements to the **alter materialized view log** command

- The new **dbms_dimension** package

Materialized View Column Aliasing

If you have an Mview that has like column names, you need to alias the commonly named SELECT columns of the Mview to avoid an error, as shown in this example:

```
CREATE MATERIALIZED VIEW mv_emp_data
ENABLE QUERY REWRITE
SELECT a.active_time employee_time,
b.active_time retiree_time
FROM employee a, retiree b
WHERE a.empid=b.empid;
```

The unfortunate side effect of this requirement is that query rewrite will likely not be possible for this view because of the aliases included in the view. This is because full text match rewrite can only occur if the text of the Mview and the SQL statement is the same, and it is probably not likely that the same aliases will be used in the query that might otherwise be rewritten.

Oracle Database 10*g* solves this problem when defining Mviews through the extension of the syntax of the **create materialized view** command. Now, the command allows you to define the column aliases as a part of the command itself, without having to attach those aliases to the actual select list. Here is an example of the new syntax in use:

```
CREATE MATERIALIZED VIEW MV_EMP_DATA
(employee_time, retiree_time)
ENABLE QUERY REWRITE
SELECT a.active_time, b.active_time
FROM employee a, retiree b
WHERE a.empid=b.empid;
```

Enhanced Materialized View Partition Maintenance Functionality

Oracle Database 10*g* now supports Enhanced Materialized View partition maintenance functions. You can now **truncate** a partition, **split** a partition, or **exchange** a partition using the **alter materialized view** command in Oracle Database 10*g*. These commands eliminate the need to use the **alter table** command to make these changes directly on the underlying tables of the materialized view being changed.

Commenting Materialized Views in Oracle Database 10*g*

In Oracle Database 10*g*, you no longer are allowed to use the **comment on table** command to define comments associated with an Mview when **compatible** is set to 10.0.1 or above. You need to start using the new **comment on materialized view** command instead. Here is an example:

```
COMMENT ON MATERIALIZED VIEW mv_all_emps
IS 'Summary employee Mview';
```

Three new views are provided to allow you to view these comments: DBA_MVIEW_COMMENTS, ALL_MVIEW_COMMENTS, and USER_MVIEW_COMMENTS. Note that when an Mview is built from a prebuilt table, the resulting Mview inherits any existing comments, and those comments will be marked in the *_MVIEW_COMMENTS views as having come from the source table. New comments will indicate that they were added after the Mview was built.

Changes to alter materialized view log Command

A force parameter has been added to the **alter materialized view log** command. This causes Oracle Database 10g to ignore any items in the add clause that have already been defined in the Mview log. Oracle Database 10g simply ignores the error, and any items in the command that can be added will be added. Some conditions will still cause errors to be signaled, however, such as if you improperly define a tablespace.

The dbms_dimension Package

The **dbms_dimension** package is new for Oracle Database 10g. This package offers new functionality to help you manage dimensions. You can use the procedure **dbms_dimension.describe_dimension** to extract the definition of a dimension. Also, the **dbms_dimension.validate_dimension** procedure allows you to validate dimensions (this is similar functionality to the **dbms_olap.validate_dimension** procedure).

New Partitioning Features

Oracle Database 10g comes with a number of new partitioning enhancements:

- Index-organized table partitioning improvements

- Hash-partitioned global indexes

- Partitioned index maintenance

- Skipping unusable indexes

Index-Organized Table Partitioning Improvements

If you use index-organized tables (IOTs), you might well be interested in some new partitioning features related to IOTs. First, prior to Oracle Database 10g, you could not use list partitioning with IOTs. This restriction has been removed. Note that an IOT still cannot be partitioned using composite partitioning.

In Oracle Database 10g, global maintenance (e.g., drop or exchange partition operations) of an IOT will not result in the indexes being marked as unusable. Instead, Oracle now maintains the indexes during the maintenance operation and maintains the UROWIDs associated with the IOTs.

If you create a mapping table on a partitioned IOT, the mapping table will be partitioned if the IOT is partitioned and those partitions will share the same name and physical attributes as the base IOT partitions. Finally, prior to Oracle Database 10g, certain types of partitioned IOT's could not contain LOB columns (e.g. hash partitioned tables). This restriction has been removed in Oracle Database 10g.

Jonathan Says...
Remember to test every assumption you make with newer features. Just
because a new feature looks like an old feature, you don't have any guarantee
that it will behave the same way. For example, you can move IOTs online:

```
Alter table IOT move online;
```

But if you try the same thing with a partition of a hash-partitioned IOT,
it doesn't work (yet):

```
SQL> alter table iot_hash move partition sys_p177 online;
alter table iot_hash move partition sys_p177 online
                                                    *
ERROR at line 1:
ORA-14020: this physical attribute may not be specified for a
table partition
```

Hash-Partitioned Global Indexes

Until Oracle Database 10*g*, you could only create global indexes as range-partitioned
objects. Oracle Database 10*g* now allows you to create global indexes as hash-
partitioned indexes. With hash-partitioned global indexes, each index partition will
contain a hashed value based on the partition key of the index and the number of
partitions in that index.

   In this section, we look at the creation of hash-partitioned global indexes, and
then we look at maintaining these indexes.

Creating Hash-Partitioned Global Indexes

Hash-partitioned global indexes can be very useful in OLTP environments with
high user activity and high contention for index leaf blocks. Hash-partitioned global
indexes may be just the thing for high-activity OLTP environments where there is
high contention for index leaf blocks, because index entries will be hashed to different
partitions, spreading the data (and the contention for that data) over the entire index.
Queries that frequently use equality and **in** predicates may benefit from a hash-
partitioned global index, because these types of queries can take advantage of
partition pruning. Hash-partitioned global indexes are simply created as demonstrated
in this example:

```
CREATE INDEX my_hash_idx ON sales_table
(invoice_number, sales_date)
```

```
GLOBAL PARTITION BY HASH (invoice_number)
(partition part_1 TABLESPACE sales_idx_part1,
 partition part_2 TABLESPACE sales_idx_part2,
 partition part_3 TABLESPACE sales_idx_part3,
 partition part_4 TABLESPACE sales_idx_part4);
```

An alternative form of the creation of this index might look like this:

```
CREATE INDEX my_hash_idx ON sales_table
(invoice_number, sales_date)
GLOBAL PARTITION BY HASH (invoice_number)
PARTITIONS 4
STORE IN (sales_idx_part1, sales_idx_part2, sales_idx_part3,
sales_idx_part4) PARALLEL;
```

Note that the only storage attribute for the individual index partitions that is allowed is the **tablespace** clause. Finally, note the use of the **parallel** clause in this **create index** command.

Maintaining Hash-Partitioned Global Indexes

Once a hash-partitioned global index is created, you need to maintain it. This might include

- Adding a partition
- Coalescing a partition
- Performing other maintenance operations

Adding a Partition   To add a partition to a hash-partitioned global index, use the **alter index add partition** command:

```
ALTER INDEX my_hash_idx ADD PARTITION part_5
TABLESPACE sales_idx_part2 PARALLEL;
```

In this case, we have added partition part_5 to the index. This index will be populated with rehashed index entries from another partition. Also note that we created this new partition using the **parallel** clause.

Coalescing a Partition   The process of coalescing a partition reduces the hash-partitioned index by one partition. Thus, the **alter index coalesce partition** command is the reverse of the **alter index add partition** command. Oracle Database 10*g* chooses the partition to be removed and will redistribute the data from that partition into a remaining partition.

Performing Other Maintenance Operations   As a DBA you may need to perform other maintenance operations on hash-partitioned indexes. This might include operations such as rebuilding a partition, renaming a partition, or dropping the hash-partitioned table. These operations are pretty much identical to like operations on range and hash global indexes, such as:

- Using the **alter index rebuild partition** to rebuild an index partition

- Using the **alter index** command to modify partition storage specifications

- Using the **alter index** command to modify the default attributes of the index

- Using the **alter index** command to mark a partition or the entire index as unusable

- Using the **alter index** command to rename a partition of the index

- Using the **drop index** command to remove the entire index

Further, some operations are not supported for hash-partitioned global indexes, including:

- Using the **alter table split index partitions** and the **alter table merge index partitions** commands to split or merge the index partitions

- Using the **alter index rebuild** command to rebuild the entire index, rather than individual partitions

- Using the **alter index** command to modify a partition, except to make it unusable

Partitioned Index Maintenance

In earlier versions of Oracle Database, database operations that would impact a table partition, such as adding, splitting, merging, or moving a partition, would cause associated index partitions to be placed in either the default tablespace or in the same tablespace as the partitions being rebuilt.

Oracle Database 10g offers a new parameter to the **alter table** clause, **update indexes**, that will cause indexes to be rebuilt automatically within the tablespace that they reside in. Note that this command will invalidate and rebuild all index partitions, not just the partitions affected by the operation. Here is an example of the use of the **update indexes** command:

```
ALTER TABLE sales_test SPLIT PARTITION s_q2 at (6)
INTO (partition s_q2_1, partition s_q2_2) UPDATE INDEXES;
```

Jonathan Says...
If **update indexes** rebuilds all index partitions in a case like this, then that seems to be a good reason to make sure that you never use it. Aren't partitioned objects supposed to be large, and isn't the ability to restrict maintenance to a small section of a large object at any one moment supposed to be one of the best reasons for using partitioning? I think we can assume that there is a suboptimal implementation (bug) here waiting to be fixed.

Skipping Unusable Indexes

ORA-01502s, you hate 'em, right? We all hate 'em. Well, has Oracle got a solution for you. Now, Oracle Database 10*g* comes with the **skip_unusable_indexes** parameter that can be set at the instance level (you could set **skip_unusable_indexes** at the session level in Oracle8*i* Database and later versions). By default, this parameter is set to TRUE, which means that Oracle Database 10*g* will not create execution plans for indexes that are marked with a status of UNUSABLE. Also, to notify you when an index is marked as UNUSABLE, Oracle Database 10*g* now puts a handy-dandy message in the alert log, as demonstrated in this snippet:

```
Wed Dec 10 21:03:43 2003
Some indexes or index [sub]partitions of table SYS.SALES_TEST
have been marked unusable
```

CHAPTER 7

Application Development

racle Database 10*g* comes with a number of new features that are designed to provide enhanced application development functionality within the Oracle database. This chapter covers the following topics related to these new features:

- Bulk bind improvements

- Collection set operations

- Database storage of natively compiled PL/SQL

- PL/SQL fine-grained debug privileges

- PL/SQL regular expressions

- User-specified quote character assignment

- The new **utl_compress** package

- The new **utl_mail** package

- PL/SQL compile-time warnings

- New PL/SQL compiler

- Improvements to the **dbms_profiler** procedure

- Table function enhancements

Bulk Bind Improvements

Bulk bind operations help to improve the performance of PL/SQL operations. Oracle Database 10*g* offers new functionality associated with bulk binds, including:

- Processing of sparse collections

- New exception handling

Processing Sparse Collections

Prior to Oracle Database 10*g*, processing of collections that contained sparse element collections was inefficient. If the **save exceptions** clause was not specified, then the statement being executed would terminate when it reached the first deleted element. When **save exceptions** was used, the operation would not fail, but if there were a number of deleted elements, the performance of the process was much worse than it would have been if **save exceptions** had not been used.

Oracle Database 10g offers a new keyword, **indices**, to allow for much faster processing of sparse collections. The performance of the statement with the use of the **indices** keyword is much improved over that with the **save exceptions** clause. Let's look at an example of this new functionality in use. In this example, we have a table called FAMILIES as our source data. From this table, we have a PL/SQL procedure that will remove all dependents from the FAMILIES table, and then populate a table called employee. Since we are likely to have a number of dependents for each employee, the bulk bind is likely to be very sparse by the time we are ready to insert our employees, so we will use the new **indices of** clause to speed up the process. Here is the example:

```
CREATE TABLE FAMILIES
( id_ssn              NUMBER,
  Last_name           VARCHAR2(30),
  First_name          VARCHAR2(30),
  Emp_dep_code        NUMBER);

CREATE TABLE employees AS
SELECT * FROM FAMILIES WHERE 1=2;

CREATE UNIQUE INDEX u_employees_idx
on EMPLOYEES(id_ssn);

-- Now, insert some records
INSERT INTO families VALUES (123456780, 'Freeman','Robert',0);
INSERT INTO families VALUES (123456781, 'Freeman','Lisa',1);
INSERT INTO families VALUES (123456782, 'Freeman','Felicia',2);
INSERT INTO families VALUES (123456783, 'Freeman','Sarah',3);
INSERT INTO families VALUES (123456784, 'Freeman','Jacob',4);
INSERT INTO families VALUES (123456785, 'Freeman','Jared',5);
INSERT INTO families VALUES (123456786, 'Freeman','Lizzie',6);
INSERT INTO families VALUES (123456787, 'Bundy','Al',0);
INSERT INTO families VALUES (123456788, 'Bundy','Peg',1);
INSERT INTO families VALUES (123456789, 'Jetson','George',0);
INSERT INTO families VALUES (123456790, 'Jetson','Jane',1);
COMMIT;

-- Now, here is the PL/SQL used to load the employee table.
DECLARE
    TYPE typ_famtyp IS TABLE OF families%ROWTYPE;
    v_fam    typ_famtyp;
BEGIN
    SELECT *
    BULK COLLECT INTO v_fam
    FROM families;
-- loop through the collection and remove
-- unneeded entries.
```

```
    FOR rec IN 1..v_fam.LAST()
    LOOP
        IF v_fam(rec).emp_dep_code!=0
        THEN
            v_fam.delete(rec);
        END IF;
    END LOOP;
    FORALL inds IN INDICES OF v_fam
        INSERT INTO employees VALUES v_fam(inds);
END;
/
```

Exception Handling

In Oracle Database 10*g*, the PL/SQL engine allows you to handle exceptions raised during the execution of a **forall** statement. This allows your code to be written in such a way that an error does not need to halt its execution. You can also save information about the error after it occurs, write it to a table, or display it. The Oracle documentation provides some good examples of this feature.

SQL and PL/SQL Regular Expressions

Regular expressions are new features in Oracle Database 10*g*. This section looks at what regular expressions are, and how regular expressions can be used in Oracle Database 10*g*, including a review of new functions that are used in association with regular expressions.

What Are Regular Expressions?

If you have done much scripting in UNIX, then no doubt you are well acquainted with regular expressions. A *regular expression* is a set of symbols and elements of syntax that allows you to match patterns of text within a given expression. Regular expressions are very powerful and allow for pattern matching that was previously only possible through a programmatic solution.

Oracle Database 10*g* now supports the use of regular expressions in SQL and PL/SQL. The definitions for these regular expressions are defined within the POSIX standard regular expression syntax. Regular expressions use a combination of metasymbols to define various matching and search criteria. Note that matching criteria are case sensitive when using regular expressions. The most commonly used metasymbols are listed and described in Table 7-1.

Using Regular Expressions in Oracle Database 10*g*

Regular expressions in Oracle Database 10*g* are supported through the use of a number of new functions, which are described in more detail in the following sections.

Metasymbol	Description	Example
*	Wildcard symbol that matches zero or more occurrences.	Ad* matches Ada, Adb, and Adcbdd but does not match Acd or add.
?	Wildcard symbol that matches one character occurrence.	A?c matches Aac, AAc, and Adc but does not match Bcc or zzc.
^	Matches the start of the line.	^abc matches abch but does not match habc.
$	Matches the end of the line.	Abc$ matches Abc but does not match Abcadd.
[]	Allows for matching of any character found within the braces.	A[a-c]b matches Aab or Acb but does not match Adb or aaa.
{m}	Allows for a match of *m* times.	Myname[0-9]{3} matches Myname9, Myname99, and Myname222 but does not match Myname2222.
{m,n}	Matches at least *m* times but no more than *n* times.	Myname[0-9]{3,5} matches Myname9, Myname99, and Myname2222 but does not match Myname222222 (because there are six 2s).
\n	This is called a back reference expression. Causes the previous expression to be repeated n times.	[aeiou] \2 matches aaron but does not match aron.

TABLE 7-1. *Common Metasymbols*

NOTE
There is much more to regular expressions in Oracle Database 10g than I could cover in this chapter. What you find here are the basics to get you started. For more complex applications, check out the Oracle Database 10g SQL Reference Guide, the Application Developers Guide, MetaLink, or OTN.

The regexp_like Function

The **regexp_like** function is akin to the SQL **like** operator. It extends the functionality of the **like** operator to allow for the use of regular expressions to do pattern matching within text. The input value can be any of the following data types: CHAR, VARCHAR2, NCHAR, NVARCHAR2, CLOB, or NCLOB. The regular expression will be converted to the same data type as the search value.

> **CAUTION**
> *During the review of this book against production Oracle Database 10g, we found a bug in the **regexp_like** function. Test it carefully before you use it.*

The **regexp_like** function comes with options that allow you to ignore case; by default, case is matched. Also, the function can treat the search string as a multiple-line string. Finally, if the regular expression is a NULL value, then the function will return an unknown value. The syntax for the **regexp_like** function is as follows:

 `Regexp_like(search_string, pattern [, match_option]);`

where:

- **search_string** is the search value.

- **pattern** is the regular expression to be used and is limited to 512 bytes.

- **match_option** is a literal text string that allows you to change the matching behavior of the function. This parameter can consist of one or more of the values described in Table 7-2.

match_option Value	Description
C	Case-sensitive matching (the default).
I	Case-insensitive matching.
N	Allows the period (.) to match any newline character.
M	Treats the source string as if it contains multiple lines. This causes Oracle Database 10*g* to interpret the ^ and $ characters as the start and end of any line anywhere in the source string, rather than treating the entire source string as one big line.

TABLE 7-2. *Valid match_option Choices*

So, let's look at some examples of this function in use. First, we are going to use a table called TEST_EXPRESSIONS, which has this format and content:

```
SQL> DESC test_expressions
 Name                    Null?    Type
 ------------------    --------  --------------
 CHAR_VALUE                       VARCHAR2(30)
 DATE_VALUE                       DATE

SQL> SELECT * FROM test_expressions;
CHAR_VALUE                          DATE_VALUE
----------------------------      ----------
abcd                                27-DEC-03
abb                                 27-DEC-03
zzz                                 27-DEC-02
zbz                                 30-JUN-03
zabz                                30-JUN-03
aaron                               30-JUN-03
```

Let's assume that we want to see all rows where the CHAR_VALUE column has characters that start with ab at the beginning of the column. We would use this query:

```
SQL>   SELECT * FROM test_expressions
  2    WHERE REGEXP_LIKE(char_value, '^ab*');
CHAR_VALUE                          DATE_VALUE
----------------------------      ----------
abcd                                27-DEC-03
abb                                 27-DEC-03
```

Here is another example. Assume that we want to find all records where b is the second character in the column. We might use this query:

```
SQL>   SELECT * FROM test_expressions
  2    WHERE REGEXP_LIKE(char_value, '^.b.');
CHAR_VALUE                          DATE_VALUE
----------------------------      ----------
abcd                                27-DEC-03
abb                                 27-DEC-03
zbz                                 30-JUN-03
```

You can also compare dates, but you need to convert them into character strings first with the **to_char** function. In this example, we look for all records that were created when the minute was 08:

```
SQL> SELECT TO_CHAR(date_value, 'mm/dd/yyyy hh24:mi:ss')
  2  FROM test_expressions
```

```
   3  WHERE REGEXP_LIKE(TO_CHAR(date_value, 'yyyy/mi'),
   4  '200[2-3]/08');

TO_CHAR(DATE_VALUE,
-------------------
12/27/2003 12:08:36
12/27/2003 12:08:43
12/27/2002 12:08:51
06/30/2003 12:08:59
```

In this final example of the **regexp_like** function, we want to find all repeated occurrences of a specific set of characters, in this case, the character z or the character a:

```
SQL>  SELECT char_value FROM test_expressions WHERE
      2 REGEXP_LIKE(char_value, '(([za]))/2', 'i');
CHAR_VALUE
-----------------------------
aaron
zzz
```

The regexp_instr Function

The **regexp_instr** function is an extension of the **instr** operator. It searches the input string for the regular expression pattern. Based on the **return_option** setting, the function then returns an integer indicating the position where the match either began or ended. The input value can be any of the following data types: CHAR, VARCHAR2, NCHAR, NVARCHAR2, CLOB, or NCLOB. The regular expression is converted to the same data type as the search value. If the regular expression is a NULL value, then the function returns an unknown value. The syntax for the **regexp_instr** function is as follows:

```
Regexp_instr(search_string, pattern [, position [, occurrence
[, return_option [, match_option]]]]);
```

where:

- **search_string** is the search value.

- **pattern** is the regular expression to be used; limited to 512 bytes.

- **position** is a positive integer that indicates where the search should begin. This value defaults to 1.

- **occurrence** defines the occurrence of the pattern to search for. The default is 1, meaning that Oracle Database 10*g* will search for the first occurrence.

- **return_option** is a numeric value that indicates which value should be returned by the function. This can be the beginning position of the match (defined by a zero value) or a non-zero option indicates that the ending position (the position after the character found) should be returned.

- **match_option** is a literal text string that allows you to change the matching behavior of the function. This parameter can consist of one or more of the values described earlier in Table 7-2.

So, let's look at some examples of this function in use. We will use the table TEST_EXPRESSIONS again. Here is our first example:

```
SQL> SELECT * FROM test_expressions
  2 WHERE REGEXP_INSTR(char_value,'b',1, 2, 0) > 0;
CHAR_VALUE                     DATE_VALU
------------------------------ ---------
abb                            27-DEC-03
```

In this example, we are looking for the second occurrence of the character b in the CHAR_VALUE column.

Of course, we are really not using a regular expression in the preceding example, so let's do so in the next:

```
SQL> SELECT * FROM test_expressions
  2   WHERE REGEXP_INSTR(char_value,'[b-c]',1, 2, 0) > 0;
CHAR_VALUE                     DATE_VALU
------------------------------ ---------
abcd                           27-DEC-03
abb                            27-DEC-03
```

In this example, we have looked for the second occurrence of the character b or c in the CHAR_VALUE column, which gives us two results. Let's look at another example:

```
SQL> SELECT REGEXP_INSTR('This is a test','[^ ]+', 1, 2)
FROM dual;
REGEXP_INSTR('THIS IS A TEST','[^]+',1,2)
-----------------------------------------
                                        6
```

Note in this example that the function returns the character position after the end of the search string, not the position of the last character in the search string.

The regexp_replace Function

The **regexp_replace** function is an extension of the **replace** function. It allows you to search the input string for the regular expression and, as an output, replace those characters with a replacement string. The input string value can be any of the following data types: CHAR, VARCHAR2, NCHAR, NVARCHAR2, CLOB, or NCLOB. The regular expression will be converted to the same data type as the search value. The syntax for the **regexp_replace** function is as follows:

```
Regexp_replace(search_string, pattern [,replacestr [, position
[, occurrence [, match_option]]]]);
```

where:

- **search_string** is the search value.

- **pattern** is the regular expression to be used; limited to 512 bytes.

- **replacestr** can be any character type and is the string that will be used to replace the search string.

- **position** is a positive integer that indicates where the search should begin. This value defaults to 1.

- **occurrence** defines the occurrence of the pattern to search for. The default is 1, meaning that Oracle Database 10*g* will search for the first occurrence.

- **match_option** is a literal text string that allows you to change the matching behavior of the function. This parameter can consist of one or more of the values described earlier in Table 7-2.

So, let's look at some examples of this function in use. Our first example is pretty basic, demonstrating how the function works. In this case, we replace the string "This is the wild west west" with the string "This is the wild west dude":

```
SELECT REGEXP_REPLACE
('this is the wild west west',
'west$','dude') FROM dual;
REGEXP_REPLACE('THISISTHEW
-------------------------
this is the wild west dude
```

The next example is a bit more complex. It converts existing phone numbers with dashes into a decimal format:

```
SQL> Select REGEXP_REPLACE('206-555-1212',
'([[:digit:]]{3})\-([[:digit:]]{3})\-([[:digit:]]{4})','\1.\2.\3')
from dual;
REGEXP_REPLA
------------
206.555.1212
```

In this example, we used what is known as a character class definition (called [:digit:]) to indicate that the range of expressions indicated are digits. So, the first part of the example [[:digit:]]{3} basically patterns three digits and is the same as [0-9]{3}. This convention (which is POSIX compliant) makes it easier to deal with character classes such as lowercase letters or only numeric values.

The regexp_substr Function

The **regexp_substr** function is an extension of the **substr** function. It allows you to search the input string for the regular expression, and the output is the replacement string. In this way, it is much like the **regexp_instr** function, except that **regexp_substr** returns the actual string rather than a starting or ending position. The input string value can be any of the following data types: CHAR, VARCHAR2, NCHAR, NVARCHAR2, CLOB, or NCLOB. The regular expression will be converted to the same data type as the search value. The syntax for the **regexp_substr** function is as follows:

```
Regexp_substr(search_string, pattern [, position [, occurrence
[, match_option]]]]);
```

where:

- **search_string** is the search value.

- **pattern** is the regular expression to be used; limited to 512 bytes.

- **position** is a positive integer that indicates where the search should begin. This value defaults to 1.

- **occurrence** defines the occurrence of the pattern to search for. The default is 1, meaning that Oracle Database 10*g* will search for the first occurrence.

- **match_option** is a literal text string that allows you to change the matching behavior of the function. This parameter can consist of one or more of the values described earlier in Table 7-2.

So, let's look at some examples of this function in use. In this first example, we are looking for any record that has a b in it as the second occurrence:

```
SQL> SELECT REGEXP_SUBSTR(char_value,'b',1, 2)
  2  FROM test_expressions
  3* WHERE REGEXP_INSTR(char_value,'b',1,2) > 0;

REGEXP_SUBSTR(CHAR_VALUE,'B',1
------------------------------
b
```

In the next example, we want to find all character values with either the letter b or c in them, and then we want to only print out characters in those strings that have b, c, or d values:

```
SQL> SELECT char_value,
  2  REGEXP_SUBSTR(char_value,'([b-d]+/?) {0,5}/?')
  3  FROM test_expressions
  4  WHERE REGEXP_INSTR(char_value,'[b-c]',1,2) > 0;
CHAR_VALUE                      REGEXP_SUBSTR(CHAR_VALUE,'([B-
------------------------------ ------------------------------
abcd                           bcd
abb                            bb
```

Case- and Accent-Insensitive Searches

Oracle Database 10*g* now allows for case- and accent-insensitive sorting. This is supported through the use of the **nls_sort** parameter, affixing the parameters **_ai** for accent insensitive and **_ci** for case insensitive to the NLS language you are using.

The **nls_sort** parameter affects a number of SQL functions and operations, including the following:

- where
- order by
- start with
- having

- in/not in
- between
- case-when

The SQL functions that compare based on byte order rather than character (operations such as **like**, **trim**, and **instr**) are not affected by the **nls_sort** settings. Also, you can

Jonathan Says...

In case you can't wait for Oracle Database 10*g* to do your regular expression search-and-replace tasks, you might want to look at the **owa_pattern** package, which has been around for several years. See $ORACLE_HOME/rdbms/admin/ pubpat.sql for details.

It's just a PL/SQL package (surely a candidate for native compilation), so it's not fast. On the other hand, I don't think anyone will be depending on regular expression handling to find data quickly even in Oracle Database 10*g*; it is more likely to be the final test applied to a small number of rows, or an occasional text-processing trawl through an individual LOB.

use the **nlssort** function within SQL operations to perform specific case-insensitive searches, which eliminates the need to set the **nls_sort** parameter. Here is an example:

```
SQL> SELECT * FROM names ORDER BY 1;
NAME
-----------------------------
FREEMAN
Freeman
Freeman
freeman
SQL> ALTER SESSION SET NLS_SORT=generic_m_ci;

SQL> SELECT * FROM names ORDER BY 1;
NAME
--------------------
freeman
Freeman
FREEMAN
Freeman
```

Note how the sorting in the second query is different from the first query. After setting the **nls_sort** parameter to indicate that case-insensitive sorting should be used, the sort order of the query changes. The same result can be retrieved without using the **nlssort** function, as shown in this example:

```
SQL> select * from names order by nlssort(name,
  2  'NLS_SORT=generic_m_ci');
NAME
--------------------
freeman
Freeman
FREEMAN
Freeman
```

Finally, you may wish to make a search accent insensitive. Append **_ai** to the **nls_sort** parameter or within the **nlssort** function call to facilitate this insensitive search. Note that the **_ai** option also includes case-insensitivity functionality within it.

Jonathan Says...

Changing how sorts occur can result in unexpected side effects that will impact some systems. Some queries may change their execution path when you use case-insensitive or accent-insensitive comparisons. For example, Robert's original query could have used an index to do a **nosort (order by)** by accessing data in sorted order through the index; but the inclusion of the **nsl_sort()** function would disable the index access path, and introduce a sort.

User-Specified Quote Character Assignment

SQL statements may contain literal single quotes in them, such as when a possessive form of a noun is used (e.g., 'Roberts's Bike'). Until now, the literal quotes had to be double quoted to make it clear to the SQL or PL/SQL engine that they were literal (e.g., 'Robert''s Bike'). This tends to start to look really ugly in code, and can cause lots of errors that are sometimes hard to find.

Oracle Database 10*g* offers a solution to this problem in the form of user-specified quote character assignment. Now, the ' symbol can be replaced by just about any single- or multibyte delimiter or the character pairs [ ], { }, ( ), or < >.

The delimiter is defined by using the quote operator, **q**, followed by a quote and then the assigned replacement quote delimiter to be used. Here is an example that uses the bracket pair ([ ]) as quote delimiters:

```
SQL> INSERT INTO record VALUES
  2 (q'[Robert's book is good isn't it?]');
SQL> SELECT * FROM record WHERE
  2* the_value=q'XRobert's book is good isn't it?X';

THE_VALUE
--------------------------------------------------
Robert's book is good isn't it?
```

In our this example, we inserted a record into the RECORD table. We used a bracket set as the delimiter. Then, we queried the same record, this time using the letter *X* as our delimiter. In both cases, there are single quotes at the beginning after the **q** operator, and at the very end after the final delimiter.

PL/SQL New Packages of Note

Oracle Database 10*g* offers a number of new PL/SQL packages that you can use. I have introduced a number of them in this book already. In this section, I introduce two additional packages. The first, **utl_compress**, allows you to compress database data to be loaded within columns. The second, **utl_mail**, allows you to manage mail within the database much easier.

The utl_compress Package

Oracle Database 10*g* introduces the ability to compress and decompress BLOB or RAW data using the Lempel Ziv compression algorithm. This is supported via the new Oracle-supplied package **utl_compress**. The **utl_compress** package provides two functions, **lz_compress** and **lz_uncompress**. Let's look at each of these packages in a bit more detail next.

The utl_compress.lz_compress Function

The **lz_compress** function of **utl_compress** provides the ability to store data in the database in a compressed format. This can significantly reduce the overall storage required in a database. Oracle Database 10g only supports compression of RAW or BLOB data. The syntax for the **lz_compress** function is as follows:

```
UTL_COMPRESS.LZ_COMPRESS
( src       IN          RAW,
  ratio     OUT         BINARY_INTEGER,
  quality   IN          BINARY_INTEGER DEFAULT 6)
 RETURN RAW;
UTL_COMPRESS.LZ_COMPRESS
( src       IN          BLOB,
  ratio     OUT         BINARY_INTEGER,
  quality   IN          BINARY_INTEGER DEFAULT 6)
 RETURN BLOB;
```

NOTE
*One limitation of **utl_compress** is that it only works on RAW and BLOB data.*

The utl_compress.lz_uncompress Function

If you have compressed your data using **utl_compress.lz_compress**, then you can uncompress it using the function **utl_compress.lz_uncompress**. Here is the definition of the **lz_uncompress** function:

```
UTL_COMPRESS.LZ_UNCOMPRESS
( src  IN  RAW ) RETURN RAW;
UTL_COMPRESS.LZ_UNCOMPRESS
( src  IN  BLOB) RETURN BLOB;
```

The utl_mail Package

Oracle Database 10g now offers a new interface to manage e-mail in the form of a PL/SQL-supplied package called **utl_mail**. The **utl_mail** package allows you to send an e-mail easily and to attach objects to that e-mail. The principle procedure in **utl_mail** is the **send** procedure. This procedure is used to actually send the e-mail. The **send** procedure allows you to define recipients, cc recipients, bcc recipients, and perform other common e-mail functions. You can also use the **utl_mail** procedures **send_attach_raw** and **send_attach_varchar2** to send e-mails with attachments.

Other New PL/SQL Packages

Oracle Database 10*g* comes with a number of other new PL/SQL packages, listed next, many of which are discussed in other chapters of this book:

dbms_advanced_rewrite	**dbms_advisor**	**dbms_datapump**
dbms_dimension	**dbms_file_transfer**	**dbms_frequent_itemset**
dbms_frequent_itemset	**dbms_monitor**	**dbms_scheduler**
dbms_server_alert	**dbms_service**	**dbms_sqltune**
dbms_stat_funcs	**dbms_streams_auth**	**dbms_streams_messaging**
dbms_streams_tablespace_adm	**dbms_warning**	**dbms_xmlstore**
utl_dbws	**utl_i18n**	**utl_lms**
utl_recomp		

Oracle Collections

Oracle collections consist of two different structures, nested tables and VARRAY columns. Oracle Database 10*g* offers the following new functionality for Oracle collections:

- The ability to create temporary tables with VARRAY columns
- The ability to change the element size of a VARRAY column
- The ability to define the tablespace of a nested table
- New ANSI-related functionality within nested tables

Creating Temporary Tables with VARRAY Columns

In Oracle Database 10*g*, you can now include VARRAY columns in a temporary table. Here is an example of such an operation:

```
Create type ty_cust_info as object
( first_name  varchar2(30),  last_name  varchar2(30),
  address     varchar2(30),  city       varchar2(30),
  state       varchar2(2),   zip        varchar2(5) )
/
create type nt_cust_info as varray(10) of ty_cust_info;
/
create global temporary table t_cust_info
```

```
(   customer_information    nt_cust_info,
    created_date            date,
    last_update_date        date );
```

Note that nested tables are still not supported in temporary tables.

Changing the VARRAY Size

Oracle Database 10g now allows you to alter the size of a VARRAY element, as shown in this example:

```
create or replace type test as object (test_id number);
/
create or replace type ty_test as varray(20) of test;
/
create table t_test_info
(   test_id_no             ty_test,
    created_date           date,
    last_update_date       date );

insert into t_test_info values
(ty_test(test(1)), sysdate, sysdate );
```

Now, if you want to modify the VARRAY so that it will be able to hold more elements, you simply issue an **alter type** command:

```
alter type ty_test modify limit 1000 cascade;
```

Two options (neither of which is a default value) are available when altering types:

- **invalidate** Invalidates all dependent objects when the operation takes place and does so without any checks. This can be dangerous, as you can inadvertently drop an attribute that is critical, so use **invalidate** carefully.

- **cascade** Propagates the change to all dependent types and tables, and an error will occur if any errors are found.

Finally, you can only increase the size of a VARRAY. An error will occur if you try to make it smaller.

Defining the Tablespace of a Nested Table

Oracle Database 10g now allows you to define a different tablespace for the storage table of a nested table. By default, the storage table will be created where the parent table has been created. You can use the **tablespace** parameter in the **store as** clause to define a different tablespace, as shown in this example:

```
create or replace type test as object (test_id number);
/
create or replace type ty_test as table of test;
/
create table t_test_info
(   test_id_no              ty_test,
    created_date            date,
    last_update_date        date )
nested table test_id_no store as test_id_tab
(tablespace users);
```

You can also alter the existing tablespace of the table of a nested table collection with the **alter table** command, as shown in this example:

```
Alter table test_id_no move tablespace new_users;
```

ANSI Support for Nested Tables and VARRAY Columns

Oracle Database 10g now offers added ANSI-related functionality (equivalent to the array and multiset ANSI functionality) to nested tables and VARRAY columns. This includes

- Support for equality and inequality predicates
- Support for **in** and **not in** operators
- New operators

Let's look at each of these in a bit more detail next.

Jonathan Says...

Don't forget to rebuild your index on the hidden NESTED_TABLE_ID column when you do this. As with all heap-table moves, the indexes become unusable.

It's a nice touch that the hidden index created against the base table can also be moved to a different tablespace and can even be renamed and rebuilt with different storage parameters. I am most unenthusiastic about objects being stored in the database, but at least Oracle Database 10g has introduced some damage-limitation features to help the DBA.

Support for Equality and Inequality Predicates

Nested tables now support the use of equality and inequality predicates via the use of the **equal** and **not equal** operators. The result of the comparison is a Boolean value that indicates the success or failure of the comparison. Here is an example:

```
CREATE OR REPLACE TYPE t_review_dates AS OBJECT
(review_date   DATE,
 MAP MEMBER FUNCTION convert RETURN DATE);
/
CREATE OR REPLACE TYPE BODY t_review_dates AS
MAP MEMBER FUNCTION convert RETURN DATE IS
BEGIN
     RETURN review_date;
END;
END;
/
CREATE OR REPLACE TYPE ty_review AS TABLE OF t_review_dates;
/
CREATE TABLE t_emp_info
(   emp_id                NUMBER PRIMARY KEY,
    review_date           TY_REVIEW,
    salary_last_increase  TY_REVIEW,
    hire_date             DATE,
    last_update_date      DATE )
NESTED TABLE review_date STORE AS emp_tab
NESTED TABLE salary_last_increase STORE AS sup_tab;

INSERT INTO t_emp_info VALUES (1,
TY_REVIEW (T_REVIEW_DATES(SYSDATE), T_REVIEW_DATES(SYSDATE-30),
T_REVIEW_DATES(SYSDATE-60), T_REVIEW_DATES(SYSDATE-90) ),
TY_REVIEW (T_REVIEW_DATES(SYSDATE-30), T_REVIEW_DATES(SYSDATE-90) ),
SYSDATE, SYSDATE);

INSERT INTO t_emp_info VALUES (2,
TY_REVIEW (T_REVIEW_DATES(SYSDATE), T_REVIEW_DATES(SYSDATE-30),
T_REVIEW_DATES(SYSDATE-60), T_REVIEW_DATES(SYSDATE-90) ),
TY_REVIEW (T_REVIEW_DATES(SYSDATE), T_REVIEW_DATES(SYSDATE-30),
T_REVIEW_DATES(SYSDATE-60), T_REVIEW_DATES(SYSDATE-90) ),
SYSDATE, SYSDATE);
```

Note that we had to create a **map** method for the object, which is required. After we have created the objects and inserted the data, we can then query the collection items in the table, as shown in this example:

```
COLUMN review_date FORMAT a20
COLUMN salary_last_increase FORMAT a20
```

```
SQL> SELECT emp_id FROM t_emp_info WHERE review_date=salary_last_increase;

    EMP_ID
----------
         2
```

Support for in and not in Operators

In Oracle Database 10g, you can use **in** and **not in** operators to determine if a given nested table appears in another nested table. The **in** and **not in** operators return a Boolean value depending on the result of the execution of the operator.

The following is an example of using this new functionality in Oracle Database 10g. In it, we re-create the T_EMP_INFO table, adding another column. We then create two records to test with. Finally, we issue two queries. In the first query, using the **in** operator, one record matches our query, because we are looking for a promotion date that is the same as either the REVIEW_DATE date or the SALARY_ LAST_INCREASE date, which is the case with EMP_ID 2. The second query, using the **not in** operator, matches the record for EMP_ID 1, because the **not in** query predicate eliminates the record that has different dates within it.

```
-- First, we are going to drop and recreate the t_emp_info
-- table from our earlier example.
DROP TABLE t_emp_info;
CREATE TABLE t_emp_info
(   emp_id                  NUMBER PRIMARY KEY,
    review_date             TY_REVIEW,
    salary_last_increase    TY_REVIEW,
    promotion_date          TY_REVIEW,
    hire_date               DATE,
    last_update_date        DATE )
NESTED TABLE review_date STORE AS emp_tab
NESTED TABLE salary_last_increase STORE AS sup_tab
NESTED TABLE promotion_date STORE AS promo_tab;

-- Insert 2 records.
INSERT INTO t_emp_info values (1,
TY_REVIEW (T_REVIEW_DATES(SYSDATE-365),
T_REVIEW_DATES(SYSDATE-300),
T_REVIEW_DATES(SYSDATE-270),
T_REVIEW_DATES(SYSDATE-200) ),
TY_REVIEW (T_REVIEW_DATES(SYSDATE-365),
T_REVIEW_DATES(SYSDATE-300) ),
TY_REVIEW (T_REVIEW_DATES(SYSDATE)),
SYSDATE, SYSDATE);

INSERT INTO t_emp_info VALUES (2,
```

```
TY_REVIEW (T_REVIEW_DATES(SYSDATE), T_REVIEW_DATES(SYSDATE-30),
T_REVIEW_DATES(SYSDATE-60), T_REVIEW_DATES(SYSDATE-90) ),
TY_REVIEW (T_REVIEW_DATES(SYSDATE), T_REVIEW_DATES(SYSDATE-30),
T_REVIEW_DATES(SYSDATE-60), T_REVIEW_DATES(SYSDATE-90) ),
TY_REVIEW (T_REVIEW_DATES(SYSDATE), T_REVIEW_DATES(SYSDATE-30),
T_REVIEW_DATES(SYSDATE-60), T_REVIEW_DATES(SYSDATE-90) ),
SYSDATE, SYSDATE);

-- Now, query using the in operator
COLUMN review_date FORMAT A20
COLUMN salary_last_increase FORMAT A20
SQL> SELECT emp_id FROM t_emp_info WHERE
promotion_date IN (review_date, salary_last_increase);

    EMP_ID
----------
         2
SQL> SELECT emp_id FROM t_emp_info WHERE
promotion_date NOT IN (review_date, salary_last_increase);

EMP_ID
----------
         1
```

New Operators

A number of new operators are available for use with collections in Oracle Database 10*g*. Table 7-3 lists these new operators and describes their use. For examples and usage, see the *Oracle Database 10*g *SQL Reference Guide* or the *Oracle Database 10*g *PL/SQL Users Guide and Reference*.

The PL/SQL Compiler

There have been changes to the PL/SQL compiler in Oracle Database 10*g*. This includes a new version of the PL/SQL compiler, changes to native compilation of PL/SQL, new fine-grained debugging capabilities, and new PL/SQL compiler warnings. Let's look at each of these features in more detail in the next few sections.

New PL/SQL Compiler

Oracle Database 10*g* comes with a new, faster PL/SQL compiler. The compiler is more efficient than the previous PL/SQL compilers, and thus generates code that runs more efficiently. In fact, Oracle reports that the new PL/SQL compiler is 50 to 75 percent faster than the Oracle9*i* compiler. Associated with the new compiler is a new parameter, **plsql_optimize_level**. When this parameter is set to 2 (the default

Operator	Description
submultiset	Tests whether a given nested table is a subset of another nested table.
multiset union	Returns a nested table that contains the values of two inputted nested tables. You can use the **all** or **distinct** option, as required, to allow for or eliminate duplicates, including NULL values.
multiset intersect	Returns a nested table that contains values that are common to the two nested tables passed in through the input operators. You can use the **all** or **distinct** option, as required, to allow for or eliminate duplicates, including NULL values.
multiset except	This operator takes the names of two nested tables as parameters. When executed it will return a nested table which contains elements listed in the first parameter of the function, that do not exist in the parameter. You can use the **all** or **distinct** option, as required, to allow for or eliminate duplicates, including NULL values.
cardinality	Returns the number of elements contained within a given nested table.
member of	Allows you to test a given value and determine whether it is a member of a nested table. The result is a Boolean value.
set	Allows you to convert a nested table into a set of elements that are distinct. This set is returned in the form of a nested table.
is a set	Allows you to determine whether a nested table is made up of distinct elements. If a duplicate value is contained in the nested table, then the operator returns FALSE; otherwise, TRUE is returned.
is empty	Allows you to determine whether a given nested table is empty.
collect	Creates a nested table from a set of elements.
powermultiset	Used on nested tables to generate multiple sets of nested table entries from a given nested table.
powermultiset_by _cardinality	Used on nested tables to generate multiple sets of nested table entries based on a specified cardinality. This restricts the depth of the resulting nested table output.

TABLE 7-3.   *New Operators for Collections*

setting) Oracle optimizes compiled PL/SQL code as much as it can. Programs that are computation intensive will benefit the most from the additional optimization, so if your PL/SQL is mostly SQL statements, you may not see as much of a performance boost.

Natively Compiled PL/SQL New Features

Natively compiled PL/SQL code executes even faster in Oracle Database 10*g*. The results of the compilation process are now stored in the database as BLOB data within the database. Also, native compilation is now available in a Real Application Clusters (RAC) environment.

In Oracle9*i* Database, the **plsql_compiler_flags** parameter was used to define specific compiler flags that would indicate how the PL/SQL compiler was supposed to operate. The **plsql_compiler_flags** parameter is obsoleted (but is still valid) by the following three new parameters:

Parameter Name	Description	Valid Settings	Default
plsql_optimize_level	PL/SQL optimization level	1 or 2	2
plsql_debug	Enables or disables debug mode	TRUE or FALSE	FALSE
plsql_code_type	Determines if the execution of PL/SQL code is based on interpreted or native compiled code execution	Interpreted or Native	Interpreted

These parameters are all dynamic at both the system and session level. They can also be set to a NULL value. These settings are used whenever the **create or replace** or **alter compile** statements are executed.

Oracle also provides columns in the *_PLSQL_OBJECT_SETTINGS data dictionary view that provide some insight into the settings used when the given object was created. An example of the use of this view is shown next:

```
SELECT owner, name, type, plsql_optimize_level,
plsql_code_type, plsql_debug
FROM dba_plsql_object_settings;
```

If you want to change the way code has been compiled, then the parameters listed in the table above will need to be altered. For example, if you wish to change interpreted code to compiled code, you first want to change the **plsql_code_type** parameter, via either an **alter session** or **alter database** command, and then recompile the code you wish to change.

Oracle provides scripts that allow you to convert all code in the database to either fully compiled or interpreted versions, if you like. Run **dbmsupgnv.sql** to change all code to be compiled, and run **dbmsupgin.sql** to change all code to interpreted code.

Fine-Grained Debug Privileges

The DBA can now grant debug privileges on specific PL/SQL program units. This allows for a more secure development environment, because the DBA can control what code the developers have access to.

PL/SQL Compile-Time Warnings

Oracle Database 10*g* provides new functionality when compiling PL/SQL programs. Rather than just dealing with unblemished success or dismal failure during PL/SQL program compiles, Oracle now provides various warnings that give you some insight into potential problems or inefficiency with your PL/SQL code. So, now your PL/SQL may compile and run just fine but have some warnings associated with it, or it might still fail to compile but have additional compiler-provided warnings available to review.

Enabling Compiler Warnings

Before you can use compiler warnings, you need to enable them by setting the parameter **plsql_warnings**, either in the database parameter file or via the **alter system** or **alter session** commands. Valid settings for **plsql_warnings** include the following:

- **ENABLE** Allows you to enable warnings. You can enable based on the type of warning (all, severe, informational, or performance) or based on a numeric value for the warning messages.

- **DISABLE** Allows you to disable warnings. You can disable based on the type of warning (all, severe, informational, or performance) or based on a numeric value for the warning messages.

- **ERROR** Allows you to define specific warnings as errors instead, which will halt compiles. You can define warnings that should be treated as errors based on the type of warning (all, severe, informational, or performance) or based on a numeric value for the warning messages.

Oracle has classified the warning message ranges (code PLW) as follows:

- PLW-5000 to 5999 are severe warnings

- PLW-6000 to 6249 are informational warnings
- PLW-7000 to 7249 are performance-related warnings

Here are some examples of enabling and disabling compiler warnings:

```
ALTER SESSION SET PLSQL_WARNINGS='enable:severe';
ALTER SESSION SET PLSQL_WARNINGS=
     'enable:severe', 'disable:informational';
ALTER SESSION SET PLSQL_WARNINGS='enable:(6000, 6010)';
ALTER SYSTEM SET PLSQL_WARNINGS='enable:performance'
     SCOPE=memory;
```

Finally, a new package, **dbms_warnings**, allows you to modify the warning settings on a more granular basis, and more incrementally within your code. For example, you can use **dbms_warnings** to enable or disable warning messages from subprograms that are called.

Reviewing Compiler Warnings

You don't need to do much of anything new to see the compiler warnings. They appear when you use the **show errors** command. Also, the compiler warnings appear in the ALL_ERRORS, USER_ERRORS, OR DBA_ERRORS data dictionary views. Within these views, the ATTRIBUTES column indicates if the message is a warning. Here is an example of a procedure that I compiled, and the resulting warning message that I got:

```
ALTER SESSION SET PLSQL_WARNINGS=
'enable:severe', 'enable: performance',
'enable:informational';

CREATE OR REPLACE PROCEDURE my_proc
(p_date_info IN OUT VARCHAR2) AS
v_return     BOOLEAN;
first_test   TY_TEST;
second_test  TY_TEST;
BEGIN
first_test   := TY_TEST(test(1, SYSDATE));
second_test := TY_TEST(test(1, SYSDATE));
v_return     := first_test = second_test;
p_date_info := 'The date is '||SYSDATE;
IF v_return THEN
dbms_output.put_line('The two are the same.');
ELSE
dbms_output.put_line('The two are not the same.');
```

```
END IF;
END;

SP2-0804: Procedure created with compilation warnings
SQL> show err
Errors for PROCEDURE MY_PROC:
LINE/COL ERROR
-------- --------------------------------------------------------
2/2      PLW-07203: parameter 'P_DATE_INFO' may benefit from
                    use of the NOCOPY compiler hint
```

We can also look at DBA_ERRORS and see this warning message, as shown in this example:

```
SQL> COLUMN message FORMAT A60 WRAP
SQL> SELECT owner||'.'||name||CHR(10)||attribute
       2 ||CHR(10)||message_number||CHR(10)||text||
       3 CHR(10) "Message"
       4 FROM dba_errors
       5 WHERE name='MY_PROC';
Message
------------------------------------------------------------
TEST.MY_PROC
WARNING
7203
PLW-07203: parameter 'P_DATE_INFO' may benefit from use of
the NOCOPY compiler hint
```

Jonathan Says...

Clearly a very useful feature—but be careful that you don't allow anything to fiddle with the **plsql_warnings** flag on a production system. Unexpected invalidations do occur from time to time on production systems, and you don't want to slow down the automatic recompilation with the overhead of unnecessary warnings being written into the data dictionary tables.

Even on a development system, you may need to take some steps to clear out old warnings—for example, recompiling a package one last time with **plsql_warnings** set to pick up errors only—otherwise, compilation times may acquire an irritating overhead.

Improvements to the dbms_profiler Procedure

The Profiler API provides services that allow you to gather and save PL/SQL run-time statistics for later analysis. The **dbms_profiler** procedure has been improved in Oracle Database 10*g*. It allows you to profile natively compiled PL/SQL code. Also, improvements have been made to ensure that the lines reported by the profiler and the actual lines in the source code are correct. Finally, **dbms_profiler** now flushes profile data out to the Oracle table faster at the end of the profile run.

Table Function Enhancements

Oracle Database 10*g* offers the following improvements to table functions:

- Projection information is passed to the table function to help it compute only the required attributes. The ODCITable interface in Oracle Database 10*g* is now improved so that it will communicate to the table function the list of referenced attributes. This makes the process much more efficient, since only referenced attributes are computed and set.

- Integration with the Extensible Optimizer helps produce better query plans.

- Support for anonymous return types for the AnyDataSet table functions. The **describe** procedure (ODCITableDescribe) now can build and return a transient anonymous type using the AnyType interfaces, such as AnyDataSet. These AnyType interfaces are generic collection types that have APIs available for both PL/SQL and C.

New Connect String Format

If you are running on a TCP/IP network, you can take advantage of a new connect string format when using Oracle Database 10*g* Oracle clients such as SQL*Plus. With this new connect string, all you need is the host, port, and service name of the database service that you wish to connect with. Once you have that information, you can easily connect to the database (no tnsnames.ora or naming service required), as shown here:

```
C:\Documents and Settings\FREEMANR>sqlplus
test/test@//rfmobile:1521/betatwo
SQL*Plus: Release 10.1.0.1.0 - Beta on Fri Dec 26 13:26:03 2003
Copyright (c) 1982, 2003, Oracle.  All rights reserved.
```

```
Connected to:
Oracle10i Enterprise Edition Release 10.1.0.1.0
With the Partitioning, OLAP and Data Mining options
SQL>
```

Note that advanced functionality, such as connect-time failover or load balancing, is not available when using this method of connecting to the database server. Also note that this functionality does not negate the need for an operational listener. Finally, this method only works in TCP/IP environments, and certain naming or security restrictions may prevent it from working.

CHAPTER
8

Other Database
New Features

e have covered a number of new features in Oracle Database 10*g*. This chapter covers some miscellaneous new features in Oracle Database 10*g*, including the following:

■ Calling remote stored procedures

■ Workspace Manager enhancements

■ SQL*Plus enhancements

■ New features in the SQL language

Calling Remote Stored Procedures

Oracle Database 10*g*, through Heterogeneous Services, can (within a number of limitations) call remote stored procedures on non-Oracle remote systems. This functionality is, of course, limited by the remote system's support for this feature. Remote sites are not likely to support such things as SQL statements with **connect by** clauses, use of ROWID, and other Oracle-specific functionality.

Workspace Manager Enhancements

Workspace Manager was introduced in Oracle9*i* Database and is improved in Oracle Database 10*g*. Workspace Manager allows you to version your tables, enabling you to create different data sets within the same logical object. Workspace Manager allows you to make a set of changes in isolation and then make them available to other users at a later time. Oracle Database 10*g* offers new functionality for Workspace Manger, including the following, each of which is discussed in turn in the following sections:

■ New functionality in the **dbms_wm** package

■ Multiparent workspaces

■ Workspace Manager events

■ Exporting, importing, and loading versioned data

■ Workspace continuous refresh

■ Other miscellaneous features

Jonathan Says...
Workspace Manager is one of the Oracle features that I view with mixed feelings. On one hand, it's strategically sensible to use the various features of the Oracle Database, including Workspace Manager, as developers may be able to work a bit closer to the database and may be able to take advantage of low-level operations that are not easily available to normal end-user code. On the other hand, it looks horribly out of place in a "proper" database; and the fact that it is built in may encourage too many people to use it unnecessarily and without considering the costs and alternatives properly.

   If you do think that using Workspace Manager might be appropriate, make sure you set up a few tests with **sql_trace** enabled so that you can see what's going on behind the scenes with all the extra tables, indexes, views, and synonyms that it produces.

New Functionality in the dbms_wm Package

The **dbms_wm** package is used to manage Workspace Manager. Oracle Database 10*g* offers new functionality in the **dbms_wm** package, including the capability to set a number of Workspace Manager–related parameters on a system-wide basis and the capability to determine the status of a versioned table. Let's look at each of these capabilities in more detail next.

Setting System-Wide Workspace Manager Parameters

Oracle Database 10*g* now allows you to enforce global Workspace Manager–related settings. These settings (or parameters) control how Workspace Manager can be used. You use the **dbms_wm.setsystemparameter** procedure, which is new in Oracle Database 10*g*, to set these global settings. Any user who is using the **dbms_wm.setsystemparameter** procedure must be granted the **wm_admin_role** role first.

NOTE
*The parameters set with the **dbms_wm.setsystemparameter** procedure are not database parameters like those found in the database parameter file.*

The **dbms_wm.setsystemparameter** procedure can be used to set a number of different parameters. These include the following:

Parameter	Use	Valid Values
allow_capture_events	Allows Workspace Manager to capture events when enabled (see more about Workspace Manager events later in this chapter). Enabling this parameter has performance issues you will want to consider.	ON/OFF (default)
allow_multi_parent_workspaces	Allows for the creation of multiparent workspaces (a new feature in Oracle Database 10*g*). Enabling this parameter has performance issues you will want to consider.	ON/OFF (default)
allow_nested_table_columns	Allows tables that contain nested tables to be version enabled. Enabling this parameter has performance issues you will want to consider.	ON/OFF (default)
cr_workspace_mode	Allows you to choose either an optimistic locking strategy or a pessimistic locking strategy.	OPTIMISTIC_LOCKING (default) or PESSIMISTIC_ LOCKING
fire_triggers_for_nondml_events	When set to ON, a version-enabled table's user-defined triggers are fired when a workspace non-DML operation is executed. Triggers set in the **dbms_ wm.settriggerevents** procedure override this parameter setting.	ON (default)/OFF

Parameter	Use	Valid Values
noncr_workspace_mode	Allows you to choose either an optimistic locking strategy or a pessimistic locking strategy.	OPTIMISTIC_LOCKING (default) or PESSIMISTIC_LOCKING
use_timestamp_type_for_history	When set to ON, the CREATETIME and RETIRETIME columns use the data type TIMESTAMP WITH TIME ZONE for Oracle database release 9.0.1 or later. Otherwise, the DATE data type is used.	ON (default)/OFF

Determining the Table Status

You can use the new **dbms_wm.getphysicaltablename** procedure to determine whether or not a table is version enabled. If the table is not version enabled, then calling this function simply returns the name of the table. If the table is version enabled, then calling the function returns the name of the table, with an _LT suffix to indicate that the table is versioned. Here is an example that indicates the table SCOTT.WMEMP is version enabled:

```
SQL> SELECT dbms_wm.getphysicaltablename('SCOTT','WM_EMP')
        2  FROM dual;
DBMS_WM.GETPHYSICALTABLENAME('SCOTT','WM_EMP')
--------------------------------------------------------
WM_EMP_LT
```

Multiparent Workspaces

A new feature in Oracle Database 10g Workspace Manager is the ability to have a child workspace with many different parents. This section first introduces multiparent workspaces, and then shows you how to configure Workspace Manager for multiparent workspaces and how to create multiparent workspaces. Finally, it introduces new data dictionary views that are related to multiparent workspaces.

Introducing Multiparent Workspaces

Prior to Oracle Database 10g, a child workspace was based on the data within a single parent workspace. Oracle Database 10g now supports multiparent workspaces. With a multiparent workspace, a given workspace can be a child of one or more parent workspaces. Any workspace starts with a single parent workspace. Once the initial workspace is created, you can add other workspaces as parent workspaces to the existing child workspace.

The top level of a workspace hierarchy is known as the *multiparent root workspace.* All ancestor workspaces are known as *multiparent leaf workspaces.* Any workspace that is a multiparent workspace must be derived from parent workspaces that have the same multiparent root workspace. Thus, multiparent workspaces are not join mechanisms; they bring together workspaces derived from the same parent workspace. For example, you cannot create a multiparent workspace from the EMP and DEPT live root workspaces. You can, however, create a multiparent workspace from two workspaces defined on EMP.

A child workspace that has multiple parents can see the data from all the parent workspaces. A child workspace can also be merged into any of the parent workspaces, and can be refreshed from any of the parent workspaces.

Configuring the Database to Use Multiparent Workspaces

Before you can create a multiparent workspace, you need to set some Workspace Manager system parameters via the **dbms_wm.setsystemparameter** procedure, which was mentioned earlier in this chapter. First, set the Workspace Manager parameter **allow_multi_parent_workspace** to a value of ON. Next, if you want the workspace to be continually refreshed (as discussed later in this section), then you need to set **cr_workspace_mode** to PESSIMISTIC_LOCKING. Otherwise, for a workspace that is not to be continually refreshed, set the Workspace Manager parameter **noncr_ workspace_mode** to PESSIMISTIC_LOCKING.

Using Multiparent Workspaces

Once configured, creating a multiparent workspace is pretty simple. You use the **dbms_wm.addasparentworkspace** procedure to add a parent workspace to an existing workspace. Here is an example:

```
-- Set parameters
SQL> exec dbms_wm.setsystemparameter
('ALLOW_MULTI_PARENT_WORKSPACES','ON');
SQL> exec dbms_wm.setsystemparameter
('NONCR_WORKSPACE_MODE','PESSIMISTIC_LOCKING');

-- The table of our workspaces
SQL> SELECT empno FROM employee;
     EMPNO
----------
      7369
      7499
      7521
      7566
```

```
--   Version Enable the table
SQL> exec dbms_wm.enableversioning
('EMPLOYEE','VIEW_WO_OVERWRITE');
--   create 2 workspaces
SQL> exec dbms_wm.createworkspace('EMPLOYEE_WS_A');
SQL> exec dbms_wm.createworkspace('EMPLOYEE_WS_B');

-- Now, change data in workspace 1
SQL> exec dbms_wm.gotoworkspace('EMPLOYEE_WS_A');
SQL> INSERT INTO employee VALUES (1,'FREEMAN','BOSS',1,sysdate,
 99999.99, 0, 10);
1 row created.
SQL> COMMIT;
SQL> SELECT empno FROM employee;
     EMPNO
----------
         1
      7369
      7499
      7521
      7566
-- Now, goto workspace 2
SQL> exec dbms_wm.gotoworkspace('EMPLOYEE_WS_B');
SQL> SELECT empno FROM employee;
     EMPNO
----------
      7369
      7499
      7521
      7566
-- add WS1 a parent workspace of WS2. This makes WS2 a
-- multiparent workspace.
SQL> exec dbms_wm.addasparentworkspace
('EMPLOYEE_WS_B','EMPLOYEE_WS_A');

-- Note the changes to the data in the current workspace.
SQL> SELECT empno FROM employee;
     EMPNO
----------
      7369
      7499
      7521
      7566
         1
```

As you can see from this example, workspace EMPLOYEE_WS_B had workspace EMPLOYEE_WS_A merged into it as a parent workspace. Now, changes in EMPLOYEE_WS_A will appear in EMPLOYEE_WS_B. However, changes that occur in EMPLOYEE_WS_B will not appear in EMPLOYEE_WS_A.

Let's revisit some new Oracle Database 10*g* terms at this point. A multiparent leaf workspace is the same thing as a multiparent workspace. Thus, EMPLOYEE_WS_B from the previous example is a multiparent leaf workspace. The multiparent root workspace is the nearest ancestor of all the parent workspaces of multiparent workspaces. In the previous example, the root workspace is the live workspace of the EMPLOYEE table. Finally, a multiparent graph workspace is any workspace that participates in the creation of multiparent workspaces, including the multiparent workspace itself. In the previous example, both workspaces EMPLOYEE_WS_B and EMPLOYEE_WS_A are the graph workspaces.

Removing parent workspaces is done through the **dbms_wm** package again, this time via the **removeasparentworkspace** procedure, as shown in this example:

```
SQL> exec dbms_wm.removeasparentworkspace
('EMPLOYEE_WS_B','EMPLOYEE_WS_A');
SQL> SELECT empno FROM employee;
    EMPNO
----------
      7369
      7499
      7521
      7566
```

Note that in this example, when the parent is removed from the workspace, the records associated with that parent are also removed.

New Workspace Manager Data Dictionary Views

The following new views are available in Oracle Database 10*g* to help you manage multiparent workspaces:

- **ALL_MP_GRAPH_WORKSPACES**   Also available in the ALL and USER varieties, these views contain information about multiparent graph workspaces.

- **ALL_MP_PARENT_WORKSPACES**   Also available in the ALL and USER varieties, these views contain information about parent workspaces as well as multiparent leaf workspaces.

Workspace Manager Events

Oracle Database 10*g* supports capturing Workspace Manager events. This can be useful in cases when an application you have written needs to be aware of certain Workspace Manager events. This event framework uses Oracle Database 10*g*'s Advanced Queuing (AQ) architecture. Messages from Workspace Manager are passed to AQ. Applications can subscribe to AQ queues and pull events from those queues.

Exporting, Importing, and Loading Versioned Data

Oracle Database 10g allows you to export/import versioned data out of and into workspaces via the **dbms_wm** procedure (though this is slightly different than using the Oracle Data Pump utility). Additionally you can use SQL*Loader to load data into versioned tables. Let's look at each of these functions in more detail next.

Using dbms_wm.export

You can export data from a version-enabled table to a staging table (which can then be exported) via the **dbms_wm.export** procedure. You can use the **where_clause** parameter of the **dbms_wm.export** procedure to define predicates that control the data that is exported.

When you export data from a workspace, the **dbms_wm.export** procedure will create the staging table for you (in other words, don't try to create the staging table yourself!). By default, it creates the staging table in the current schema. If you want the staging table to be created in another schema, then that schema must have the **create any table** and **insert any table** privileges assigned. The staging table can be used for subsequent export operations as long as certain DDL operations have not occurred, such as alteration of column names or data types or modification or removal of a primary key constraint. In these cases, you should remove the staging table and allow the export procedure to re-create it.

Something else to be aware of is that if you want to overwrite data in the staging table during later exports, you need to use the **overwrite_existing** data parameter of the **dbms_wm.export** procedure. If you do not select this parameter, then the export will fail if data to be exported already exists in the staging table. Here is an example of exporting workspace data with the **dbms_wm_export** procedure:

```
Exec dbms_wm.export(table_name=>'EMPLOYEE',
staging_table=>'EMPLOYEE_STAGE', workspace=>'EMPLOYEE_WS_A');
```

The result of this export will be the creation of the EMPLOYEE_STAGE table, and it will be populated with the EMPLOYEE table data within the EMPLOYEE_WS_A workspace. The next example exports data only where EMPNO is less than 1000 and overwrites any data that exists in the staging table:

```
Exec dbms_wm.export(table_name=>'EMPLOYEE',
staging_table=>'EMPLOYEE_STAGE', workspace=>'EMPLOYEE_WS_A',
where_clause=>'empno<1000', overwrite_existing_data=>TRUE);
```

Using dbms_wm.import

You can import data into a workspace from a staging table created by the **dbms_wm.export** procedure. You can choose to import either all data or just modified data into the workspace through the use of the **import_scope** parameter. This process allows you to easily move data between like versioned tables in different schemas.

Here is an example of using the **dbms_wm.export** procedure to import data into one workspace from another:

```
Exec dbms_wm.import(staging_table=>'EMPLOYEE_STAGE',
to_table=>'EMPLOYEE',
from_workspace=>'EMPLOYEE_WS_A', to_workspace=>'EMPLOYEE_WS_B',
import_scope=>DBMS_WM.IMPORT_MODIFIED_DATA_ONLY,
where_clause=>'empno>1000');
```

Note in this example that we are moving data from the EMPLOYEE_STAGE staging table into the EMPLOYEE_WS_B workspace. Note that we have also listed the workspace that the data in the EMPLOYEE_STAGE table came from via the **from_ workspace** parameter. This is required if the data in the staging table is versioned (that is, it comes from another workspace rather than the live workspace).

> **NOTE**
> *If the Workspace Manager locking modes are set to PESSIMISTIC_LOCKING (which is required to continuously refresh multiparent workspaces, discussed next), you might receive errors (e.g., ORA-20254) when trying to import data. To eliminate these errors, set the* **cr_workspace_mode** *and* **noncr_workspace_mode** *Workspace Manager parameters to OPTIMISTIC_LOCKING.*

Using SQL*Loader with Versioned Tables

You can use SQL*Loader to perform both conventional path and direct path bulk data loads into version-enabled tables. You can load into either the root (or live) workspace or the latest version of any workspace. When you load data into the root workspace, it will be visible to all the other child workspaces. If those child workspaces have changed the data being imported, then that data will not appear in that workspace.

The bulk loading of data into a workspace requires special procedures when loading the data, including the use of a few **dbms_wm** procedures, including the **dbms_wm.getbulkloadversion** and **dbms_wm.beginbulkloading** procedures. Bulk loading into a workspace takes four steps:

1. Use the **dbms_wm.getbulkloadversion** function to fetch the version number that the bulk-loaded data will need to be tagged with. This function returns a version number that you need in Step 3.

2. Use the **dbms_wm.beginbulkloading** procedure to prepare the table for the bulk load.

3. Modify the SQL*Loader control file with the version number fetched in Step 1. Also, modify the SQL*Loader control file so that the table name being loaded into ends with the _LT extension (which is the extension that Workspace Manger affixes to any version-enabled tables). Execute the load with SQL*Loader.

4. Once the SQL*Loader load is complete, execute the **dbms_wm.commitbulkloading** procedure to complete the load. You can also use the **dbms_wm.rollbackbulkloading** procedure to roll back the data loaded.

Workspace Continuous Refresh

When you create a workspace, it is initially populated with data from the parent workspace. Prior to Oracle Database 10*g*, if the parent workspace was updated, that update was done manually using the **dbms_wm.refreshworkspace** procedure. Now, with Oracle Database 10*g*, you can configure a workspace so that it will be automatically refreshed when its parent workspace is refreshed.

If a workspace is configured to be continually refreshed, then it will be refreshed with any change to the parent workspace, including merge operations into the parent workspace from another child workspace. To create a workspace that will be continuously refreshed, set the **isrefreshed** parameter to TRUE when you create the workspace. If the workspace is already created, use the **changeworkspacetype** procedure, as shown in this example:

```
Exec dbms_wm.changeworkspacetype('EMPLOYEE_WS_A');
```

You also use the **changeworkspacetype** procedure to take a workspace out of continuous refresh mode. If the workspace is in continuous refresh mode, then the **changeworkspace** call will take it out of continuous refresh mode; otherwise, the procedure will put the workspace in continuous workspace mode.

Other Improvements for Workspace Manager

There are a few other new features in Workspace Manager that you will want to know about. This section looks at support for table-level constraints, support for Virtual Private Database, the DBA_WM_SYS_PRIVS view, and new DDL functionality.

Table-Level Constraint Support

Previous to Oracle Database 10*g*, a table had to have a primary key constraint defined on it before it could be version enabled. Oracle Database 10*g* now supports creation of version-enabled tables if there is a unique constraint defined on the table. The unique constraint should be defined on one or more columns and may be enforced either by the definition of a unique constraint on those columns or by the presence of a unique index on those columns.

Workspace Manager Support for Virtual Private Database

Oracle Database 10*g* now supports Virtual Private Database (VPD) functionality when using Workspace Manager. This allows you to define policies that will be enforced by VPD. VPD policies are defined on the tables that are created during versioning process. This includes the table itself, and the _LOCK, _CONF, _DIFF, and _HIST tables that get created.

The DBA_WM_SYS_PRIVS View

The DBA_WM_SYS_PRIVS data dictionary view provides information about all users that have Workspace Manager–related privileges. This view is available to any database user account that has the WM_ADMIN_ROLE role assigned.

New DDL Functionality

Oracle Database 10*g* supports a number of new DDL operations on version-enabled tables, including the following:

- Changing the scale and/or precision of a NUMBER data type

- Changing the length of VARCHAR2, VARCHAR, CHAR, NCHAR, NVCHAR, and NVCHAR2 columns

- Adding, dropping, or enabling unique constraints

Additionally, the **dbms_wm.commitddl** procedure now allows you to enforce unique constraints through the **enforce_unique_constraints** parameter. If this parameter is set to TRUE, then the unique constraints on the version-enabled table are enforced. Also, setting the **enforce_rics** parameter to TRUE causes referential integrity constraints to be enforced.

Streams Enhancements

There are a number of enhancements with Oracle Streams in Oracle Database 10*g*. We simply don't have enough pages to share a great deal of detail on these enhancements, but here is a quick summary:

- The **dbms_streams_auth** package has been added to make it easier to configure and manage the Streams administrator.

■ You can now define negative rule sets, which simplifies the ability to discard changes so that the Streams client will not process them.

■ A new feature, Downstream Capture, allows you to run the capture process on a database other than the source database.

■ You can define subset rules for the capture process, propagation, and apply process.

■ You can now define a Streams pool, which allows you to allocate memory in the SGA for use by Streams. This is done via the STREAMS_POOL_SIZE database initialization parameter.

■ New dynamic performance views are available in Oracle Database 10*g* for monitoring.

■ A new procedure, **dbms_streams_adm.set_rule_transform_function**, allows for easier-to-use rule-based transformations.

■ You can now use the new **dbms_apply_adm** procedure, **set_enqueue_ destination**, to specify a destination queue for events that satisfy a certain rule. Also, the **set_execute** procedure of the **dbms_streams_adm** procedure allows you to define processes that do not execute events based on certain rules.

■ New data types are supported in Streams, including:

  ■ NCLOB

  ■ BINARY_FLOAT

  ■ BINARY_DOUBLE

  ■ LONG

  ■ LONG RAW

■ Streams capture and apply processes now support index-organized tables, function-based indexes, and descending indexes.

■ You can remove the entire Streams configuration from your database now with the new **dbms_streams_anm.remove_streams_configuration** package.

■ New supplemental logging options are available that make it easier to define and manage supplemental logging at the source database.

■ Transportable tablespaces and RMAN can now be used for Streams instantiations.

> **Jonathan Says...**
> Streams clearly looks like a strategic direction for Oracle. Some of the enhancements in this release (particularly, I think, the changes regarding supplemental logging) promise to make the logical standby database a viable option in the near future.

■ A new procedure, **dbms_repcat.streams_migration**, is available to assist in migrating from Advanced Replication to Streams.

■ A new package called **dbms_streams_messaging** is available to ease the process of enqueueing and dequeueing messages from a sys.AnyData queue.

SQL*Plus Enhancements

Prior to its release, there were some rumors floating around about Oracle Database 10*g*. One of these was that the SQL*Plus client would be done away with. I'm happy to report that the rumors of the demise of SQL*Plus were premature and that it is very much alive and well. In fact, some enhancements are present in SQL*Plus in Oracle Database 10*g*:

■ Enhancements to the **describe** command

■ Enhancements to the **spool** command

■ Changes to behavior of the SQL*Plus profile files

■ New **define** variables

■ The ability to do variable substitution at the SQL prompt

■ The new SQL*Plus **compatibility** command

■ Support for whitespace in filenames and paths

Enhancements to the describe Command

If you use rules in the database, you will want to know that the SQL*Plus **describe** command is now enhanced to describe rules, rule sets, and rule evaluation contexts. Thus, you can quickly look up rule specifications, rather than having to reference the data dictionary views themselves.

Enhancements to the spool Command

The **spool** command in SQL*Plus has new functionality that allows you to append to an existing spool file. Simply use the **spool append** command to use this functionality, as shown in this example (I removed the query output for brevity):

```
SQL> spool myspool.txt
SQL> select * from emp;
SQL> spool off;
SQL> spool myspool.txt append
SQL> select * from emp;
```

Also note that in Oracle Database 10g the default action for the **spool** command is to replace any existing spool file.

Changes to the Behavior of the SQL*Plus Profile Files

Profile files allow you to customize your SQL*Plus environment as you see fit. Oracle offers the **glogin.sql** site profile file (which is located in the default location of $ORACLE_HOME/sqlplus/admin, and the login.sql profile file (which is searched for in the local directory) for individual user profiles. Oracle also searches the path set by the environment variable SQLPATH for these files if they are not in their default locations.

In Oracle Database 10g, the site and user profile files are executed after each successful database connection, rather than just when SQL*Plus is started. You can enable or disable this behavior through the use of the new SQL*Plus **compatibility** command (described later, in the section "The New SQL*Plus compatibility Command"). By default, in Oracle Database 10g, this new functionality is enabled.

Jonathan Says...
This may look like an insignificant detail, but personally I find it very convenient, particularly for running tests. A lot of the code I run in SQL*Plus is of the following form: prepare data – produce output – modify environment – produce second output. It's basically iterative in nature. The ability to switch spooling off and on between the two sets of output and get both sets into the same file is very useful.

New define Variables

SQL*Plus offers three new **define** variables in Oracle Database 10*g*:

- _date
- _privilege
- _user

The _date Variable

The _date variable is a dynamic variable that provides the date based on the current NLS_DATE_FORMAT setting. You can also override the variable nature of _date by setting your own fixed string with the **define _date** command. If you set the _date variable manually, you can reset it by using the **define _date** command to set _date to an empty string, as in this example:

```
DEFINE _DATE=""
```

The _date variable can be used in a number of places, such as **ttitle**. When prefixed with an & character, the time reported by _date will be the time that the command is executed; otherwise, it is reevaluated for each page. Here is an example of the use of the _date variable:

```
SQL> TTITLE CENTER 'Report generated on ' _DATE
SQL> SELECT empno FROM emp;
                          Report generated on 01-JAN-04
    EMPNO
----------
      7369
      7499
      7521
      7566
```

The _privilege and _user Variables

The _privilege variable is a new predefined variable in Oracle Database 10*g* that contains the privilege level of the currently connected user. The _user variable contains the username of the user currently connected to the database. These variables can be used when defining the SQL prompt, described next.

Capability to Do Variable Substitution at the SQL Prompt

Run-time variable substitution is now supported in SQL*Plus. You do not need to prefix the variable with the & sign. Here is an example:

```
SCOTT 01-JAN-04 >DEFINE database=betatwo
SCOTT 01-JAN-04 >SET SQLPROMPT 'database _user _date >'
betatwo SCOTT 01-JAN-04 >
```

The New SQL*Plus compatibility Command

You can now start SQL*Plus, setting the SQL*Plus compatibility variable (defined by a **–c** at the SQL*Plus command line) when you execute the SQL*Plus client. This allows you to set this variable before the global or local parameter files are executed. This is done when the SQL*Plus client is started via the use of the **-c** command-line parameter, followed by the Oracle Database version you wish the SQL*Plus session to be compatible with. Here is an example:

```
C:\ sqlplus -c 9.2 "sys as sysdba"
```

Support for Whitespace in File- and Pathnames

In Oracle Database 10*g*, whitespace can be included in file- and pathnames. Commands such as **spool**, **@**, **@@**, and **run** all can benefit from this new functionality. Here is an example:

```
SPOOL "output report.txt"
```

Other SQL*Plus Enhancements and New Features

There are a number of other new features in SQL*Plus. The SQL*Plus **copy** command has new error messages associated with it. The new **show recyclebin** command will display items that are currently in the recycle bin and available for purging. Also, the **pagesize** default in Oracle Database 10*g* has been changed from 24 to 14.

SQL Language New Features

Oracle Database 10*g* provides new SQL language functionality. This section highlights some of these new features, including the following:

- Data type enhancements
- Moving data between BFILEs and LOB data types
- The ability to create **before insert** and **update** triggers on LOB columns
- New functionality for the **returning** clause
- The new SQL **model** clause

Data Type Enhancements

Oracle Database 10*g* offers new floating-point data types that are based on the ANSI/IEEE 754 standard. Floating-point numbers differ from NUMBER data types in the way that Oracle stores the number internally. The result is that the floating-point number data types are more efficient than the NUMBER data type. Floating-point numbers do not have a scale associated with them like a NUMBER data type does. Floating-point numbers can be defined using the BINARY_FLOAT and BINARY_ DOUBLE data types. Also, floating-point numbers are fixed in length, unlike a NUMBER data type, which is variable. A BINARY_FLOAT data type is a 32-bit, single-precision floating-point data type that requires 5 bytes of storage. A BINARY_ DOUBLE is a double-precision floating-point data type that requires 9 bytes of storage (including the length byte).

Moving Data from BFILEs to a LOB

Moving data from a BFILE to a LOB data type can be tricky. Oracle Database 10*g* provides the **loadfromfile2()** procedure to simplify this process. The **loadfromfile2()** procedure replaces the existing **loadfromfile()** procedure. It allows you to copy data from the BFILE to a LOB. The **loadfromfile2()** procedure allows you to define the character set of the BFILE using the **csid** parameter of the procedure. If required, the data is converted from that character set into the database character set when the data is moved.

LOBs and the before row insert Trigger

Oracle Database 10*g* now allows you to modify a LOB in a **before row insert** trigger. This allows you to modify the value of any LOB column within a trigger after an **insert** or **update** operation has occurred.

New Functionality for the returning Clause

Oracle Database 10*g* now allows you to return a summary function in the **returning** clause. The following example updates the salaries of all employees and returns the average resulting salary for those employees:

```
SQL> VARIABLE a NUMBER
SQL> UPDATE employee
  2  SET sal=sal*1.10 RETURNING AVG(sal) INTO :a;
SQL> PRINT a
         a
   --------
     655.22
```

SQL Modeling

Oracle Database 10*g* offers a new **model** clause, which offers more power and flexibility to SQL calculations. The **model** clause allows you to create a "spreadsheet," or a multidimensional array, from query results. You can also apply formulas to the results and calculate new values. In essence, this functionality can replace some PC-based spreadsheets.

The **model** clause offers a great amount of power and flexibility, and it supports Oracle's security features. Modeling offers spreadsheet-like functionality such as symbolic cell addressing, array computation, and the ability to insert cell values and update existing cell values.

Because of the **model** clause's flexibility, covering its wealth of features is beyond the scope of this discussion. You will find much more information on this feature of Oracle Database 10*g* in the *Oracle10*g *Database Data Warehousing Guide*.

Using Aggregates in the returning Clause

Oracle Database 10*g* now allows you to return a summary function in the **returning** clause. The following example updates the salaries of all employees and returns the average resulting salary for those employees:

```
SQL> VARIABLE a NUMBER
SQL> UPDATE employee
  2  SET sal=sal*1.10 RETURNING AVG(sal) INTO :a;
SQL> PRINT a
         a
   --------
     655.22
```

Here is an example of using this functionality within PL/SQL:

```
Declare
    a       number;
begin
    update employee set sal=sal*1.10 returning avg(sal) into a;
    dbms_output.put_line(a);
end;
```

In this case, the query returns the average of the SAL column. Keep in mind that the **returning** clause only has an effect on the rows actually touched by the query, so the average is the average of the rows inserted, and does not include in that average rows that are already in the table. Single-set aggregate operations are also possible on **insert** and **delete** operations as seen in this example:

```
Declare
     a      number;
begin
     delete from employee where sal > 1000 returning avg(sal) into a;
     dbms_output.put_line(a);
end;
```

Grouped Table Outer Joins

Normally, data is stored in a fairly dense format. However, in certain cases, this is not the case and data may be sparse in its nature. An example might be in an inventory report, we might not have inventoried a specific product over the period (perhaps there was none of that product in stock), but we might still want to reflect a 0 inventory for that product rather than a NULL.

A grouped table outer join (or partitioned outer join) allows you to improve the performance of SQL statements (and create easier-to-read SQL statements) that involve time-based calculations. The grouped table outer join allows you to fill in missing (or sparse) data in your joins. Here is an example of using a partitioned outer join:

```
SELECT emp_name, dname, t.sales_date, NVL(amount,0) dense_sales
FROM
  (SELECT SUBSTR(e.ename,1,15) emp_name, d.dname,
   s.sales_date sales_date, SUM(Amount) amount
   FROM Sales s, dept d, emp e
   WHERE s.empno = e.empno AND e.deptno=d.deptno
   AND s.sales_date > sysdate - 365
   AND d.deptno=30
   GROUP BY SUBSTR(e.ename,1,15), d.dname, s.sales_date ) v
PARTITION BY (v.emp_name)
RIGHT OUTER JOIN
  (SELECT DISTINCT sales_date
   FROM sales
   WHERE sales_date > sysdate - 365 ) t
ON (v.sales_date = t.sales_date)
ORDER BY t.sales_date;
```

And here is an example of the output from this query:

EMP_NAME	DNAME	SALES_DATE	DENSE_SALES
ALLEN	SALES	02/01/2004	100
WARD		02/01/2004	0
ALLEN		02/02/2004	0
WARD	SALES	02/02/2004	200

Jonathan Says...
I love it when a clear and concise addition to the language makes entire classes of a problem much easier to solve. Of course, you do have to keep an eye on the effects this has on execution plans, and test what happens with more complex queries and views, but the initial impressions are good.

    I understand that this feature has recently been accepted for inclusion in the next SQL standard.

Here we see that Allen had sales on 2/1 of $100, but that Ward had no sales. Conversely, we see that Allen had no sales on 2/2, but that Ward had $200 of sales.

Removal of Aggregate and SQL Statement Length Limitations

Oracle Database 10g removes previous restrictions on the number of aggregates allowed in the **group by** clause. Also, Oracle Database 10g removes the 64K SQL statement size limitation.

New connect by Functionality

Oracle Database 10g offers new functionality using the **connect by** clause of the **select** command. These changes specifically apply to hierarchical queries, allowing the return of not only parent-child pairs but also ancestor-dependent pairs. Three new clauses are available when using the **connect by** clause:

- **connect_by_iscycle**   Determines whether the current row has a child row that is also its ancestor

- **connect_by_isleaf**   Determines whether the current row is a leaf in the tree defined by the **connect by** operation

- **connect_by_root**   Returns the column value from the root row

The following sections discuss some examples of using each of these operators.

Example Using connect_by_iscycle

Here is an example of using the **connect_by_iscycle** operator:

```
SELECT ename "Emp", CONNECT_BY_ISCYCLE leaf,  mgr "Manager",
    LEVEL-1 "Pathlen", SYS_CONNECT_BY_PATH(empno, '/') "Path"
FROM employee
Where level-1 < 3
CONNECT BY NOCYCLE PRIOR empno = mgr;
```

Example Using connect_by_isleaf

Here is an example of using the **connect_by_isleaf** operator:

```
SELECT ename "Emp", CONNECT_BY_ISLEAF leaf,  mgr "Manager",
    LEVEL-1 "Pathlen", SYS_CONNECT_BY_PATH(empno, '/') "Path"
FROM employee
Where level-1 < 3
CONNECT BY NOCYCLE PRIOR empno = mgr;
```

Example Using connect_by_root

Finally, here is an example of using the **connect_by_root** operator:

```
SELECT ename "Emp", CONNECT_BY_ROOT mgr "Manager",
    LEVEL-1 "Pathlen", SYS_CONNECT_BY_PATH(empno, '/') "Path"
FROM employee
Where level-1 < 3
CONNECT BY NOCYCLE PRIOR empno = mgr;
```

CHAPTER
9

Oracle Enterprise Manager 10g

- **Introducing the Redesigned OEM Architecture**
- **Changes to OEM Installation**
- **Key New Features in OEM**
- **Introducing the Revamped OEM Home Page**
- **Key New Management Features**
- **New OEM Administration and Maintenance Features**
- **Introducing Oracle EM2Go**
- **Other New OEM Related Features**

racle Enterprise Manager 10*g* is newly revamped for Oracle Database 10*g* and introduces a great deal of new functionality, much of which revolves around new features in Oracle Database 10*g*. This chapter will talk all about the new features in Oracle Enterprise Manager 10*g*, including the following:

- Introducing the redesigned OEM architecture

- Changes to installation of OEM

- Key new features in OEM

- Introducing the revamped OEM home page

- New OEM administration and maintenance features

- Introducing Oracle EM2Go

- Other OEM new features

Introducing the Redesigned OEM Architecture

Most of OEM is now redesigned in an Internet-enabled three-tier architecture based on HTML (as of this writing, some aspects remain Java based). You can now connect to OEM from any web browser and manage all of your databases and systems from the browser interface. You can even connect to OEM via your PDA! The Java console is gone, and thus the necessity of installing a client software is removed.

OEM comes in two basic flavors. The first, Oracle Enterprise Manager Database Control, is installed with every Oracle database. If you are using Oracle Real Application Clusters 10*g*, then you may want to install the second flavor, Oracle Enterprise Manager Grid Control, a separate product installed on separate media. Figure 9-1 depicts the basic architectural overview.

There are several components associated with OEM in Oracle Database 10*g*, including the following:

- The server tier

- The client tier

- The middle tier

- Communication components

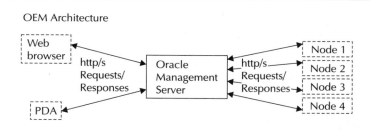

FIGURE 9-1. *OEM basic architectural overview*

Server Tier

As with the earlier releases of OEM, the server tier is a distributed, lightweight agent installed at each of the nodes, which are managed by OEM. A node can be any component of your database grid, such as a database server or an application server. Only one agent is installed at each node, irrespective of the number of database instances or application servers that the node comprises.

Client Tier

With the new web-based architecture that is robust, reliable, and globally scalable, the OEM Console can be deployed and operated in a number of forms, thus giving you "manage from anywhere" flexibility. The client tier can take several forms:

■ **Web browser**   This thin client alleviates the necessity of installing any application to access the OEM Console.

■ **PDA**   The Console can be accessed via EM2Go using a PDA device capable of browsing the Internet.

■ **Portal**   Oracle has designed a reporting framework, which can be used by portals to report on the health of the database to the end user.

Middle Tier

The middle tier is Oracle Management Service (OMS), a powerful J2EE web application. OMS works in conjunction with the Oracle database repository (called Management Repository) for its persistent data store.

Communication Components

Communication between the Console and OMS, and between OMS and the agent(s), is via HTTP, thus making it easy to deploy OEM within firewall-protected environments. Secure Sockets Layer (SSL) can be enabled to allow secure communication between tiers.

Changes to OEM Installation

OEM Database Control is installed at the time you install the base Oracle software. You can choose to install it into the same ORACLE_HOME location, or give it its own ORACLE_HOME location. If you wish to install OEM Grid Control, you need to do that as a separate operation.

If you create the database via the Oracle Database Configuration Assistant (DBCA), then OEM Database Control will be installed and preconfigured along with the database. If you are manually creating the database, then you will want to run a script to install OEM Database Control in the database. The name of this script at the time of this writing is DBConsole.pm, and it appears to be a pearl on the Windows NT platform. Both the name of the script and the type of script may differ on various platforms (and versions of Oracle Database 10*g*), so check the OEM documentation to make sure which script you need to run on your platform.

An Apache HTTP server is included with the database server so you can start working with the OEM out of the box, thus requiring zero startup time. The Oracle Enterprise Manager repository, job, and event subsystems are now configured automatically, eliminating the need for manual setup.

OEM can be deployed in a number of ways, depending on the complexity of your system and the options that you want. If you create your databases using the DBCA, you are given an option to determine whether you wish to use Grid Control (shown in the figure below as central management) or Database Control (shown as local management), as shown in Figure 9-2.

Let's look at these deployment options in a bit more detail next.

NOTE
*The screens you see in your version of Oracle Database 10*g* may be somewhat different than those shown in the figures in this chapter. The look and feel of the OEM may change significantly between minor releases of the software.*

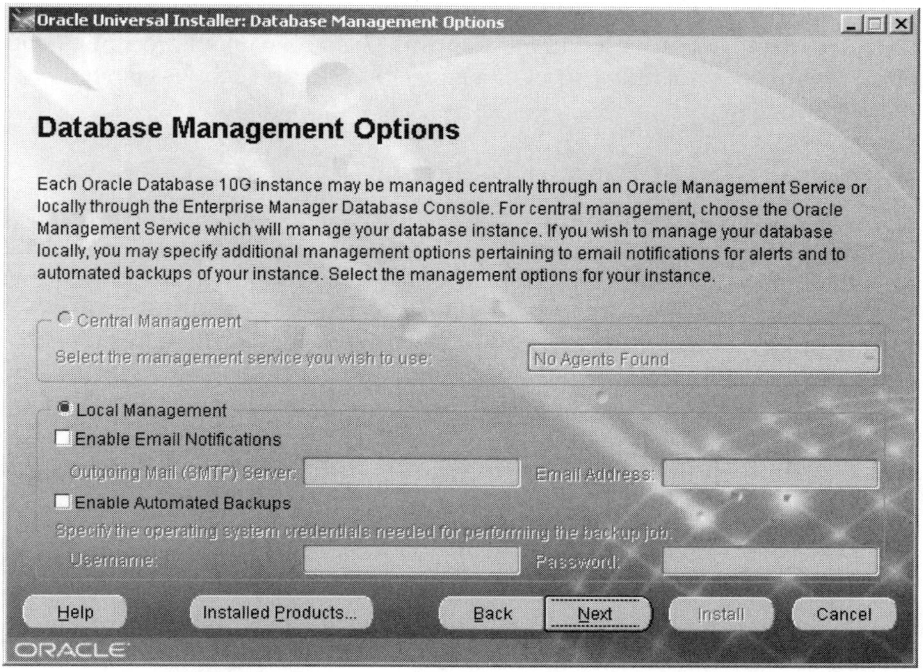

FIGURE 9-2. *DBCA window for database management*

Grid Control

Grid Control deployment is used to manage multiple hardware nodes, databases, application servers, and other targets by grouping them into single logical entities. By executing jobs, enforcing standard policies, monitoring performance, and automating many other tasks across a group of targets, instead of on many systems individually, Grid Control enables you to scale with a growing grid. Because of this feature, you can manage the low-cost hardware comprising the grid in an efficient and affordable manner.

Database Control

Database Control deployment is used to manage a single database instance. It is a much less complex method of deploying OEM. Also, since Database Control manages only a single instance, this offers much less enterprise-wide flexibility than Grid Control. Finally note that Database Control does require the creation of an OEM repository.

Studio Control

This type of deployment is used to manage any database, without preconfiguration. Studio Control does not require an OEM repository and, as such, has limited functionality.

Connecting to OEM

If you create your databases using the DBCA, OEM is automatically installed at port 5500 and can be accessed via a web browser from http://localhost.localdomain:5500/em. At the end of database creation, you will see the URL of OEM, as shown in Figure 9-3. The port information is also stored in the file $ORACLE_HOME/install/portlist.ini, where ORACLE_HOME is the path of your Oracle software, such as /u01/app/oracle/product/10.1.0.

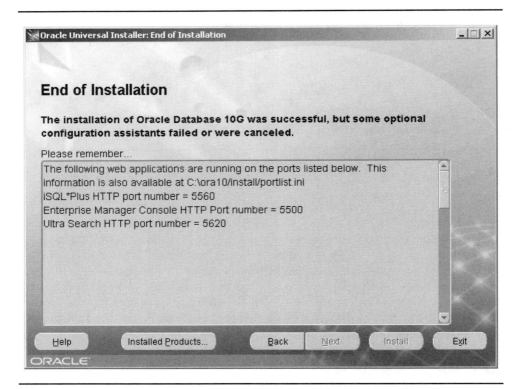

FIGURE 9-3. *DBCA displaying the OEM URL*

Key New Features in OEM

OEM in Oracle Database 10g offers a number of key improvements:

- *Much easier to use.* OEM makes management, monitoring, and tuning of a database much easier for the beginning and intermediate DBA. With preconfigured SQL queries, DBAs can dive in and manage the Oracle Database. Experienced DBAs will find OEM an adjunct to their own scripts and processes.

- *Lower cost to implement.* OEM is preconfigured and ready to use out of the box.

- *Complete solution.* OEM is a much more complete solution and offers much improved functionality over the previous version. The following table compares and contrasts functional areas of OEM in Oracle9i and OEM in Oracle Database 10g:

Area	OEM 9i	OEM 10g
Oracle Database	Yes	Yes
Administration and monitoring	Yes	Yes
Oracle e-Business Suite	Yes	Yes
Oracle9iAS	No	Yes
Oracle Collaboration Suite	No	Yes
Operating system	Yes	Yes
Storage	No	Yes
Network	No	Yes
Server load balancers	No	Yes
Hardware	No	Yes

- *Integrated.* Administration, tuning, software/hardware configuration, etc. source from one single console. OEM does not attempt to manage the operating system and hardware, but rather attempts to reduce the overall workload of the DBA. The focus is to look from the perspective of the application/end user.

- *Scalable.* OEM can manage thousands of systems with ease.

Jonathan Says...
When you see a comment like "OEM can manage thousands of systems with ease," don't you really want to see the whitepaper that describes the test case and gives you a clue about which bits of what software were actually exercised, and how often? Oracle Corporation has produced some very informative whitepapers of this type (e.g., Data Guard), and should be encouraged to do more.

Introducing the Revamped OEM Home Page

One of the finest improvements of OEM Console is its capability to show consolidated target information in the home page. This is particularly useful when you want to quickly check the health of your database system, at a glance. The following two sections look at OEM Home Page features in a bit more detail.

Consolidated Management with Target Home Pages

Each managed target has a "home page." The home page provides you with a view of the current state of the database by displaying a series of metrics that portray the overall health of the database. Summary metrics are displayed on the home page. If you find a metric of interest, you can bring up a comprehensive set of performance and health metrics via drill-down menus. Thus, the home page helps the DBA to quickly isolate and diagnose the root cause of problems facing the target. In addition, target home pages provide DBAs with direct access to configuration information as well as quick access to administrative functions. The target home page feature also promotes a consistent look and feel, irrespective of the type of target being monitored and managed.

Here is the basic information that you can view on the home page:

- General status information
- CPU information
- Availability
- Space usage
- Advice/advice from ADDM (new feature in Oracle Database 10g)
- Job information
- Alerts

Figures 9-4 and 9-5 provide an example of the database home page. Note that OEM is deployed with the Database Control option in this case.

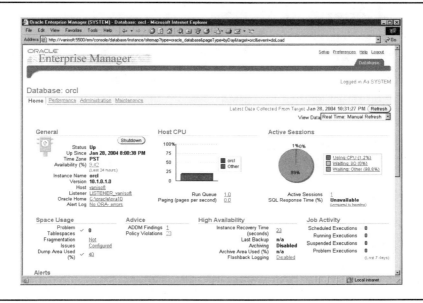

FIGURE 9-4. *OEM Home Page, top half*

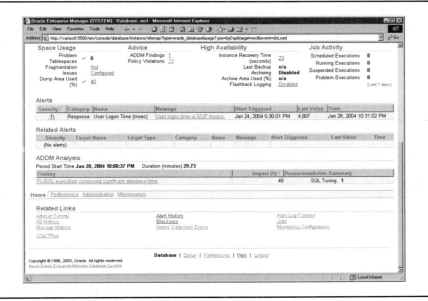

FIGURE 9-5. *OEM Home Page, bottom half*

Server-Generated Alerts

The agent on each targeted host monitors the status, health, and performance of all targets on that host. If the target goes down, or if a performance metric crosses a warning or critical threshold, an alert is generated and sent to the OEM Console (which may be on the administrator's desktop, laptop, and/or PDA) and is e-mailed to any administrators who have registered interest in receiving such notifications.

Key New Management Features

Several new management features are introduced in OEM 10g:

- Provisioning
- Job Scheduler

Provisioning

This section addresses two different kinds of provisioning associated with OEM: hardware provisioning and software provisioning.

Hardware Provisioning

OEM simplifies the management of your entire enterprise by providing a centralized view of the health of your hosts. This view summarizes key performance metrics to allow administrators to quickly assess the health of the host. OEM provides detailed system configuration information covering hardware components, applications, and the underlying operating system. Also, it can dynamically provision resources on-the-fly, based on policies defined in the database.

Software Provisioning

Because of the potentially large number of physical nodes, it's especially important in a grid environment to ensure that installation and configuration of the software running on those nodes is fast and requires no human intervention. Manually installing software on hundreds or thousands of nodes would be time consuming and cumbersome. Administrators would certainly find ways to work around a manual installation, but the workarounds could lead to unsupportable upgrade situations and lost information about the configuration of the system. With Grid Control, Oracle 10g automates installation, configuration, and cloning of Oracle Application Server 10*g* and Oracle Database 10*g* across multiples nodes. OEM provides a common framework for software provisioning and management, allowing administrators to create, configure, deploy, and utilize new servers with new instances of the application server and database as they are needed. This framework is used not only to provision new systems but also to apply patches and upgrade existing systems.

In Oracle Application Server 10*g*, applications can be deployed once to a single application server instance, registered with the central repository, then automatically deployed to all relevant nodes in the grid. As changes are made to the application and as new nodes are added to the grid, nodes can be kept in sync.

Job Scheduler

The Job Scheduler in Oracle Database 10*g* runs jobs from within the database. As job information is stored in the database, you will have more direct/consolidated information on all the jobs being run in the database. OEM provides a graphical user interface (GUI) to the Job Scheduler, in contrast to the packaged interface **dbms_scheduler**.

OEM, with the help of the Job Scheduler, can manage the following job types:

■ Executables, including shell scripts, that execute with the permissions of "oracle" or a similar user at the operating system level

■ PL/SQL or Java procedures

Also, Database Resource Manager functionality is extended to job scheduling. Resource Manager can prioritize and allocate resources for jobs, based on configured priority. You can group jobs into *job classes* and configure resource allocation for the classes for enhanced convenience. For example, you can divide your jobs into two classes, Payroll Jobs and HR Jobs, and allocate 70 percent and 30 percent of resources, respectively, to each class. You can also dynamically change the resource allocation for the classes based on time frames, called *windows*. For example, you can configure the database to dynamically change the allocation to 30 percent and 70 percent from 6 P.M. to 6 A.M., if you expect more nightly jobs for HR Jobs.

Figure 9-6 provides an example of using OEM to create a job through the OEM Job Scheduler. Figure 9-7 provides a look at the window used to manage existing jobs in OEM.

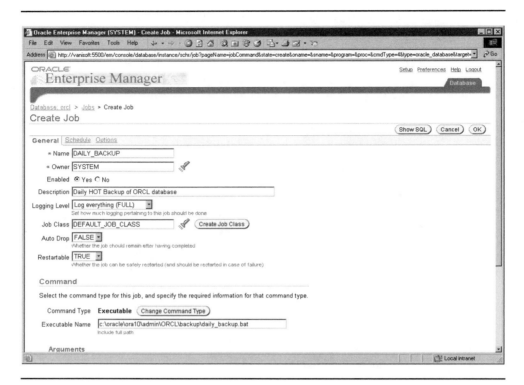

FIGURE 9-6. *Creating a job with OEM*

New OEM Administration and Maintenance Features

OEM facilitates the complete life cycle management for your database system, by supporting all the activities performed during the life of your database. Enterprise Manager provides database storage administration tools that make it easier for administrators to optimize database performance. Using these tools, you can administer operations on control files, tablespaces, and datafiles, rollback segments, redo log groups, and archive logs, as shown in Figure 9-8.

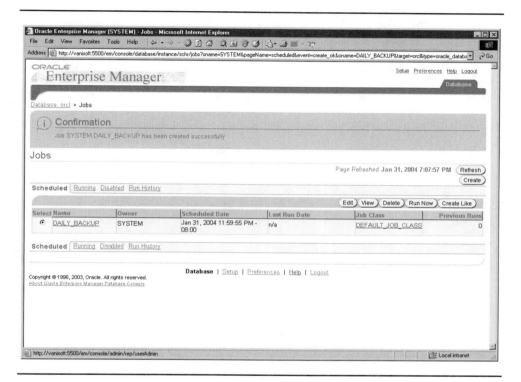

FIGURE 9-7.   *Using the OEM Job Scheduler management window*

As with the earlier releases, OEM makes regular management of tablespaces, datafiles, redo logs, and archive logs an easy task for DBAs. The Oracle Database File Topology page displays the graphical view of files, to give you a quick overview and to facilitate easy maintainability. Also, OEM supports Oracle Managed Files.

Oracle Enterprise Manager 10*g* has introduced support for Automatic Storage Management (ASM), which is an integrated volume manager and database file system. Using OEM you can perform various ASM tasks such as disk group configuration, capacity provisioning, RAID configuration, and disk rebalancing.

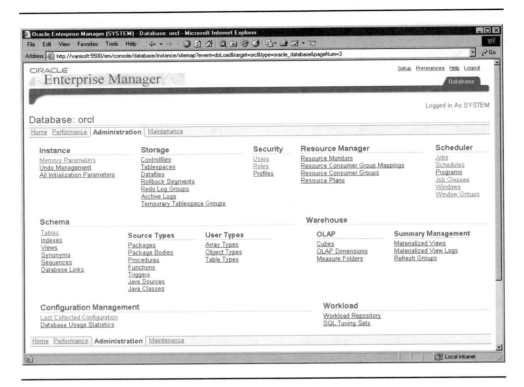

FIGURE 9-8. *The OEM Administration window*

The Enhanced Partition Management feature provides a user-friendly, intuitive GUI for complete management of the wide range of partitioning options provided by Oracle. OEM also provides various utilities that assist you in managing your data, performing backups and recoveries and patching the database. Figure 9-9 shows the available options.

NOTE
The ability to download and apply patches is one of the cooler new features in Oracle Database 10g OEM.

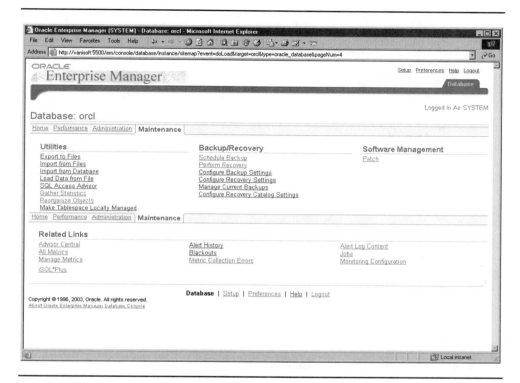

FIGURE 9-9.   *Available OEM Maintenance options*

Performance Tuning

While diagnosing and correcting a problem, it is imperative for the administrator to monitor the health of various targets, namely, operating systems and databases. Using OEM, administrators will be able to gather real-time performance data from as many targets as they need to. OEM automatically detects all the targets to which you have access and keeps polling these targets to return your real-time data.

The enhanced Oracle Enterprise Manager HTML interface provides a central point of access to all database performance-related statistics and facilitates complete monitoring and diagnostics, as shown in Figure 9-10 and Figure 9-11.

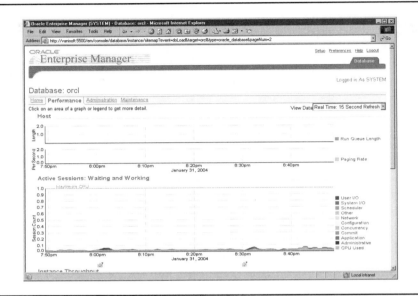

FIGURE 9-10. *Example OEM enterprise performance monitoring window, top half*

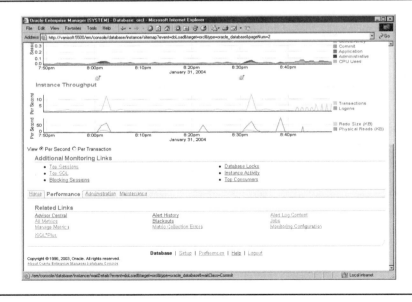

FIGURE 9-11. *Example OEM enterprise performance monitoring window, bottom half*

Several different performance interfaces are available in OEM. Let's look at those next.

OEM Grid Control

OEM Grid Control views the availability and performance of the grid infrastructure as a unified whole, as a user would experience it, rather than as isolated storage units, processing boxes, databases, and application servers. An administrator can trace a performance or availability problem as experienced by a user from end to end, from the user-visible web page, through external and internal networks, to application code, application server, and database access. Grid Control then allows an administrator to trace the root cause of the problem down to the individual Java class, for example, or the individual system configuration parameter.

On the Database Performance page, you can view activity trends for CPU, memory, and disk I/O for both the database and the underlying host. Additional powerful real-time diagnostic capabilities include identification of the most resource-consuming sessions and SQL statements, the top wait events, and any blocking and waiting database sessions. Thus, OEM merges administration, diagnostics, and tuning into one task. Also, OEM supports the use of policy violations that allow alerts to be sent if certain target thresholds are violated.

Top Sessions

Our old friend Top Sessions is still available in OEM. Top Sessions will display the most time- and resource-consuming sessions, waits, and SQL statements to help you pinpoint the most problematic areas on which to focus your database tuning efforts. You can use Top Sessions to assist you in identifying performance bottlenecks within your system and database environment. Top Sessions displays database sessions that are contributing most heavily to database activity. You can display various details for these sessions, including the SQL statements, and resource usage. You can obtain an overview of session activity by displaying the top sessions sorted by a statistic of your choosing. For any given session, you can drill down for more detail or, if you choose, terminate the session by using the Kill Session option.

Top SQL Assessment

Top SQL Assessment allows OEM to automatically identify the most resource-intensive SQL statements, as shown in Figure 9-12. Suspect SQL statements are evaluated and areas for possible tuning are identified in a plain-language SQL Assessment. In addition, the user can view the statement together with its execution statistics and execution plan, by running SQL Tuning Advisor. This analysis is available for SQL statements currently being executed as well as for executions over the last 24 hours.

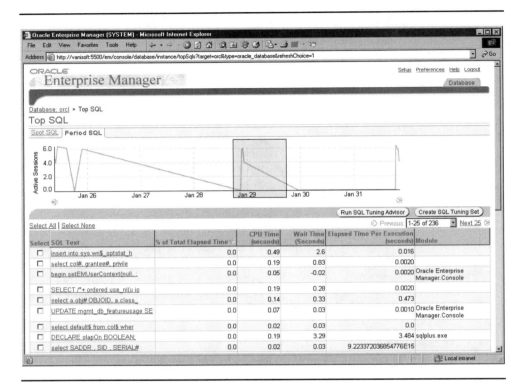

FIGURE 9-12. *Top SQL Assessment window*

Jonathan Says...

There goes the "lightweight" feature, if you're not careful. It doesn't matter how efficient the rest of the system is; if you start *regularly* (note the stress on regularly) probing the SGA for the most expensive SQL, then you've introduced a heavy hitter into your system. Use it, but use it cautiously. Don't, for example, set it up to refresh the Top 10 screen every 15 seconds.

Introducing Oracle EM2Go

The mobile version of OEM, called EM2Go, is a subset of OEM functionality that fulfills the information and administration requirements of a mobile user. After fielding that frantic call or page, administrators can resolve problems on the spot, even if they are away from the office. EM2Go leverages the architecture of OEM and shares the same OC4J instance, so no additional infrastructure is required to use EM2Go.

Like the OEM Console, EM2Go provides a very intuitive interface that makes enterprise management much like clicking on a set of web links from your PDA. Performance is one of EM2Go's best features, as ease of use results not only from the layout but also from how quickly one is able to reach the desired information.

EM2Go Home Page

After entering preferred credentials on the EM2Go login page, a personal console home page is displayed, with a consolidated overview of your enterprise's health, as shown in Figure 9-13. This page is a useful starting point to quickly assess the availability and health of your Oracle environment. It provides high-level data to isolate and repair availability and performance problems. The Alerts and Availability section displays the number of critical, warning, and error alerts generated by all the managed targets, providing the ability to drill down so that you can investigate the problem that generated the alert.

FIGURE 9-13.   *The EM2Go home page*

Other New OEM Related Features

OEM offers these additional new features in Oracle Database 10*g*:

- Baselining
- History
- An interface to Oracle Data Pump
- Links to related information
- The alert log viewer

Baselining

A baseline is a set of metrics stored at a certain point of time. If you take a baseline for your database when it is in good health, you can use it to compare the metrics when you have a database performance issue. OEM supports the collection of baselines for later comparison and troubleshooting purposes.

History

Database-related performance metrics are stored automatically and graphs can be drawn for various parameters. History is a great diagnostic tool for detecting and identifying performance bottlenecks. Metrics are stored in the repository and are purged automatically based on defined policies.

Oracle Data Pump

OEM provides an interface to Oracle Data Pump, which is a new feature of Oracle Database 10*g*. The Oracle Data Pump interface in OEM allows you to stop or suspend Oracle Data Pump import or export operations, and manage Oracle Data Pump operations.

Related Links

OEM adds a great little feature to the bottom of many of the OEM windows. Hyperlinks are now available that enable you to access additional, related information to the topic at hand. For example, when you are in the Response Time window, you see links for Compare Targets and Manage Metrics.

Alert Log Viewer

OEM provides a convenient way to access the alert log file. The user can view the latest alert from the instance alert log file directly on the OEM home page.

APPENDIX

Oracle Database 10g
New Processes

everal new operating system processes are introduced in Oracle Database 10*g*. Many of these processes are not well documented yet. This appendix provides you with a list of these new processes and describes their purpose.

Process Name	Description
ARB	This process is related to Automatic Storage Management (ASM).
ASMB	This process is related to ASM.
CTWR	The Change Tracking Writer process supports the RMAN change tracking file.
MMAN	The Memory Manager process serves as the SGA memory broker that coordinates the sizing of the different memory components, keeps track of the sizes of the different SGA components, and coordinates resize operations.
MMNL	The Memory Monitor Light process works with the Automatic Workload Repository (AWR) to write out database statistics to disk as required.
MMON	The Memory Monitor process works with the AWR features that are responsible for problem detection and database self tuning.
RBAL	This process is related to ASM.
RVWR	The Recovery Writer process supports Flashback Database, a new feature in Oracle Database 10*g*. This process writes flashback logs to the flash recovery area.

Index

References to figures and illustrations are in italics.

options, 3
other methods, 5–6
rolling upgrades for RAC, 14–15
Upgrade Information Tool (UIT), 4
versions to upgrade from, 3
See also downgrading
user-configurable default tablespaces, 33
user-specified quote character
assignment, 174
utl_compress package, 174–175
utl_mail package, 175

V

V$ALERT_TYPES, 61
V$ASM_ALIAS, 12
V$ASM_CLIENT, 12–13
V$ASM_DISK, 13
V$ASM_DISKGROUP, 13
V$ASM_FILE, 13
V$ASM_OPERATION, 13
V$ASM_TEMPLATE, 13
V$DATABASE view, 96
V$DISPATCHER_CONFIG, 66
V$EVENT_HISTOGRAM, 43
V$EVENT_NAME view, 40–41
V$EVENTMETRIC, 49
V$FILE_HISTOGRAM, 43
V$FILEMETRIC, 49
V$FILEMETRIC_HISTORY, 49
V$FLASHBACK_DATABASE_LOG view, 96
V$FLASHBACK_DATABASE_STAT
view, 96
V$JAVA_LIBRARY_CACHE_MEMORY, 59
V$JAVA_POOL_ADVICE, 59
V$LIBRARY_CACHE_MEMORY, 58
V$METRICGROUP, 49
V$METRICNAME, 49
V$SERVICEMETRIC, 49
V$SESSION, 41, 42
V$SESSMETRIC, 49
V$SHARED_POOL_ADVICE, 58
V$SYSMETRIC, 49, 60
V$SYSMETRIC_HISTORY, 49, 61
V$TEMP_HISTOGRAM, 43
V$WAITCLASSMETRIC, 49
V$WAITCLASSMETRIC_HISTORY, 49

variables
define variables in SQL*Plus, 204
run-time variable substitution,
204–205
VARRAY columns
ANSI support for, 178–181
changing the element size, 177
creating temporary tables with,
176–177
versioned data, 197–199
views
flash recovery area, 81
Flashback Database, 96
histogram, 42–43
Virtual Private Database
column-level privacy, 68–69
new policies, 69–70
support for parallel query, 70
Workspace Manager support for, 200
VPD. *See* Virtual Private Database

W

wait interface, improvements to, 40–43
windows, 27, 221
workload repository (WR), 45–48
See also Automatic Workload
Repository
Workspace Manager, 190–191
continuous refresh, 199
data dictionary views, 196
DBA_WM_SYS_PRIVS view, 200
DDL functionality, 200
events, 196
exporting, importing and loading
versioned data, 197–199
multiparent workspaces, 193–196
new functionality in dbms_wm
package, 191–193
setting system-wide parameters,
191–193
support for Virtual Private
Database, 200
table-level constraint support,
199–200
using SQL*Loader with versioned
tables, 198–199

INTERNATIONAL CONTACT INFORMATION

AUSTRALIA
McGraw-Hill Book Company
Australia Pty. Ltd.
TEL +61-2-9900-1800
FAX +61-2-9878-8881
http://www.mcgraw-hill.com.au
books-it_sydney@mcgraw-hill.com

CANADA
McGraw-Hill Ryerson Ltd.
TEL +905-430-5000
FAX +905-430-5020
http://www.mcgraw-hill.ca

GREECE, MIDDLE EAST, & AFRICA
(Excluding South Africa)
McGraw-Hill Hellas
TEL +30-210-6560-990
TEL +30-210-6560-993
TEL +30-210-6560-994
FAX +30-210-6545-525

MEXICO (Also serving Latin America)
McGraw-Hill Interamericana Editores
S.A. de C.V.
TEL +525-1500-5108
FAX +525-117-1589
http://www.mcgraw-hill.com.mx
carlos_ruiz@mcgraw-hill.com

SINGAPORE (Serving Asia)
McGraw-Hill Book Company
TEL +65-6863-1580
FAX +65-6862-3354
http://www.mcgraw-hill.com.sg
mghasia@mcgraw-hill.com

SOUTH AFRICA
McGraw-Hill South Africa
TEL +27-11-622-7512
FAX +27-11-622-9045
robyn_swanepoel@mcgraw-hill.com

SPAIN
McGraw-Hill/
Interamericana de España, S.A.U.
TEL +34-91-180-3000
FAX +34-91-372-8513
http://www.mcgraw-hill.es
professional@mcgraw-hill.es

UNITED KINGDOM, NORTHERN,
EASTERN, & CENTRAL EUROPE
McGraw-Hill Education Europe
TEL +44-1-628-502500
FAX +44-1-628-770224
http://www.mcgraw-hill.co.uk
emea_queries@mcgraw-hill.com

ALL OTHER INQUIRIES Contact:
McGraw-Hill/Osborne
TEL +1-510-420-7700
FAX +1-510-420-7703
http://www.osborne.com
omg_international@mcgraw-hill.com

Sound Off!

Visit us at **www.osborne.com/bookregistration** and let us know what you thought of this book. While you're online you'll have the opportunity to register for newsletters and special offers from McGraw-Hill/Osborne.

We want to hear from you!

Sneak Peek

Visit us today at **www.betabooks.com** and see what's coming from McGraw-Hill/Osborne tomorrow!

Based on the successful software paradigm, Bet@Books™ allows computing professionals to view partial and sometimes complete text versions of selected titles online. Bet@Books™ viewing is free, invites comments and feedback, and allows you to "test drive" books in progress on the subjects that interest you the most.

GET YOUR FREE SUBSCRIPTION
TO ORACLE MAGAZINE

Oracle Magazine is essential gear for today's information technology professionals. Stay informed and increase your productivity with every issue of *Oracle Magazine*. Inside each free bimonthly issue you'll get:

- Up-to-date information on Oracle Database, Oracle Application Server, Web development, enterprise grid computing, database technology, and business trends
- Third-party vendor news and announcements
- Technical articles on Oracle and partner products, technologies, and operating environments
- Development and administration tips
- Real-world customer stories

IF THERE ARE OTHER ORACLE USERS AT YOUR LOCATION WHO WOULD LIKE TO RECEIVE THEIR OWN SUBSCRIPTION TO ORACLE MAGAZINE, PLEASE PHOTOCOPY THIS FORM AND PASS IT ALONG.

Three easy ways to subscribe:

① Web
Visit our Web site at otn.oracle.com/oraclemagazine. You'll find a subscription form there, plus much more!

② Fax
Complete the questionnaire on the back of this card and fax the questionnaire side only to +1.847.763.9638.

③ Mail
Complete the questionnaire on the back of this card and mail it to P.O. Box 1263, Skokie, IL 60076-8263

ORACLE

FREE SUBSCRIPTION

○ **Yes, please send me a FREE subscription to *Oracle Magazine*.**   ○ **NO**

To receive a free subscription to *Oracle Magazine*, you must fill out the entire card, sign it, and date it (incomplete cards cannot be processed or acknowledged). You can also fax your application to +1.847.763.9638.
Or subscribe at our Web site at otn.oracle.com/oraclemagazine

○ From time to time, Oracle Publishing allows our partners exclusive access to our e-mail addresses for special promotions and announcements. To be included in this program, please check this circle.

○ Oracle Publishing allows sharing of our mailing list with selected third parties. If you prefer your mailing address not to be included in this program, please check here. If at any time you would like to be removed from this mailing list, please contact Customer Service at +1.847.647.9630 or send an e-mail to oracle@halldata.com.

signature (required)   date

X

name   title

company   e-mail address

street/p.o. box

city/state/zip or postal code   telephone

country   fax

YOU MUST ANSWER ALL TEN QUESTIONS BELOW.

① WHAT IS THE PRIMARY BUSINESS ACTIVITY OF YOUR FIRM AT THIS LOCATION? (check one only)
- □ 01 Aerospace and Defense Manufacturing
- □ 02 Application Service Provider
- □ 03 Automotive Manufacturing
- □ 04 Chemicals, Oil and Gas
- □ 05 Communications and Media
- □ 06 Construction/Engineering
- □ 07 Consumer Sector/Consumer Packaged Goods
- □ 08 Education
- □ 09 Financial Services/Insurance
- □ 10 Government (civil)
- □ 11 Government (military)
- □ 12 Healthcare
- □ 13 High Technology Manufacturing, OEM
- □ 14 Integrated Software Vendor
- □ 15 Life Sciences (Biotech, Pharmaceuticals)
- □ 16 Mining
- □ 17 Retail/Wholesale/Distribution
- □ 18 Systems Integrator, VAR/VAD
- □ 19 Telecommunications
- □ 20 Travel and Transportation
- □ 21 Utilities (electric, gas, sanitation, water)
- □ 98 Other Business and Services

② WHICH OF THE FOLLOWING BEST DESCRIBES YOUR PRIMARY JOB FUNCTION? (check one only)
Corporate Management/Staff
- □ 01 Executive Management (President, Chair, CEO, CFO, Owner, Partner, Principal)
- □ 02 Finance/Administrative Management (VP/Director/ Manager/Controller, Purchasing, Administration)
- □ 03 Sales/Marketing Management (VP/Director/Manager)
- □ 04 Computer Systems/Operations Management (CIO/VP/Director/ Manager MIS, Operations)
IS/IT Staff
- □ 05 Systems Development/ Programming Management
- □ 06 Systems Development/ Programming Staff
- □ 07 Consulting
- □ 08 DBA/Systems Administrator
- □ 09 Education/Training
- □ 10 Technical Support Director/Manager
- □ 11 Other Technical Management/Staff
- □ 98 Other

③ WHAT IS YOUR CURRENT PRIMARY OPERATING PLATFORM? (select all that apply)
- □ 01 Digital Equipment UNIX
- □ 02 Digital Equipment VAX VMS
- □ 03 HP UNIX

- □ 04 IBM AIX
- □ 05 IBM UNIX
- □ 06 Java
- □ 07 Linux
- □ 08 Macintosh
- □ 09 MS-DOS
- □ 10 MVS
- □ 11 NetWare
- □ 12 Network Computing
- □ 13 OpenVMS
- □ 14 SCO UNIX
- □ 15 Sequent DYNIX/ptx
- □ 16 Sun Solaris/SunOS
- □ 17 SVR4
- □ 18 UnixWare
- □ 19 Windows
- □ 20 Windows NT
- □ 21 Other UNIX
- □ 98 Other
- 99 □ None of the above

④ DO YOU EVALUATE, SPECIFY, RECOMMEND, OR AUTHORIZE THE PURCHASE OF ANY OF THE FOLLOWING? (check all that apply)
- □ 01 Hardware
- □ 02 Software
- □ 03 Application Development Tools
- □ 04 Database Products
- □ 05 Internet or Intranet Products
- 99 □ None of the above

⑤ IN YOUR JOB, DO YOU USE OR PLAN TO PURCHASE ANY OF THE FOLLOWING PRODUCTS? (check all that apply)
Software
- □ 01 Business Graphics
- □ 02 CAD/CAE/CAM
- □ 03 CASE
- □ 04 Communications
- □ 05 Database Management
- □ 06 File Management
- □ 07 Finance
- □ 08 Java
- □ 09 Materials Resource Planning
- □ 10 Multimedia Authoring
- □ 11 Networking
- □ 12 Office Automation
- □ 13 Order Entry/Inventory Control
- □ 14 Programming
- □ 15 Project Management
- □ 16 Scientific and Engineering
- □ 17 Spreadsheets
- □ 18 Systems Management
- □ 19 Workflow

Hardware
- □ 20 Macintosh
- □ 21 Mainframe
- □ 22 Massively Parallel Processing
- □ 23 Minicomputer
- □ 24 PC
- □ 25 Network Computer
- □ 26 Symmetric Multiprocessing
- □ 27 Workstation
Peripherals
- □ 28 Bridges/Routers/Hubs/Gateways
- □ 29 CD-ROM Drives
- □ 30 Disk Drives/Subsystems
- □ 31 Modems
- □ 32 Tape Drives/Subsystems
- □ 33 Video Boards/Multimedia
Services
- □ 34 Application Service Provider
- □ 35 Consulting
- □ 36 Education/Training
- □ 37 Maintenance
- □ 38 Online Database Services
- □ 39 Support
- □ 40 Technology-Based Training
- □ 98 Other
- 99 □ None of the above

⑥ WHAT ORACLE PRODUCTS ARE IN USE AT YOUR SITE? (check all that apply)
Oracle E-Business Suite
- □ 01 Oracle Marketing
- □ 02 Oracle Sales
- □ 03 Oracle Order Fulfillment
- □ 04 Oracle Supply Chain Management
- □ 05 Oracle Procurement
- □ 06 Oracle Manufacturing
- □ 07 Oracle Maintenance Management
- □ 08 Oracle Service
- □ 09 Oracle Contracts
- □ 10 Oracle Projects
- □ 11 Oracle Financials
- □ 12 Oracle Human Resources
- □ 13 Oracle Interaction Center
- □ 14 Oracle Communications/Utilities (modules)
- □ 15 Oracle Public Sector/University (modules)
- □ 16 Oracle Financial Services (modules)
Server/Software
- □ 17 Oracle9i
- □ 18 Oracle9i Lite
- □ 19 Oracle8i
- □ 20 Other Oracle database
- □ 21 Oracle9i Application Server
- □ 22 Oracle9i Application Server Wireless
- □ 23 Oracle Small Business Suite

Tools
- □ 24 Oracle Developer Suite
- □ 25 Oracle Discoverer
- □ 26 Oracle JDeveloper
- □ 27 Oracle Migration Workbench
- □ 28 Oracle9i AS Portal
- □ 29 Oracle Warehouse Builder
Oracle Services
- □ 30 Oracle Outsourcing
- □ 31 Oracle Consulting
- □ 32 Oracle Education
- □ 33 Oracle Support
- □ 98 Other
- 99 □ None of the above

⑦ WHAT OTHER DATABASE PRODUCTS ARE IN USE AT YOUR SITE? (check all that apply)
- □ 01 Access
- □ 02 Baan
- □ 03 dbase
- □ 04 Gupta
- □ 05 IBM DB2
- □ 06 Informix
- □ 07 Ingres
- □ 08 Microsoft Access
- □ 09 Microsoft SQL Server
- □ 10 PeopleSoft
- □ 11 Progress
- □ 12 SAP
- □ 13 Sybase
- □ 14 VSAM
- □ 98 Other
- 99 □ None of the above

⑧ WHAT OTHER APPLICATION SERVER PRODUCTS ARE IN USE AT YOUR SITE? (check all that apply)
- □ 01 BEA
- □ 02 IBM
- □ 03 Sybase
- □ 04 Sun
- □ 05 Other

⑨ DURING THE NEXT 12 MONTHS, HOW MUCH DO YOU ANTICIPATE YOUR ORGANIZATION WILL SPEND ON COMPUTER HARDWARE, SOFTWARE, PERIPHERALS, AND SERVICES FOR YOUR LOCATION? (check only one)
- □ 01 Less than $10,000
- □ 02 $10,000 to $49,999
- □ 03 $50,000 to $99,999
- □ 04 $100,000 to $499,999
- □ 05 $500,000 to $999,999
- □ 06 $1,000,000 and over

⑩ WHAT IS YOUR COMPANY'S YEARLY SALES REVENUE? (please choose one)
- □ 01 $500, 000, 000 and above
- □ 02 $100, 000, 000 to $500, 000, 000
- □ 03 $50, 000, 000 to $100, 000, 000
- □ 04 $5, 000, 000 to $50, 000, 000
- □ 05 $1, 000, 000 to $5, 000, 000

100103